10.00

THE **Woodsmith** COLLECTION™

DESKS, TABLES & CHAIRS

From the Editors and Staff of
Woodsmith® Magazine

AUGUST HOME PUBLISHING COMPANY
DES MOINES, IOWA

AUGUST HOME
PUBLISHING COMPANY

Publisher Donald B. Peschke

August Home Books

Executive Editor	Douglas L. Hicks
Art Director	Linda F. Vermie
Senior Graphic Designer	Chris Glowacki
Graphic Design Intern	Vu Nguyen
Copy Editor	David Stone
Contributing Book Designer	Ted Kralicek

Contributing Staff

Editor, *Woodsmith*	Terry J. Strohman
Art Director, *Woodsmith*	Todd Lambirth
Editor, *ShopNotes*	Tim Robertson
Art Director, *ShopNotes*	Cary Christensen
Editor, *Workbench*	Chris Inman
Art Director, *Workbench*	Robert Foss
Project Design Developer	Ken Munkel
Project Designers	Kent Welsh
	Ted Wong
	Kevin C. Boyle
Project Builders	Steve Curtis
	Steve Johnson
Editors	Vincent S. Ancona
	Jon Garbison
	Bryan Nelson
	Phil Totten
Illustrators	Mark Higdon
	David Kreyling
	Erich Lage
	Mike Mittermeier
	Roger Reiland
	Kurt Schultz
	Cinda Shambaugh
	Dirk Ver Steeg
Photographers	Lark Smothermon
	Crayola England
Production Director	George Chmielarz
Production	Douglas M. Lidster
	Troy A. Clark
	Susan Dickman
V.P. Planning & Finance	Jon Macarthy
Sales & Marketing	Bob Baker
	Kent A. Buckton
	Glenda Battles
New Media Manager	Gordon C. Gaippe
Technical Service	Matt TeRonde

If you have any comments about this book or would like subscription information about *Woodsmith*, *ShopNotes*, or *Workbench* magazines, please write:

August Home Publishing Co.
2200 Grand Ave.
Des Moines, IA 50312

Or call: 1 800–444–7527
Internet: http://www.augusthome.com
E-Mail: books@augusthome.com

 ISBN: 0-9634375-5-0

Printed in the United States of America.

INTRODUCTION

It seems like every woodworker has a dream of some day building a project based around a classic design feature. Maybe it's an "S-shaped" tambour door for a roll-top desk. Or the elegant cabriole legs used on a Queen Anne table.

But somewhere along the way, there's a nagging fear that the technique needed to build the project will be too difficult. For me, it was the cabriole legs. When I first started in woodworking, I figured making them would mean a lot of hand carving or turning on the lathe. So I was surprised when I found out that it's easy to make a cabriole leg by cutting to a line on a band saw and then shaping it with a file.

Making the tambour door for a roll-top desk isn't difficult either. Basically, you just glue a bunch of thin slats to a piece of canvas and then rout a groove for them to run in. (Well, there's a little more to it than that; see page 74.)

I guess what I'm saying is that classic techniques and designs such as these aren't exclusively for "master craftsmen." By breaking them down one step at a time they're not all that mysterious.

What we've tried to do in this book is present these techniques (and others) in a step-by-step manner. Once you know the techniques, you can use them to build some great desks, tables, and chairs.

Doug

NOTE: This is a special "Heavy-Duty Shop Edition" of *Classic Cabinets*. We've printed it with the following features to make it easier to use in your shop:

- UNIQUE "LAY-FLAT" BINDING — It's strong, but not attached at the spine. Don't be afraid to press down hard at the center between the pages. Open it anywhere and try it. It will stay flat and won't flap shut.
- COLD RESISTANT — The special cold-set glue used in the binding stays strong and flexible. Even in a below-freezing garage shop.
- LAMINATED COVER — Resists dirt, liquids, stains, and many finishes.
- LOW-GLARE, HEAVY-DUTY PAPER — It's easy-to-read, even under bright shop lights.

CONTENTS

Page 12

Page 39

Page 51

Page 83

COFFEE TABLE

The diagonal grain on the top of this table may be the first thing seen.
But it's the way the legs are built that will interest a woodworker.

When I built this coffee table, I did something different with the legs. Traditionally, table legs are square posts connected by stretchers with mortise and tenon joinery. Solid construction. The base on this table is solid, too — it just doesn't involve square posts or cutting mortises and tenons.

BUILT-UP LEGS. The legs are built up from ³/₄"-thick oak. But they're not put together the way you might think. First, two pieces are glued together to form an outside corner. Then a third piece is beveled to fit behind the inside corner. This creates a triangular leg.

But the beveled piece isn't just to give the leg an interesting triangular shape. It's there to "trap" a half-lap joint on the end of the table aprons. The half lap acts like a tenon that fits inside a built-up "mortise." This gives the table strength and the appearance of a piece made with traditional joinery.

GRAIN DIRECTION. One thing to consider when making built-up legs is the wood grain. To achieve the look of a one-piece leg, it's important to select the mating pieces of each leg from the same section of stock; see the Cutting Diagram on the facing page. Then, when the corner is rounded over, the color and grain direction make the built-up leg look like one piece.

TOP. The table top is made from three sections of oak plywood. To make the top more interesting, I cut the panel so the grain runs diagonally. This way the grain direction alternates from one panel to the next; see photo above.

FINISH. I lightly stained the table and finished it with polyurethane for protection; see the box on page 10.

EXPLODED VIEW

OVERALL DIMENSIONS:
16¼H x 23D x 47L

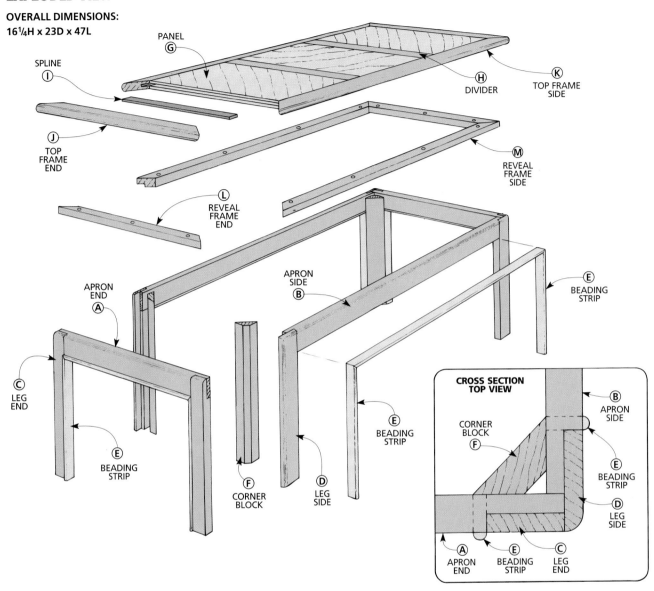

PANEL
Ⓖ

SPLINE
Ⓘ

Ⓙ
TOP
FRAME
END

Ⓗ
DIVIDER

Ⓚ
TOP FRAME
SIDE

Ⓜ
REVEAL
FRAME
SIDE

Ⓛ
REVEAL
FRAME
END

APRON
END
Ⓐ

APRON
SIDE
Ⓑ

Ⓔ
BEADING
STRIP

Ⓒ
LEG
END

Ⓔ
BEADING
STRIP

Ⓔ
BEADING
STRIP

Ⓕ
CORNER
BLOCK

Ⓓ
LEG
SIDE

**CROSS SECTION
TOP VIEW**

CORNER
BLOCK
Ⓕ

Ⓑ
APRON
SIDE

Ⓔ
BEADING
STRIP

Ⓓ
LEG
SIDE

Ⓐ
APRON
END

Ⓔ
BEADING
STRIP

Ⓒ
LEG
END

MATERIALS LIST

TABLE BASE

A	Apron - Ends (2)	¾ x 2 - 21¾
B	Apron - Sides (2)	¾ x 2 - 45¾
C	Leg - Ends (4)	¾ x 1⅝ - 15
D	Leg - Sides (4)	¾ x 2 - 15
E	Beading Strips	¼ x ⅞ - 26' rough
F	Corner Blocks (4)	¾ x 2³⁄₁₆ - 14¾

TABLE TOP

G	Panels (3)	¾ ply - 13 x 19
H	Dividers (2)	¾ x 2 - 19
I	Splines	¼ x ¹⁵⁄₁₆ - cut to fit
J	Frame Ends (2)	¾ x 2 - 23
K	Frame Sides (2)	¾ x 2 - 47
L	Reveal - Ends (2)	¾ x 1⅜ - 23 rough
M	Reveal - Sides (2)	¾ x 1⅜ - 47 rough

HARDWARE SUPPLIES

(14) No. 8 x 1¼" Fh woodscrews

CUTTING DIAGRAM

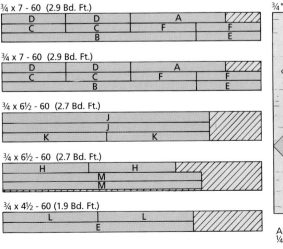

¾ x 7 - 60 (2.9 Bd. Ft.)

D	D	A	
C	C	F	F
B			E

¾ x 7 - 60 (2.9 Bd. Ft.)

D	D	A	
C	C	F	F
B			E

¾ x 6½ - 60 (2.7 Bd. Ft.)

J	
J	
K	K

¾ x 6½ - 60 (2.7 Bd. Ft.)

H	H	
M		
M		

¾ x 4½ - 60 (1.9 Bd. Ft.)

L	L	
E		

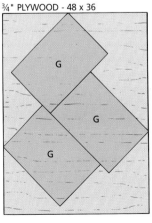

¾" PLYWOOD - 48 x 36

G
G
G

ALSO NEED:
¼" HARDBOARD FOR SPLINES (I)

TABLE BASE

There are two main parts to the coffee table — the table base and the top. I built the base first, then made the top to fit. But instead of starting out by building four legs and connecting them with aprons, I began by building four "U-shaped" assemblies; see Figs. 1 and 2. Then the assemblies are glued together to form the base; see Fig. 4.

APRONS. Start by ripping two apron ends (A) and two apron sides (B) to the same width (2") from ¾" stock; see Figs. 1 and 2. Then trim all four aprons to finished lengths (21¾" and 45¾").

LEGS. Now the legs can be added to the aprons to complete the four assemblies. The legs (C) for the end assemblies will later be joined to the legs (D) for the side assemblies. So for the best grain match when the assemblies are joined, try to cut the mating pieces (C & D) from the same section of ¾" stock; see the Cutting Diagram. (Shop Note: Mark the mating pieces so they can be assembled into the same leg unit later.)

First cut four blanks to rough width (4") and finished length (15"). Next, rip these four blanks to produce four leg ends (C) 1⅝" wide; see Fig. 1, and four leg sides (D) 2" wide; see Fig. 2.

HALF LAPS. The legs are joined to the aprons by means of half-lap joints. These half laps can be cut with a dado blade on the table saw. But to end up with the cleanest cuts possible, I used a straight bit in the router.

To make routing the half laps easier, I made an edge guide for my router. (For more on this jig, see page 11.)

Note: Half laps are cut *half* the thickness of the mating pieces (⅜" deep).

Using an edge guide to rout half laps involves two different fence setups. First, the laps on the top of the leg pieces are routed 2" wide (to accept the 2"-wide aprons); see Figs. 1 and 2. Then, 1⅝"-wide laps are routed on the ends of each apron.

U-SHAPED ASSEMBLIES. When the half laps have been cut on all twelve base pieces, the pieces can be glued up into four U-shaped assemblies.

Note: The apron sides will *not* lap completely over the leg sides; see Fig. 2a. That's okay because the legs and ends of the aprons are rabbeted next.

RABBETS. Now the four U-shaped leg assemblies are joined with rabbet joints to form the table base. Rabbets are cut *only* on the legs of the side assemblies — not the end assemblies; see Fig. 3. Again I used the edge guide with the router.

ASSEMBLY. When the rabbets have been cut on the side assemblies, all four assemblies can be glued together to form the table base; see Fig. 4.

ROUNDOVERS. To help the leg pieces blend together, I rounded over the *outside* corners of the side legs; see Figs. 5 and 5a. I also rounded over the top *outside* edge of each apron.

EDGE BEADING. After the legs and aprons are rounded over, beading strips are attached to the inside edges of the legs to soften the look. The beading strips (E) start out as 2"-wide blanks of ¾"-thick stock.

Cut two of these blanks to a rough

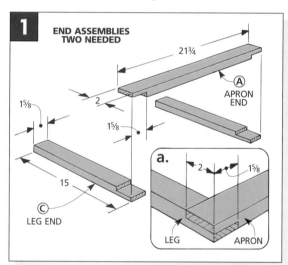

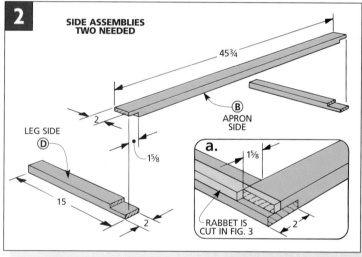

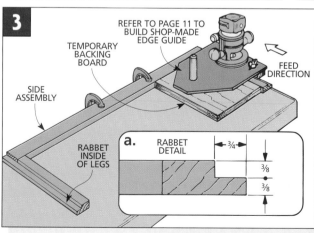

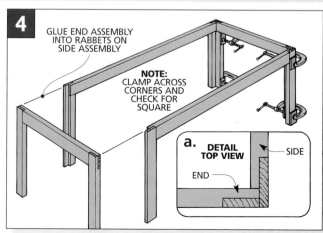

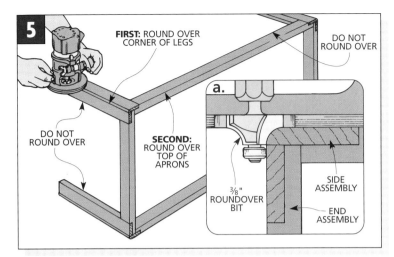

5

FIRST: ROUND OVER CORNER OF LEGS

DO NOT ROUND OVER

DO NOT ROUND OVER

SECOND: ROUND OVER TOP OF APRONS

a.

⅜" ROUNDOVER BIT

SIDE ASSEMBLY

END ASSEMBLY

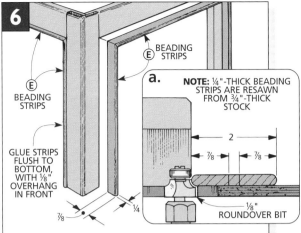

6

BEADING STRIPS

BEADING STRIPS

E

E

GLUE STRIPS FLUSH TO BOTTOM, WITH ⅛" OVERHANG IN FRONT

⅞"

¼

a.

NOTE: ¼"-THICK BEADING STRIPS ARE RESAWN FROM ¾"-THICK STOCK

2

⅞"

⅞"

⅛" ROUNDOVER BIT

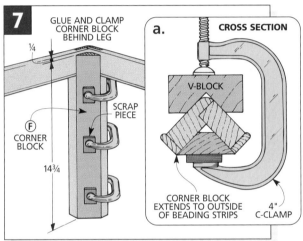

7

GLUE AND CLAMP CORNER BLOCK BEHIND LEG

¼

F

CORNER BLOCK

14¾

SCRAP PIECE

a. CROSS SECTION

V-BLOCK

CORNER BLOCK EXTENDS TO OUTSIDE OF BEADING STRIPS

4" C-CLAMP

length of 14" for the table legs. (You'll get four strips from each of these blanks.) Then cut another blank to a rough length of 42" for the end and side aprons. (You'll only need two strips from this blank.)

Now turn the blanks on edge and resaw them to produce ¼"-thick strips (2" wide). Both edges of these strips are rounded over on the router table with a ⅛" roundover bit; see Fig. 6a. Then the strips are ripped to produce the final width of ⅞".

ATTACH BEADING. To mount the beading strips, first miter one end of each short strip to fit on the inside edge of each leg; see Fig. 6. Then glue the strip in place so the square edge is flush to the back of the leg. (The rounded front edge should stick out ⅛".)

Finally, miter both ends of the long beading strips, sneaking up on the length to fit between the upright beading strips. Then glue them to the bottom edge of the aprons; see Fig. 6.

CORNER BLOCKS. To complete the legs, I cut corner blocks (F) to give the legs their triangular shape. To make these blocks, first cut four pieces of ¾" stock to a width of 2½". Then cut the blocks to length — ¼" *shorter* than the table legs; see Fig. 7.

Now the corner blocks can be beveled to fit behind each leg assembly; see Fig. 7 and the box below.

ATTACH CORNER BLOCKS. To glue the blocks in place, I used a V-block and C-clamps; see Fig. 7a.

Safe Bevel Ripping

Bevel-ripping both edges of a narrow workpiece using the table saw is a delicate operation. To make this safer, I use a narrow shop-made push stick, and the eraser end of a pencil as a hold-down.

The procedure I used to make the corner block for the coffee table was to rip a 45° bevel along one edge; see left drawing below.

Then rip another bevel on the opposite edge; see right drawing. Sneak up on the final width just until the triangular block fits in the back corner of the leg; see Fig. 7a above.

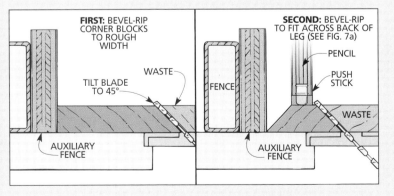

FIRST: BEVEL-RIP CORNER BLOCKS TO ROUGH WIDTH

TILT BLADE TO 45°

WASTE

AUXILIARY FENCE

SECOND: BEVEL-RIP TO FIT ACROSS BACK OF LEG (SEE FIG. 7a)

PENCIL

PUSH STICK

FENCE

WASTE

AUXILIARY FENCE

TABLE TOP PANELS

Once the table base is assembled, work can begin on the table top. The top consists of three plywood panels and two dividers surrounded by an oak frame. The parts are joined with spline and groove joints.

The panels for the top can be cut from less than half a sheet (4'x4') of hardwood plywood. I used ³/₄" oak plywood for the panels; see the Cutting Diagram on page 5.

PLYWOOD PANELS. To make the top more interesting to look at, I cut the panels with the grain oriented 45° to the outside frame.

The problem was finding the best way to cut a piece of plywood into the three panels with diagonal grain. The procedure I used involved following a number of steps.

LAY OUT PANELS. The first thing to do is draw a pencil line at a 45° angle across one of the corners; see Fig. 8. This line indicates one edge of each panel. Then use a framing square to lay out all three panels, working off the first pencil line.

Shop Note: Lay out the panels oversize (14" wide x 20" long) to allow extra room for cleaning up the rough cuts; see Fig. 8.

SABRE SAW ROUGH. Start cutting out the panels by making a single straight cut along the first layout line. To do this, I used the sabre saw guided by a straightedge; see Fig. 8. After this first cut, use the sabre saw freehand to cut out each panel, carefully following the pencil lines.

SAW A CLEAN EDGE. Next I moved to the table saw. The goal of the first cut on the table saw is simply to get a clean, straight edge. (The sabre saw probably

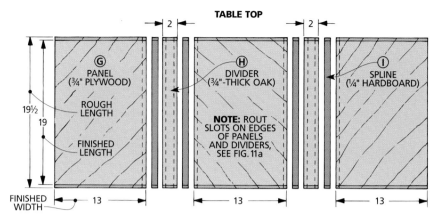

TABLE TOP

G PANEL (³/₄" PLYWOOD) ROUGH LENGTH FINISHED LENGTH

H DIVIDER (³/₄"-THICK OAK) **NOTE:** ROUT SLOTS ON EDGES OF PANELS AND DIVIDERS, SEE FIG. 11a

I SPLINE (¹/₄" HARDBOARD)

19¹/₂ · 19 · FINISHED WIDTH · 13 · 13 · 13 · 2 · 2

left some splinters.) So run each panel through the table saw with the straightest sabre-sawn edge against the rip fence, making a straight cut along the opposite edge; see Fig. 9.

Shop Note: When cutting plywood on the table saw, use a good sharp blade designed for plywood cutting. Also make all the cuts with the good side facing *up*. This way any chipout will be on the bottom side of the panels where it won't be visible after assembly.

SAW ADJACENT EDGE. The next step is to establish one square corner on each panel. Here I switched to the miter gauge and squared up a corner by holding the table-sawn edge against the miter gauge; see Fig. 10.

Shop Note: A panel-cutting jig for the table saw would make this step go a little smoother.

You should now have one clean, straight long edge, and one clean, straight short edge on each panel, with a square corner in between.

SAW TO SIZE. Now the panel can be cut to finished width; refer to drawing at the top of the page. To do this set the rip fence 13" from the blade and trim the sabre sawn edge off each piece.

After the panels are cut to width, they can be cut to length. Here I set the rip fence to cut the panels a little long (19¹/₂"). This extra ¹/₂" will allow room for trimming the uneven edges after the panels are assembled; refer to Fig. 12. Once they're cut to rough length, all three panels should be the exact same width and length.

PANEL DIVIDERS

After the plywood panels have been cut to rough size, the next step is to cut two panel dividers (H). The dividers are ripped from ³/₄"-thick hardwood to a width of 2", and crosscut to the same length as the plywood (19¹/₂"); see drawing above.

INSIDE SLOTS. Now slots can be cut on both edges of the dividers and the panels; see Fig. 11. I used a ¹/₄" slot cutter in the router to cut the slots, and centered the them on the thickness of the dividers; see Fig. 11a.

The important thing here is that all slots are cut with the router riding on the *top* face of each piece. The reason for this is that the dividers and plywood panels probably won't be the exact

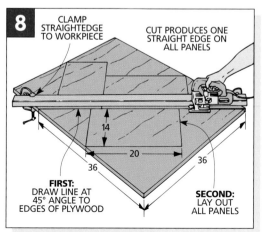

8 CLAMP STRAIGHTEDGE TO WORKPIECE · CUT PRODUCES ONE STRAIGHT EDGE ON ALL PANELS · 14 · 20 · 36 · 36 · **FIRST:** DRAW LINE AT 45° ANGLE TO EDGES OF PLYWOOD · **SECOND:** LAY OUT ALL PANELS

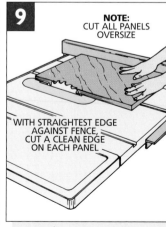

9 **NOTE:** CUT ALL PANELS OVERSIZE · WITH STRAIGHTEST EDGE AGAINST FENCE, CUT A CLEAN EDGE ON EACH PANEL

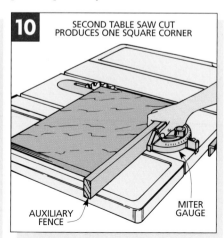

10 SECOND TABLE SAW CUT PRODUCES ONE SQUARE CORNER · AUXILIARY FENCE · MITER GAUGE

same thickness. But by indexing off the top face they will all be flush with the top; see Fig. 11b.

So I marked the top face of each piece in advance, then always routed with the marked face up; see Fig. 11. Shop Note: Once you've got the router adjusted for this, don't change the set-up — you'll need it later.

SPLINES. Next, cut the splines for attaching the panels to the dividers (and also the outside frame). I made the splines (I) from 1/4"-thick hardboard. To allow for easier assembly in the two 1/2"-wide slots, rip the splines to a width of 15/16"; see Fig. 11b.

You'll need six splines 19 1/2" long for the long edges of the plywood panels. Later, you'll use two splines 43 3/4" long

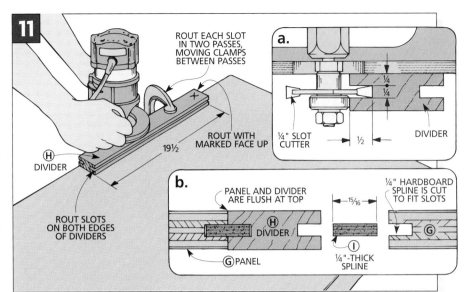

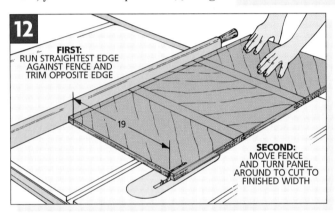

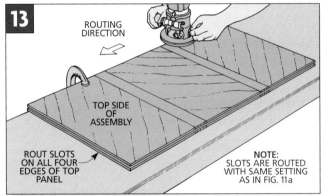

for attaching the long outside frame sections. So it's easiest to cut all the splines at one time from the end of a single four-foot wide sheet.

ASSEMBLY. When the slots have been routed on the dividers and plywood panels, the pieces can be glued together as a unit.

After the assembly is dry, trim it to finished width in two passes on the table saw; see Fig. 12. The first cut gives you one straight edge. Turn the piece around for the second cut. This cut produces the finished width, and another straight edge.

OUTSIDE SLOTS. Now slots are cut along the outside edges for attaching the outside frame; see Fig. 13. Again, I cut these slots with the router and a slot cutter adjusted the same as before; see Fig. 11a.

OUTSIDE FRAME

There are just a few more steps to complete the table. First, the top is surrounded by an oak frame. Then a

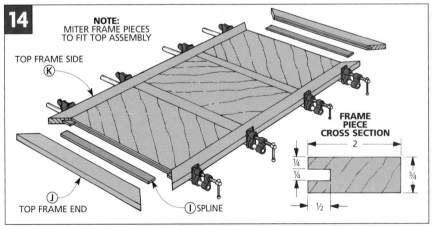

"reveal" frame is made for attaching the top to the base.

TOP FRAME. The mitered frame around the plywood top hides the edges of the plywood panels. It's attached to the edges of the plywood with splines glued into slots; see Fig. 14.

To make the frame, start by ripping two pieces for the frame ends (J) and two frame sides (K) the same width as the panel dividers (2" wide); see Fig. 14.

Now miter both ends of each piece so the finished length (long-point to long-point) equals the distance along the plywood edge *plus* the width of two frame pieces (4").

Next, rout a slot on the inside edge of each frame piece to align with the slot around the plywood assembly. Then glue splines into the slots in the panels, and glue the frame pieces onto the splines; see Fig. 14.

ROUND OVER THE EDGES. Before attaching the top to the base, I softened the top and bottom edges of the frame with a ³⁄₈" roundover bit; see Fig. 15.

Shop Note: I used my shop-built edge guide to rout the roundovers on both edges of the frame. There's a good reason for this — the fence on the edge guide keeps the bit cutting uniform roundovers on the top and bottom edges of the frame; see Fig. 15a. Without the edge guide fence, the router bit would cut deeper on the second pass, since some of the surface the pilot bearing runs against is removed on the *first* pass.

REVEAL FRAME

The next step is to build the reveal frame. This visually "lifts" the table top from the base; see Fig. 16. To build this frame, first rip the ends (L) and sides (M) to finished width (1³⁄₈") and rough length from ³⁄₄" stock; see Fig. 16.

Next, cut an ¹¹⁄₃₂"-wide rabbet on the lower outside edge of each frame section to fit on the top edge of the aprons; see Fig. 16a.

To determine the length of the pieces, measure the *inside* dimensions of the top of the table base and add ¹¹⁄₁₆". Now miter the pieces to length.

Before gluing the reveal frame to the base, I drilled a series of ³⁄₁₆" countersunk shank holes in each frame section for attaching the top.

SCREW TOP TO FRAME. Once the reveal frame sections are glued in place, turn the table top upside down on a flat surface to attach the top to the base; see Fig. 17. (Center the base on the top.)

Then, drill ¹⁄₈" pilot holes into the underside of the top frame through the holes in the reveal frame. Now screw the base unit to the top; see Fig. 17a.

FINISH. The final step is to apply the finish; see the box below. ■

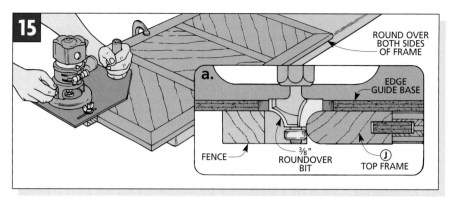

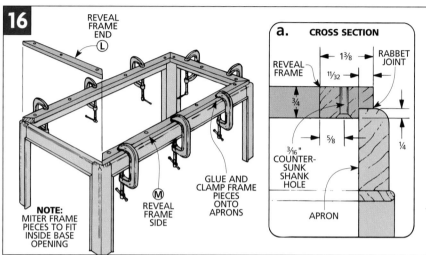

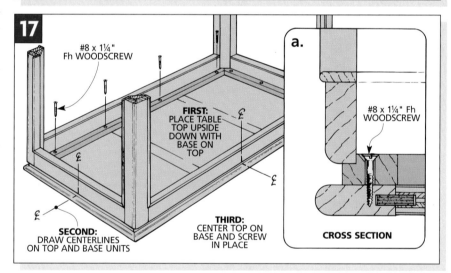

Finishing the Table

To finish the coffee table, I wanted to bring out just a bit of color, so I stained it using a homemade stain. I made it by mixing one teaspoon of burnt umber artists' oil color into a quart of boiled linseed oil.

The most important finish on any table is the protective top coat. On a coffee table (or any table that will take a lot of abuse), I use a finish that can build up a thicker film such as polyurethane.

Brush a first coat on all the surfaces of the table (even under the top) and allow it to dry following the instructions on the can.

Once it's dry, sand lightly with 320-grit sandpaper. Then apply a second coat,

(and third, if necessary) sanding between coats.

I like to top it off with a coat of paste wax applied with 0000 steel wool and buffed with a clean rag. This smoothes the surface and gives more protection.

To easily cut the half laps on the ends of the long aprons on the coffee table, I built an edge guide for a hand-held router; see photo. The guide is similar to store-bought edge guides, but I think it's more versatile.

HALF LAPS. The aprons on the coffee table connect to the legs with half-lap joints. But the aprons are too long to stand on end on the table saw and be cut easily. With this edge guide, I was able to clamp the aprons to my bench and run the router over the workpiece; see photo.

RABBETS. Another thing I liked about this edge guide is that it can be used to cut the $3/4$"-wide rabbets on the coffee table's leg units after they're assembled. For that matter it can be adjusted to cut just about any size rabbet on any workpiece.

ROUNDOVERS. This edge guide also came in handy when I was routing a roundover on the edge of the frame that surrounds the coffee table top. Using this jig made the job safer than balancing the assembled top on the router table. And it allowed me to uniformly round over the top and bottom edges.

After drilling holes for the mounting screws, bore a series of holes in the base to form two slots for adjusting the fence; see Fig. 1. Then screw a dowel handle to the other end. Finally, attach the base to the router.

FENCE. I made the fence from a piece of $3/4$"-thick hardwood with a notch in the center and holes in both ends for countersunk bolts; see Fig. 1. Two machine bolts with wing nuts hold the fence to the base.

BUILDING THE GUIDE

The edge guide has two main parts. There's a base of $1/4$" hardboard with a hole at one end for a router bit, and a handle at the other end for controlling the jig. Also, there's an adjustable fence with a notch in the middle that lets you rout with a bit recessed into the fence.

BASE. When the base is cut to size (see Fig. 1), bore a 1"-dia. hole through one end for the router bit to extend through. Then, remove the existing base from your router and use it as a template to locate the mounting holes on the new base.

USING THE GUIDE

To use the edge guide, first adjust the distance between the fence and the outside edge of a straight router bit; see Fig. 2.

This distance determines the width of the cut. The depth of the cut is determined by the height of the router bit.

To rout a half lap with this guide, make the first cut (to establish the shoulder) with the fence butted to the end of the workpiece; see Fig. 3. Then clean out the waste between the shoulder and the end of the workpiece; see Fig. 4.

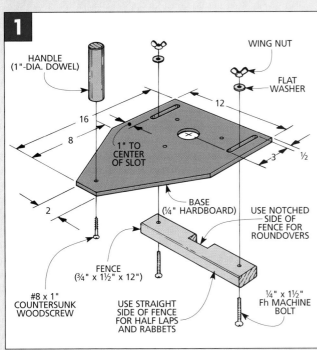

1

HANDLE (1"-DIA. DOWEL)

WING NUT

FLAT WASHER

16

12

8

1" TO CENTER OF SLOT

2

BASE ($1/4$" HARDBOARD)

USE NOTCHED SIDE OF FENCE FOR ROUNDOVERS

3

$1/2$

#8 x 1" COUNTERSUNK WOODSCREW

FENCE ($3/4$" x 1 $1/2$" x 12")

USE STRAIGHT SIDE OF FENCE FOR HALF LAPS AND RABBETS

$1/4$" x 1 $1/2$" Fh MACHINE BOLT

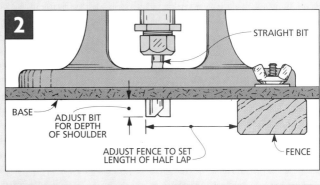

2

STRAIGHT BIT

BASE

ADJUST BIT FOR DEPTH OF SHOULDER

ADJUST FENCE TO SET LENGTH OF HALF LAP

FENCE

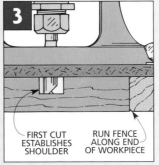

3

FIRST CUT ESTABLISHES SHOULDER

RUN FENCE ALONG END OF WORKPIECE

4

WASTE

CLEAN OUT WASTE TO COMPLETE HALF LAP

SOFA TABLE

This table features everything you'd expect of a craftsman-style table:
quartersawn oak, square spindles, and mortise and tenon joinery.

Plywood or solid wood? That's the choice you have to make when a project includes a wide panel such as the top and shelf on this Craftsman-style sofa table. Often, I'll choose plywood since it doesn't expand and contract with changes in humidity as much as solid wood.

But I decided against using plywood on this project for a couple of reasons. For one thing, I wanted to build it out of quartersawn oak which is typical of Craftsman-style (or Mission) furniture.

And quartersawn oak is hard to find in plywood. Also beveling the top edge wouldn't work without framing the edges with hardwood.

Since solid wood was the best option, I had to come up with a way to allow the panels to expand and contract. This wasn't a problem with the table top. I used some simple Z-shaped fasteners.

I was also able to use these fasteners on the front and back of the shelf. But the ends of the shelf were a concern.

The problem here is that the shelf fits between the legs. So when the panel expands, it will tend to push the legs apart, and when it contracts, there will be a gap. To solve this problem, I made a pocket for the shelf by extending the groove on the rails into the legs. This is all explained on page 17.

FINISH. I stained the sofa table with a light cherry stain and then topped this off with two coats of General Finishes' Royal Finish (oil and urethane). Finally, I rubbed on paste wax and buffed it out to a satin sheen with a soft, clean rag.

EXPLODED VIEW

OVERALL DIMENSIONS:
28H x 50L x 17D

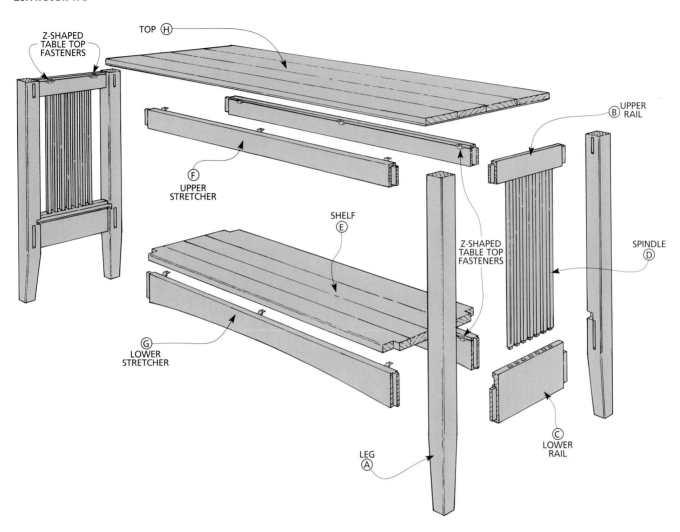

Z-SHAPED TABLE TOP FASTENERS

TOP Ⓗ

UPPER RAIL Ⓑ

Ⓕ
UPPER STRETCHER

SHELF
Ⓔ

Z-SHAPED TABLE TOP FASTENERS

SPINDLE
Ⓓ

Ⓖ
LOWER STRETCHER

LEG
Ⓐ

Ⓒ
LOWER RAIL

MATERIALS LIST

WOOD

A	Legs (4)	1¾ x 1¾ - 27¼
B	Upper Rails (2)	¾ x 2 - 11¼
C	Lower Rails (2)	¾ x 4⅛ - 11¼
D	Spindles (14)	½ x ½ - 15⅛
E	Shelf (1)	¾ x 12¾ - 40
F	Upr. Stretchers (2)	¾ x 2 - 39¾
G	Lwr. Stretchers (2)	¾ x 3 - 39¾
H	Top (1)	¾ x 17 - 50

HARDWARE SUPPLIES

(16) Z-shaped table top fasteners
(16) No. 8 x ⅝" Rh woodscrews

CUTTING DIAGRAM

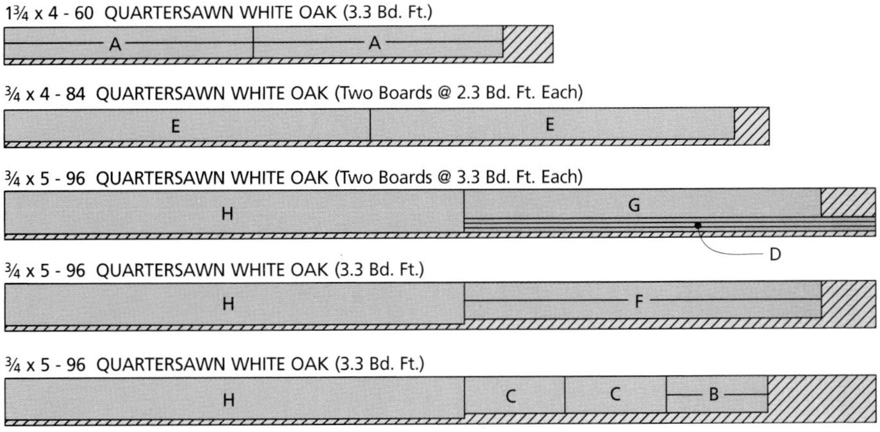

1¾ x 4 - 60 QUARTERSAWN WHITE OAK (3.3 Bd. Ft.)
A   A

¾ x 4 - 84 QUARTERSAWN WHITE OAK (Two Boards @ 2.3 Bd. Ft. Each)
E   E

¾ x 5 - 96 QUARTERSAWN WHITE OAK (Two Boards @ 3.3 Bd. Ft. Each)
H   G
D

¾ x 5 - 96 QUARTERSAWN WHITE OAK (3.3 Bd. Ft.)
H   F

¾ x 5 - 96 QUARTERSAWN WHITE OAK (3.3 Bd. Ft.)
H   C   C   B

LEGS

To build the sofa table, I started by building the end assemblies — the legs, rails, and spindles. And the first thing to work on is the legs.

With some projects, keeping all of the legs oriented correctly in relation to each other requires some mental gymnastics. But it's easy on this table since the four legs (A) are identical.

They legs are cut from 8/4 stock to a length of $27\frac{1}{4}$" and $1\frac{3}{4}$" square; see Fig. 1.

MORTISES. Once the legs were cut to size, I worked on cutting centered mortises for the rails and stretchers; see Figs. 1a and 1b. To do this, first drill overlapping $\frac{1}{4}$"-dia. holes $\frac{11}{16}$" deep on adjacent faces of the legs. Then square up the sides and ends with a chisel.

TAPERS. Finally, I tapered the inside faces of each leg. (Taper the same faces that the mortises are on.) Start the tapers 6" up from the bottom end of each leg; see Fig. 2a.

To do this, I made a simple jig that works on the table saw; see Fig. 2 and 2b. It's just a scrap piece with a tapered edge and a small cleat attached to one end. The jig acts as an angled spacer between the rip fence and the leg. You push the leg through the blade, and the cleat causes the jig to simply ride along.

When one taper is cut, rotate the leg so the other mortised face is toward the blade and make a second pass.

RAILS

Now the legs can be set aside and work can begin on the rails that will join the legs at the ends of the table.

The upper and lower rails (B, C) are cut from $\frac{3}{4}$"-thick stock and are the same length ($11\frac{1}{4}$"). But the upper rail isn't as wide (2") as the lower one ($4\frac{1}{8}$"); see Fig. 1. The extra width on

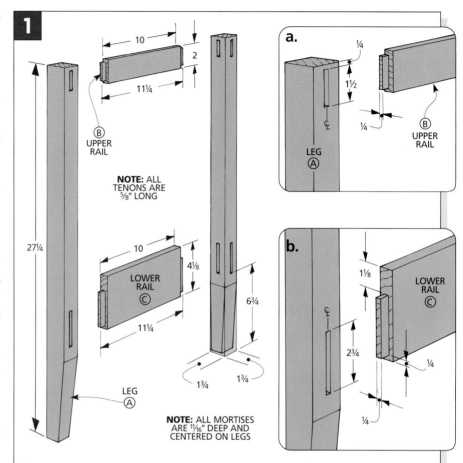

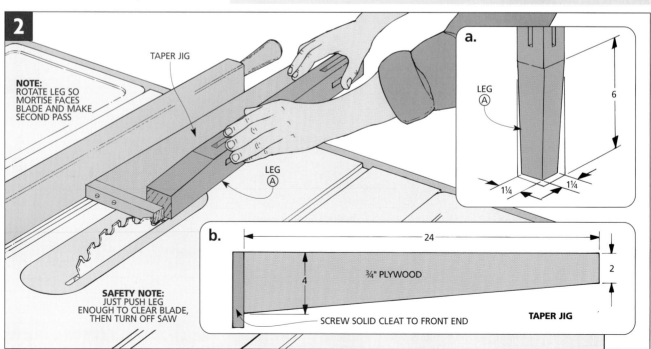

the lower rail allows room for a groove to accept the shelf that's added later.

TENONS. After cutting the rails to final size, tenons can be cut on the ends of the rails. Since the tenons are centered, I cut them on the table saw with a dado blade, flipping the rails between passes to sneak up on the thickness.

Then I cut the shoulders on the tenons, which are all $1/4''$ except the upper shoulder on the lower rail (C). Here, it's $1\frac{1}{8}''$ because of the shelf groove that's added later; see Fig. 1b.

SPINDLE MORTISES. With the tenons cut, it's time to lay out the mortises for the spindles. There are seven square mortises in each rail. For a good fit, these mortises should line up between the top and bottom rails. To ensure this, I clamped the four rails together and laid out the centers of all the mortises, see Figs. 3 and 3a.

Next, unclamp the rails and set up the drill press to bore a $3/8''$-dia. hole $5/16''$ deep that's centered on the thickness of the rail, see Fig. 4. Then drill a single hole for each mortise.

Finally, I squared up the mortises with a chisel. To keep these identical, I built a chisel guide; see box below.

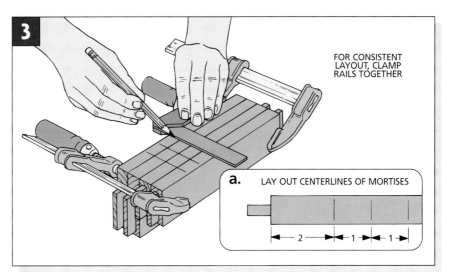

FOR CONSISTENT LAYOUT, CLAMP RAILS TOGETHER

a. LAY OUT CENTERLINES OF MORTISES

2 — 1 — 1

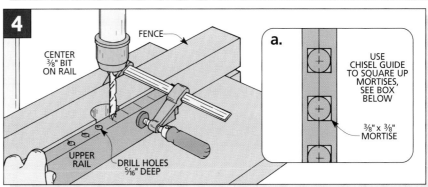

FENCE

CENTER $3/8''$ BIT ON RAIL

UPPER RAIL

DRILL HOLES $5/16''$ DEEP

a.

USE CHISEL GUIDE TO SQUARE UP MORTISES, SEE BOX BELOW

$3/8''$ x $3/8''$ MORTISE

Chisel Guide

It can be difficult to get all the holes on the sofa table rails squared up accurately for the tenons on the spindles. To speed up the process, I made a simple jig to guide my chisel.

This jig is just a piece of aluminum angle with a square hole filed in the middle. The secret to making this jig is cutting

the square hole so it's centered perfectly over the drilled holes in the rails.

This is easy to do. Once the holes for the mortises are drilled (Fig. 1), clamp the aluminum angle to the front of your workpiece; see Fig. 2. Don't move the fence on the drill press , but change to a twist bit to drill the aluminum.

Now drill the hole and square it up with a small file until it's the size needed for the mortise ($3/8$" x $3/8$"); see Fig. 3.

To use the jig, simply position it over the holes and clamp it in place; see photo. The jig guides your chisel to accurately cut square mortises that match the tenons on the spindles.

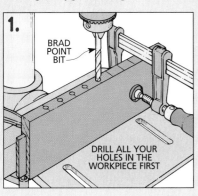

1.

BRAD POINT BIT

DRILL ALL YOUR HOLES IN THE WORKPIECE FIRST

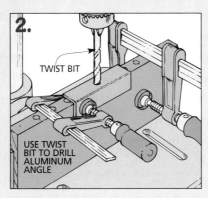

2.

TWIST BIT

USE TWIST BIT TO DRILL ALUMINUM ANGLE

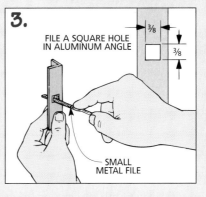

3.

FILE A SQUARE HOLE IN ALUMINUM ANGLE

$3/8$

$3/8$

SMALL METAL FILE

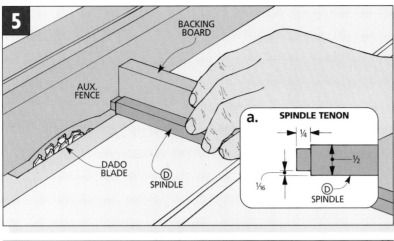

5

BACKING BOARD

AUX. FENCE

DADO BLADE

SPINDLE (D)

a. SPINDLE TENON

¼

½

¹⁄₁₆

SPINDLE (D)

SPINDLE (D)

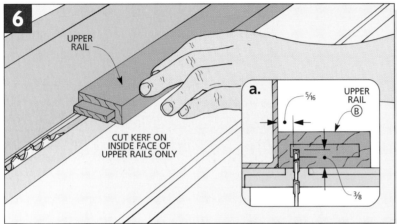

6

UPPER RAIL

CUT KERF ON INSIDE FACE OF UPPER RAILS ONLY

a. UPPER RAIL (B)

⁵⁄₁₆

³⁄₈

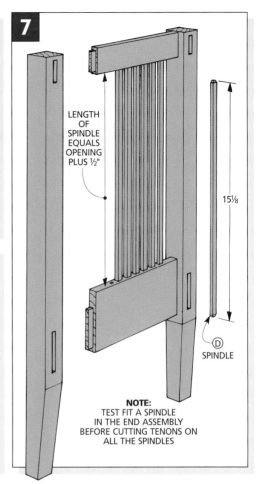

7

LENGTH OF SPINDLE EQUALS OPENING PLUS ½"

15⅛

SPINDLE (D)

NOTE: TEST FIT A SPINDLE IN THE END ASSEMBLY BEFORE CUTTING TENONS ON ALL THE SPINDLES

SPINDLES

At this point the rails are ready for the square spindles.

CUT TO SIZE. To find the length of the spindles, you need to dry assemble the rails and legs into an end unit. Then measure the distance between the rails; refer to Fig. 7. This will be the shoulder-to-shoulder distance of the spindles. Now add ¹⁄₂" to this measurement to allow for the tenons on each end. (My spindles ended up 15¹⁄₈" long.)

Next, to cut the spindles (D) to size, I began with ¹⁄₂"-thick stock cut to finished length. Then I ripped ¹⁄₂"-square spindles from the blank.

Shop Note: It's always a good idea to make a few extra spindles to help set up the cut for the tenons.

TENONS. Now, square tenons can be cut on the spindles to fit the square mortises in the rails. I like to do this on the table saw with a dado blade buried in an auxiliary fence. Leave ¹⁄₄" of the blade exposed and raise it ¹⁄₁₆" above the table; see Fig. 5.

But before cutting the tenons in all the pieces, start with a test piece and check the fit carefully. This means more than just trying the tenon in the mortise. It also means making sure the spindles are the correct length to fit between the upper and lower rails.

KERF IN RAIL. Now, to complete the *upper* rails (B), I cut a ¹⁄₈" kerf in each rail's top, inside edge; see Figs. 6 and 7. This is for the hardware used to attach the top panel later.

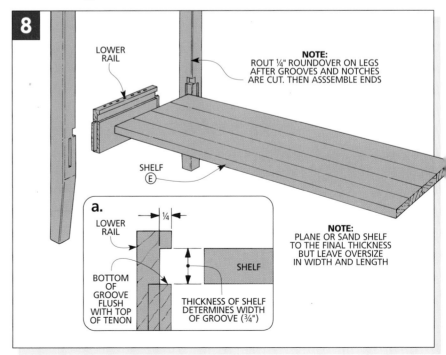

8

LOWER RAIL

NOTE: ROUT ¹⁄₄" ROUNDOVER ON LEGS AFTER GROOVES AND NOTCHES ARE CUT. THEN ASSSEMBLE ENDS

SHELF (E)

a.

LOWER RAIL

¼

SHELF

BOTTOM OF GROOVE FLUSH WITH TOP OF TENON

THICKNESS OF SHELF DETERMINES WIDTH OF GROOVE (¾")

NOTE: PLANE OR SAND SHELF TO THE FINAL THICKNESS BUT LEAVE OVERSIZE IN WIDTH AND LENGTH

SHELF JOINERY

There's just a couple more steps before the end units of the table can be assembled. First, there has to be some way to hold the shelf in place between the ends. It's done a little different than the table top.

To support the shelf and prevent it from cupping, I cut a groove in the lower rails. Easy enough. But since the shelf will be notched to fit between the legs, I had to come up with a way to allow the panel to easily expand and contract. If it were just glued in the groove, the shelf would likely split or leave gaps with changes in humidity.

The solution is to extend the groove into the legs so there's a notch in each leg for the shelf to expand into; refer to Figs. 8 and 9.

SHELF. Creating the groove for the shelf isn't difficult. But since the final thickness of the shelf (E) determines the width of the grooves, I glued the shelf up now and planed and sanded it down to final thickness; see Fig. 8a. (You can leave it at rough width and length for now.)

GROOVE. After determining the thickness of the panel, the first step is to lay out the location of the groove in the rail. Mark the bottom edge of this groove so it will be flush with the top edge of the tenon on the rail; see Fig. 8a. Then cut the groove $1/4$" deep.

NOTCH. Now dry assemble the legs

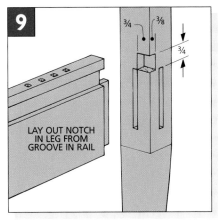
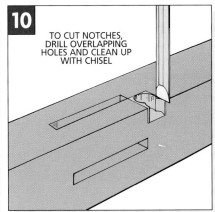

and rails again and transfer the depth and height of the groove to the leg, see Fig. 9. Then lay out the notch on the leg. Once the layout is complete, you can notch the leg. To remove most of the waste, I used my drill press to drill $3/8$"-deep overlapping holes. Then I pared up to the layout lines with a sharp chisel; see Fig. 10.

Now you can test the fit of the shelf in the grooves and notches.

ROUND OVER LEGS. Once the shelves fit in the grooves and notches, there's one more step before the ends can be assembled. Use the router table and a fence to rout a $1/4$" roundover on all four edges of the legs.

ASSEMBLE ENDS. At this point, the ends of the table can be assembled. I positioned the spindles in their mortises between the rails. Then I glued the legs to the rails.

STRETCHERS

Next, the stretchers (F,G) can be made; see Fig. 11. They're the same length ($39^3/4$"), but the upper stretchers are 2" wide, while the lower ones are 3"; see Fig. 11a.

TENONS. Next, cut $5/8$"-long tenons centered on the stretchers to fit the mortises in the legs. Note that the tenons on the lower stretchers don't have a shoulder along their top edge. That's because the shelf sits directly on top and will hide any gap.

KERFS AND ARCS. There are two more steps to complete the stretchers. First, the hardware that holds the shelf and top in place requires a kerf cut along the inside faces of the stretchers; see Fig. 11b. The second step is to lay out and cut an arc on the lower stretchers; see Fig. 11.

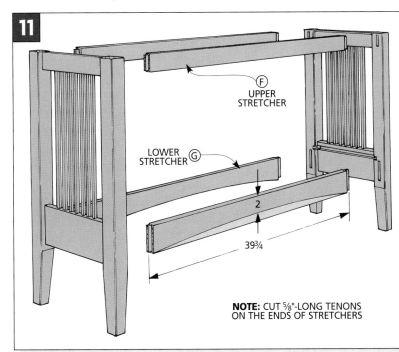
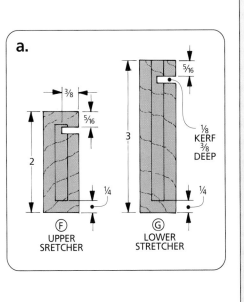

SHELF AND TOP

Before connecting the end assemblies with the stretchers, you need to cut the shelf panel to final size. To do this, you'll have to dry assemble the table again; see Fig. 12.

The overall length of the shelf equals the distance between the bottoms of the grooves in the rails. (Mine was 40" long.) The overall width equals the distance across the stretchers plus $1/8$" overhang on each side; see Fig. 12a. (Mine ended up $12^3/4$" wide.)

NOTCHES. After the shelf is cut to size, the corners need to be notched to fit around the legs (and into the notches in the legs); see Fig. 12b. Finding the depth of the shelf notch is easy. Measure from the bottom of the groove in the rail to the inside edge of the leg. (Mine was $3/4$".)

The width of the notch is a little more tricky. First measure from the outside edge of the stretcher to the edge of the notch in the leg ($7/8$"); see Fig. 12b. Add $1/8$" for the overhang on the outside of the stretcher. Then add another $1/8$" for a gap inside the notch that allows the shelf to expand and contract. (My notch was $1^1/8$" wide.)

Note: It's a good idea to double-check your measurements before cutting the notches on the shelf. The

length between the legs should equal the length between these notches. Then once the notches are cut, dry assemble the table one last time to make sure everything fits.

ASSEMBLY. When everything fits, rout a $1/16$" chamfer on the top edge of the shelf; see Fig. 12a. Then glue up the table. (Don't glue in the shelf panel.)

TOP. Now all that's left is to add the top (H). Glue up a $3/4$"-thick panel and cut it to finished size, see Fig. 13. Then rout a bevel around the bottom edge; see opposite page.

Finally, to attach the top (and the front and back of the shelf), I used table top fasteners, see Fig. 13a. These fit into the kerfs in the stretchers and rails. ■

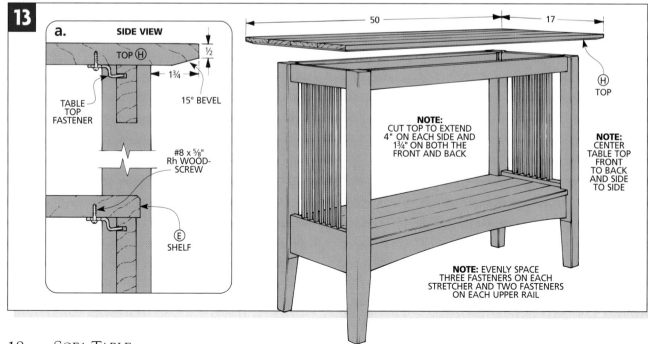

Typically, I use a table saw to cut a bevel on a workpiece. But trying to bevel the bottom side of the sofa table top, created a problem. It just wasn't safe to stand this large panel on end and use the table saw.

The solution was a shop-made jig that holds a router at an angle; see Fig. 1. With a straight bit in the router, it's easy to rout the bevel. Note: The flute length on the bit has to be long enough to cut the full width of the bevel. Mine was 1¼" long.

JIG CONSTRUCTION. The jig consists of four pieces: a fence, bit guard, auxiliary base, and a handle, see drawing below. To build the jig, start with

the fence and bit guard. First, cut a notch at the center of the fence to provide clearance for the bit. Then glue the bit guard and fence together.

To make this jig work, simply cut an angle on one end of the fence and bit

guard that matches the bevel you need on your workpiece. Then when you add the auxiliary base, it tips your router to match the bevel. The auxiliary base is simply screwed into the fence. Finally, screw a handle to the fence.

SETTING DEPTH. Since this jig is designed to cut the bevel in several passes, you adjust the depth of cut by pivoting the auxiliary base; see Fig. 2. The arched slot allows the router to swing down to the required depth before locking it in position with a screw.

USING THE JIG. Start with the depth set shallow. Then increase the depth gradually until your bevel is complete.

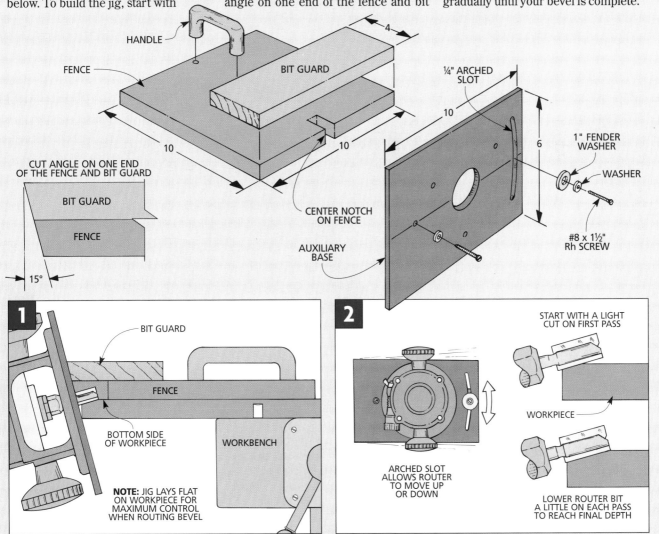

HANDLE

FENCE

BIT GUARD

4

¼" ARCHED SLOT

10

10

6

1" FENDER WASHER

WASHER

10

10

CUT ANGLE ON ONE END OF THE FENCE AND BIT GUARD

BIT GUARD

FENCE

15°

CENTER NOTCH ON FENCE

AUXILIARY BASE

#8 x 1½" Rh SCREW

1

BIT GUARD

FENCE

BOTTOM SIDE OF WORKPIECE

WORKBENCH

NOTE: JIG LAYS FLAT ON WORKPIECE FOR MAXIMUM CONTROL WHEN ROUTING BEVEL

2

START WITH A LIGHT CUT ON FIRST PASS

WORKPIECE

ARCHED SLOT ALLOWS ROUTER TO MOVE UP OR DOWN

LOWER ROUTER BIT A LITTLE ON EACH PASS TO REACH FINAL DEPTH

QUEEN ANNE END TABLE

This graceful walnut table with cabriole legs and a dovetailed drawer is one project that's sure to become a family heirloom.

There are a few pieces of furniture that every woodworker would love to build . . . someday. This Queen Anne end table is one of those pieces. Besides the beauty of the design, the attraction of this table seems to be related to the skill required to build it.

I'm not saying that you have to be a master craftsman to build it. You don't. But there is the challenge of learning several woodworking techniques and pulling them all together to produce one piece of heirloom furniture.

The primary technique of course is making the cabriole legs. They're not as

difficult as you might imagine. No turning on the lathe. No carving. They can be easily cut with a band saw and finished off with a little hand filing. (Okay, I did use a spokeshave, but you could use a file or rasp.) The step-by-step details of this technique are described starting on page 27.

There are a number of other techniques to building this table as well. For the drawer, I cut half-blind dovetail joints by hand. The aprons and legs are assembled with traditional mortise and tenon joinery. In addition there's an interesting chamfer cut around the top of the table.

WOOD. I think a formal-looking project like this should be built from a dark wood such as walnut. Mahogany and cherry would also work, but you may want to consider staining them dark.

I used 3"x3" turning squares to make the legs; see Sources on page 95.

FINISH. To finish the table, I started with a paste wood filler to fill the pores. Then I used McCloskey's High Gloss Varnish as a top coat. Start with a thinned coat (50/50) to seal the surface. Then finish it off with four full-strength coats. Finally, I rubbed it out to a glass-smooth surface with 600-grit sandpaper, pumice, and rottenstone.

EXPLODED VIEW

OVERALL DIMENSIONS:
22H x 20W x 24D

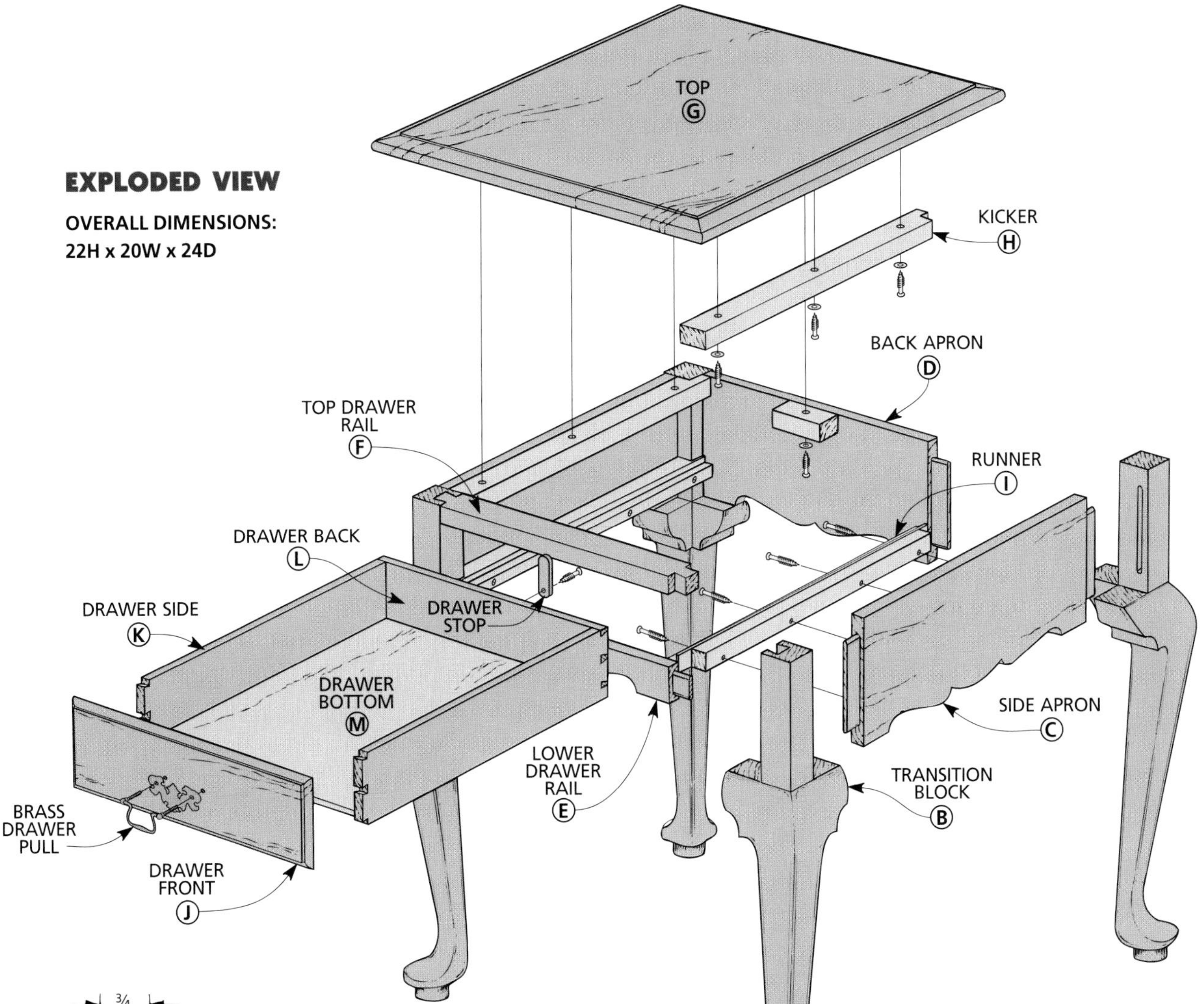

TOP
G
KICKER
H
BACK APRON
D
TOP DRAWER RAIL
F
RUNNER
I
DRAWER BACK
L
DRAWER SIDE
K
DRAWER STOP
DRAWER BOTTOM
M
SIDE APRON
C
LOWER DRAWER RAIL
E
TRANSITION BLOCK
B
BRASS DRAWER PULL
DRAWER FRONT
J
LEG
A

DOVETAIL DETAIL

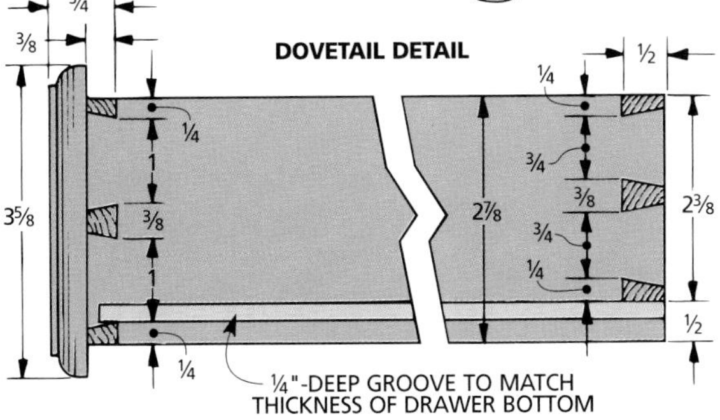

3/4
3/8
1/4
1
3/8
1
1/4
3 5/8
1/2
1/4
3/4
3/8
3/4
1/4
2 7/8
2 3/8
1/2
1/4"-DEEP GROOVE TO MATCH THICKNESS OF DRAWER BOTTOM

MATERIALS LIST & CUTTING DIAGRAM

WOOD

A	Legs (4)	$2^3/_4 \times 2^3/_4$ - $21^1/_4$
B	Transit. Blocks (8)	$2^3/_4 \times 2^3/_4$ - 2
C	Side Aprons (2)	$^3/_4 \times 5^1/_4$ - 20
D	Back Apron (1)	$^3/_4 \times 5^1/_4$ - 16
E	Lwr. Drwr. Rail (1)	$^3/_4 \times 1^1/_2$ - 16
F	Top Drwr. Rail (1)	$^3/_4 \times 1^3/_4$ - $15^1/_2$
G	Top (1)	$^3/_4 \times 20$ - 24
H	Kickers (2)	$^3/_4 \times 1^1/_2$ - $18^{13}/_{16}$
I	Runners (2)	$^3/_4 \times 1^1/_2$ - $19^3/_4$
J	Drawer Front (1)	$^3/_4 \times 3^5/_8$ - $14^1/_2$
K	Drawer Sides (2)	$^1/_2 \times 2^7/_8$ - 18
L	Drawer Back (1)	$^1/_2 \times 2^3/_8$ - $13^3/_4$
M	Drawer Btm. (1)	$^1/_4$ ply - $17^7/_8 \times 13^1/_4$

HARDWARE SUPPLIES

(1) 3" Smooth face cast plate handle
(1) No 6 x 3/4" Flathead woodscrew
(8) No. 8 x 1 3/4" Flathead woodscrews
(8) No. 8 x 1" Roundhead woodscrews
(8) No. 8 (7/16" O.D.) Washers
(2) 3/4" Wire brads
For sources of pre-made cabriole legs, see page 95

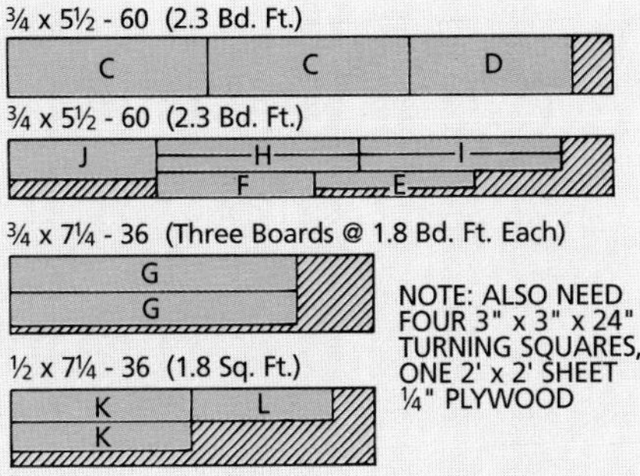

3/4 x 5 1/2 - 60 (2.3 Bd. Ft.)
C
C
D
3/4 x 5 1/2 - 60 (2.3 Bd. Ft.)
J
H
I
F
E
3/4 x 7 1/4 - 36 (Three Boards @ 1.8 Bd. Ft. Each)
G
G
1/2 x 7 1/4 - 36 (1.8 Sq. Ft.)
K
L
K

NOTE: ALSO NEED FOUR 3" x 3" x 24" TURNING SQUARES, ONE 2' x 2' SHEET 1/4" PLYWOOD

CABRIOLE LEGS

Each leg starts out as a block of walnut $2^3/4''$ square by roughly 28" long. This length includes enough for one leg (A) plus the two transition blocks (B) that are glued on near the knee; see Fig. 1.

Note: You can buy pre-made cabriole legs; see mail order sources on page 95. But I like to make my own.

If you decide to make your own legs, I don't recommend gluing them up from four pieces of $3/4''$-thick stock. The glue lines will become very obvious when the leg is shaped. Instead I like to start with a 3" x 3" turning square and trim it down to the $2^3/4''$ square size. Again, this is all explained in the article starting on page 27.

After squaring up the stock to $2^3/4''$ (see box on the opposite page), cut off a $21^1/4''$ length for the leg and two 2" lengths for the transition blocks.

PATTERN. Before gluing the transition blocks on, the first step is to mark the pattern on two adjacent faces of the leg blank.

To do this, make a pattern from the grid drawing in Fig. 1, or order the cabriole leg pattern; see "Woodsmith Project Supplies" on page 95. It's best to use carbon paper to trace this pattern onto a piece of posterboard or hardboard. Then cut out the shape and lay it over the printed pattern to make sure the shapes are the same.

Now use the cut-out pattern to mark the outline on the legs; refer to Step 1 on page 28. Since I was working with walnut, it was difficult to see a pencil line. Instead, I used a felt-tip marker to draw the pattern on the leg blank.

REFERENCE LINES. After the pattern is marked on the blank, use a square to mark a reference line right where the corner post meets the top of the knee; see Fig. 1.

Mark this line around all four faces of the leg. (These lines are used later when cutting the leg to shape and when gluing on the transition blocks; refer to Fig. 13 on page 24.)

MORTISES IN THE LEGS

Before cutting the legs to shape, the mortises are laid out. The mortises are marked on the two *inside* faces of the legs — the faces with the patterns marked on them.

However, because the mortise layout is different on the front legs and back legs, it helps to mark each leg to indicate the position it will be in when the table is assembled; refer to Fig. 6.

MORTISES ON BACK LEGS. The mortises on the *back* legs are the same on both faces — $1/4''$ wide by $3^3/4''$ long by $1^1/16''$ deep and centered $1^1/4''$ from the inside corner; see Fig. 2. This position (centered $1^1/4''$ from the corner) is such that there will be a small shoulder ($1/8''$ wide) between the face of the apron and the face of the corner post of the leg; see Fig. 5.

MORTISES ON FRONT LEGS. The mortises on the two *front* legs are a little trickier because the two mortises are different sizes and positioned differently. One side has a $3^3/4''$-long mortise for the side apron (that's positioned exactly the same as on the back legs); see Fig. 3.

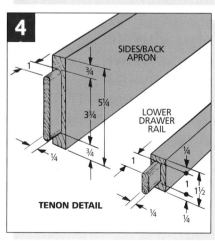

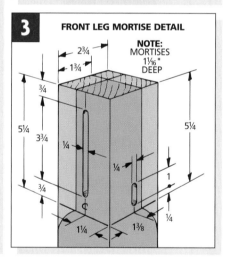

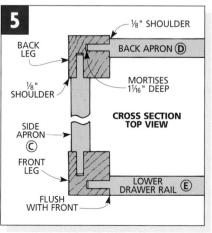

But the other side has a mortise only 1" long for the lower drawer rail (E); refer to Fig. 6. This mortise is also positioned differently — it's centered $1^3/8$" from the inside corner instead of $1^1/4$"; see Fig. 3. This way the rail will be flush with the corner post.

After the mortises were marked on all four legs, I drilled them out on a drill press by drilling a series of overlapping holes. Then I cleaned up the cheeks with a sharp chisel.

APRONS

When the mortises were complete, I proceeded to make the three aprons and the lower drawer rail out of $3/4$"-thick stock. The two side aprons (C) and the back apron (D) are all cut to a common width of $5^1/4$"; see Fig. 4.

Then the side aprons (C) are trimmed to a length of 20". This allows a shoulder-to-shoulder length of 18", and 2" for the two 1"-long tenons on each

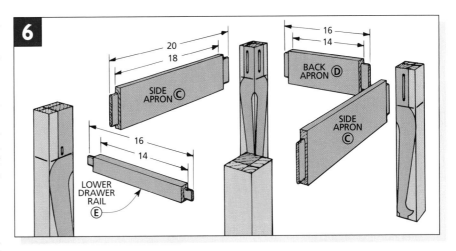

end; see Fig. 6. The back apron (D) is 16" long (with a shoulder-to-shoulder length of 14").

DRAWER RAIL. Next, the lower drawer rail (E) is cut $1^1/2$" wide and to a length of 16". This length should match the back apron (D); see Fig. 6.

TENONS. After all four pieces are cut to size, cut tenons centered on the ends

of each piece to fit the mortises in the legs; see Fig. 4.

When the tenons fit, dry-assemble the table and check to see that the top edges of the three aprons are flush with the top ends of the corner post. Also, the bottom edges of these aprons and the lower drawer rail should be aligned on the reference lines on the legs.

Squaring Up Leg Blanks

I used turning squares to make the cabriole legs. Though they're called turning *squares*, I've rarely seen one with two square (90°) faces over its entire length. The easiest way to square one up is with a jointer. But it can also be done on a table saw.

To cut the blanks square, I built a jig out of a couple pieces of scrap. The jig keeps the blank from rocking and twisting while it's being ripped.

To make the jig, nail a piece of hardboard at 90° to a scrap of $3/4$" stock. The hardboard should be about as long as the blank.

After the jig is nailed together, position the turning square in the *inside* corner of the jig and tack it in place; see Fig. 1. (Note: Tack toward the ends where the nail holes can be cut off when cutting out the leg profiles.)

Next I followed a sequence of four cuts until the four sides were 90° to one another. First, place the jig on the table saw with the jig against the rip fence; see Step 1 in Fig. 3.

Now set the fence so the blade will make a cut along face A. For a clean cut, I ripped this face in increments, raising the blade

slightly between passes.

A 10" blade can't be raised high enough to cut all the way through a 3" turning square. So I removed the square from the jig and planed down the extra lip; see Fig. 2.

Next, turn the square (Step 2), nail it to the jig, and adjust the rip fence to cut the next surface (B).

Once again make the cut in increments and plane it flat. At this point surfaces A and B should be square to one another.

To make the final two cuts, the jig won't be needed. Just set the rip fence for the finished width and cut surface C (Step 3) and finally surface D (Step 4).

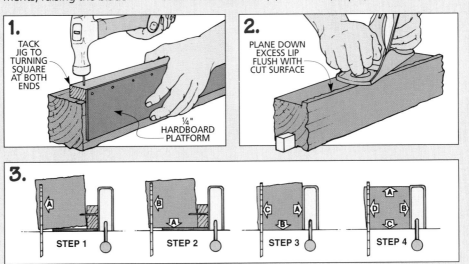

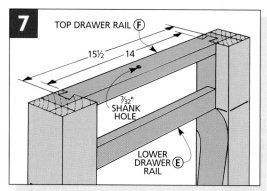

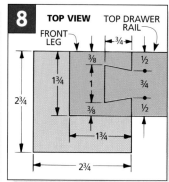

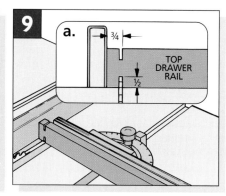

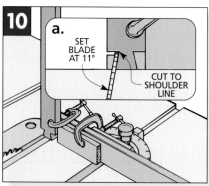

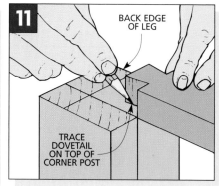

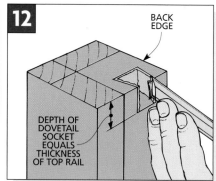

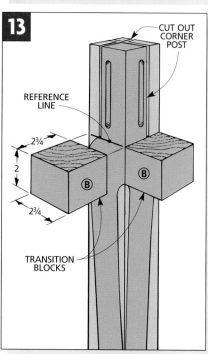

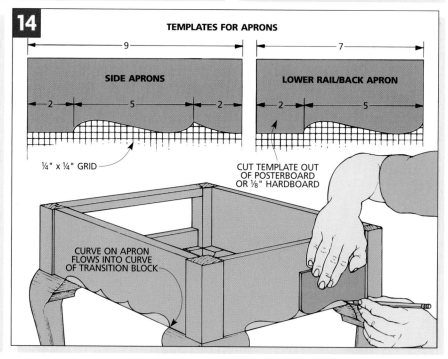

TOP DRAWER RAIL

There's one more rail to add to the table — the top drawer rail (F); see Fig. 7. It's mounted with a single dovetail joint.

Start by cutting the rail from $3/4$"-thick stock to a width of $1\,3/4$" and a length of $15\,1/2$"; see Figs. 7 and 8.

CUT DOVETAIL. To make the dovetail on a table saw, first make $1/2$"-deep shoulder cuts, $3/4$" in from both ends;

see Fig. 9. This will establish a shoulder-to-shoulder length of 14" (equal to the lower rail). Then, make 11° cuts with the rail on end; see Fig. 10.

CUT SOCKET. Now use the dovetail to mark the socket on the corner posts of the two front legs; see Fig. 11. Then chop out the socket; see Fig 12.

Also, drill a counterbored shank hole at the center of the rail; see Fig. 7. (It's the same size as the one in Fig. 15a.)

CABRIOLE LEGS

The basic parts of the table are complete, so now comes the fun part — cutting the cabriole legs to shape. (See the technique section starting on page 27.)

The procedure is to make the two face cuts for the corner posts first. Then glue the transition blocks (B) to the legs; see Fig. 13. Finally, cut and file the cabriole legs to shape.

SHAPE THE APRONS

After the legs are shaped, dry assemble the table to mark the curved pattern on the bottom of the aprons; see Fig. 14.

Position the pattern so the curve of the apron blends into the curve of the transition block on the leg. After the pattern is marked, remove the aprons and cut them to shape on a band saw.

ASSEMBLY. To assemble the table, I glued the side aprons to their corresponding legs first. Then I joined these units to the back apron and front rails.

DRAWER RUNNERS

When the table is assembled, drawer runners and kickers can be added.

KICKERS. First, kickers (H) are glued to the inside of the aprons. Cut them to length to fit between the front leg and the back apron; see Fig. 15.

Notch out the back end of the kicker to fit around the post. But before mounting it, drill oversized shank holes for the screws that hold the top in place; see Fig. 15a. (The oversized holes allow the top to expand/contract.)

RUNNERS. Next, cut the runners (I) to fit between the front rail and the back apron; see Fig. 15. Notch the ends to fit around the posts; see Step 1 in Fig. 16.

Also, rabbets are cut in the runners to guide the drawer; see Step 2. To prevent the drawer side from rubbing against the post, cut the rabbet so its shoulder sticks out a $^1/_{16}$" from the face of the corner post; see Fig. 17.

Now trim off the small sliver next to the front notch; see Step 3. Then screw (don't glue) the runner to the aprons so the bottom of the rabbet is flush with the lower drawer rail.

SCREW BLOCK. The last piece to add is a screw block centered on the top edge of the back apron; see Fig. 15.

DRAWER

The drawer is built the old-fashioned way: with half-blind dovetails on the front, and through dovetails on the back; see Fig. 18 and the Dovetail Detail on page 21. (Of course, other joinery could be used, but this might change the length of the drawer parts.)

FRONT. Start by cutting the drawer front (J) to size. To determine its length, measure the distance between the shoulders of the rabbets on the run-

ners, less $^1/_8$" (for clearance), plus $^3/_4$" (for the $^3/_8$"-wide lipped edges). The width is equal to the height of the opening, less $^1/_8$", plus $^3/_4$".

Now cut $^3/_8$" x $^3/_8$" rabbets on all four edges of the drawer front. Then the pins (sockets) of the dovetail can be cut. To complete the drawer front, rout a profile on the front face; see Fig. 18a.

SIDES. Next, cut the drawer sides (K) to size out of $^1/_2$"-thick stock. Then

cut dovetails on the ends to fit the sockets in the drawer front. Also, cut a groove for the $^1/_4$" plywood drawer bottom in the front and sides; see Fig. 18.

BACK. The drawer back (L) is joined to the sides with through dovetails. I also made a turnbutton to stick above the drawer back as a stop; see Fig. 18.

BOTTOM. Finally, glue the drawer together. Then cut the plywood bottom (M) to fit and slip it in place; see Fig. 18.

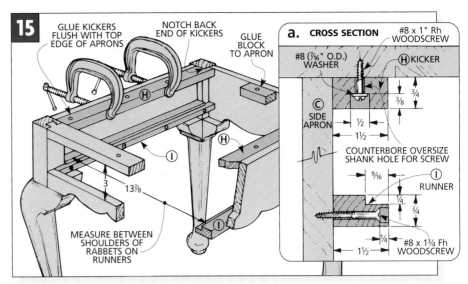

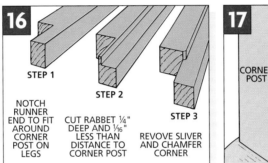

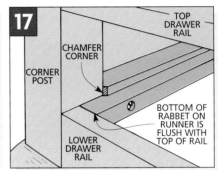

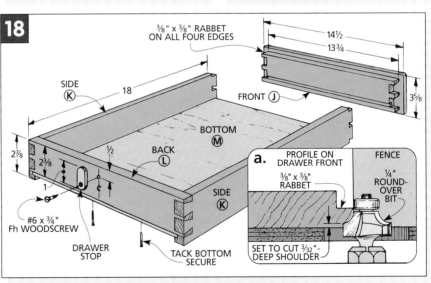

TABLE TOP

The table is complete now except for the top (G). To make the top, glue up ³⁄₄"-thick stock to get a blank that's roughly 21" by 25"; see Fig. 20.

Once the glue is dry on the blank, sand or plane both faces down so they're smooth and flat.

When it's flat, trim the blank to a final size of 20" wide by 24" long. (This produces a 1¼" lip on all four sides of the assembled table.)

PROFILE THE EDGES. After the table top was trimmed to final size, I cut the edge profiles.

Shop Note. It's best to cut the profiles immediately after planing the top smooth. If you wait overnight or a few days, the top will have a chance to warp. Even if the warp is very slight, it will cause problems when cutting the profiles to shape.

CHAMFER CUT. The first cut to make is a wide chamfer. To do this, tilt the saw blade to 11° and raise the height to 1"; see Fig. 21. Then adjust the fence so the saw blade cuts a chamfer that leaves a ³⁄₃₂" shoulder.

SQUARE SHOULDER CUT. After making the 11° chamfer cut on all four edges, reset the saw blade to 90° and lower the blade so it just barely cuts a square shoulder up to the chamfered surface; see Fig. 22.

ROUND THE EDGES. When the chamfer is complete, all four edges are rounded over with a ¼" roundover bit on a router table. First, round over the bottom edge; see Fig. 23.

Next, round over the chamfered edge; see Fig. 24. Sneak up on this cut raising the bit in small increments. What you're trying to do is round as much of the corner as possible without allowing the corner of the bit to hit the chamfered surface; see Fig. 24a. Then smooth the edge with sandpaper.

MOUNT THE TOP. When the top is complete, mount it to the table. First, remove the drawer runners so they're not in the way. Then, to ensure that the top is centered on the table, mark a centerline on the underside of the top and on the aprons and top drawer rail; see Fig. 25.

With the table centered on the top, drill pilot holes in the top, and temporarily screw the top in place with 1" roundhead screws. Then remove the screws so the table can be finished. ■

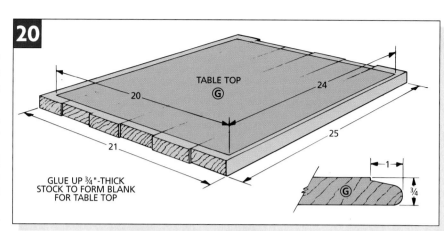

20

TABLE TOP
G

20   24

25

21

GLUE UP ³⁄₄"-THICK STOCK TO FORM BLANK FOR TABLE TOP

1

³⁄₄

G

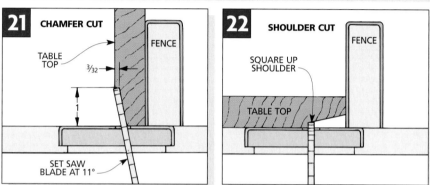

21   **CHAMFER CUT**

FENCE

TABLE TOP

³⁄₃₂

1

SET SAW BLADE AT 11°

22   **SHOULDER CUT**

FENCE

SQUARE UP SHOULDER

TABLE TOP

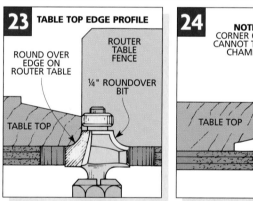

23   **TABLE TOP EDGE PROFILE**

ROUTER TABLE FENCE

ROUND OVER EDGE ON ROUTER TABLE

¼" ROUNDOVER BIT

TABLE TOP

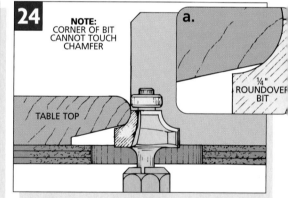

24

NOTE: CORNER OF BIT CANNOT TOUCH CHAMFER

a.

¼" ROUNDOVER BIT

TABLE TOP

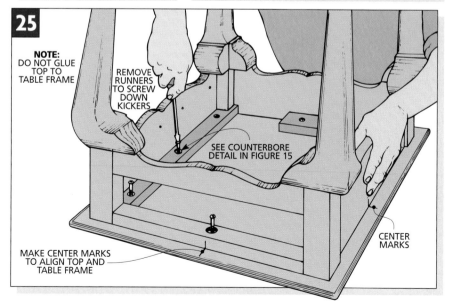

25

NOTE: DO NOT GLUE TOP TO TABLE FRAME

REMOVE RUNNERS TO SCREW DOWN KICKERS

SEE COUNTERBORE DETAIL IN FIGURE 15

MAKE CENTER MARKS TO ALIGN TOP AND TABLE FRAME

CENTER MARKS

It's easy to be convinced that making a cabriole leg is a form of sculpture — that you have to visualize the leg in a block of wood, then carve away everything that isn't a leg.

But the truth is that a cabriole leg almost evolves by itself. As an experiment, try gluing up some scraps of 2x4 to get a block with a rough size of 3"x3". Then draw the leg profile on two adjacent sides of this stock, and cut along the lines with the band saw.

When the waste falls away, you have the basic shape of a cabriole leg (as shown on the left in the photo). Okay, it's a little rough maybe — but all it takes from there is some filing and sanding to refine the shape of the leg.

LEG HEIGHT. One thing I particularly like about this method for making a cabriole leg is that you can use it no matter how tall the leg is. Sure, you will need a different pattern for the taller legs on a dining table than you would for an end table or a footstool. But the steps to make the leg are the same. The section between the knee and the ankle is just "stretched" out for a taller leg.

(Note: You might have noticed that the photo above and the drawings on the next few pages are for a *shorter* leg than is needed on the end table in this book. It was easier to clearly show the steps in the drawings on a shorter leg. Again, the procedure is the same no matter the length.)

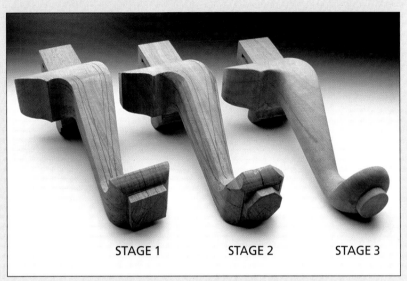

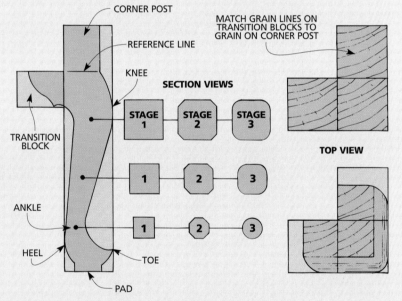

There are three steps in making a cabriole leg. In Stage 1 the blank is cut on the band saw to its basic shape. Next, in Stage 2 the corners are filed off. Finally, the corners are rounded over and the leg sanded smooth in Stage 3.

START WITH A BLANK. Basically, a cabriole leg starts out as a square piece of stock. Depending on the pattern you're using, this blank is usually a 3"x 3" square.

To get a blank this size, you can glue four pieces of 3/4"-thick stock together. However, the glue lines will show when the leg is formed. Also, because of changes in the grain patterns, there may be some problems during the shaping process. What works much better is to use a 3"x3" "turning" square (the kind used for turning on the lathe). If you can't find them locally, they're available through mail order catalogs; see page 95. I buy the squares extra long, so I can also cut transition blocks from the blank.

EARLY WORK. Even before any cutting starts, there is some preparatory work to be done. Usually, there are mortises that have to be cut in the blank to attach aprons or rails that run between the cabriole legs.

Also, the curved transition blocks are glued in place.

STAGE ONE. Once all of the preliminary work is completed, the blank goes through three stages to become the finished leg. First, the leg is bandsawn to basic shape. (This is shown on the left in the photo.)

Although the leg has a lot of curves at this point, the cross sections at various points along the leg are all squares. (This is shown in the three Section Views labeled "Stage 1" in the diagram at left.)

SECOND STAGE. In the second stage, the corners of the squares are filed or rasped to a 45° angle to give the leg an eight-sided cross section; see Section Views labeled "Stage 2".

THIRD STAGE. In the third stage, the corners are rounded to produce the final shape of the leg. In its finished form, the ankle cross section is a circle and the cross sections at other points are squares with their corners rounded to the same radius as at the ankle.

Although it certainly doesn't look like it, all you're really doing is making a square leg with rounded corners.

Cabriole Legs . . . *Step-by-Step*

The process of making a cabriole leg should always start with a good squared-up blank. If you're using a rough turning square, you may want to follow the procedure shown in the box on page 23 for squaring it up.

Once the blank is squared up, the next step is to make a full-size pattern of the cross section of the leg. (I like to cut the pattern out of hardboard.) The same pattern is used for laying out two adjacent faces of the leg (Step 1).

CUT MORTISES. After the pattern is drawn on the blank and reference lines for the corner post (Step 2), mortises for aprons are cut in the two sides of the blank marked with the patterns. I cut the mortises on the drill press (Step 3).

CUT CORNER POSTS. Next, two cuts are made to form the faces of the corner post (Step 4).

TRANSITION PIECES. Here I break with tradition. The method traditonally shown is to cut the legs first and glue on

the transition blocks later. I've found that gluing curved transition blocks to a curved leg is very awkward. Instead, I glue square transition blocks to the square legs (Step 5) and then bandsaw the whole thing to final shape at once.

Note: For the best appearance, turn the blocks so the end grain on the blocks looks like it flows into the end grain on the leg; see Top View on page 27.

FINAL LAYOUT. The final steps before cutting are to lay out cuts on the

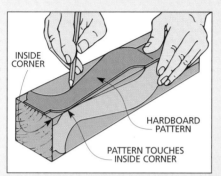

1 To draw the leg pattern, position template so back edge of corner post and heel align with inside corner of stock. Flip template and repeat on adjacent side.

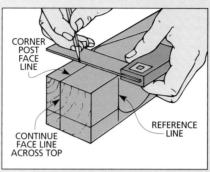

2 Draw reference lines around all four sides where the corner post meets knee. Also draw lines on top end that continue the face lines of the corner post.

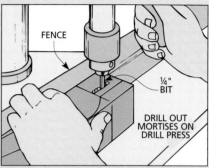

3 Cut mortises on two faces of the corner post. Drill a series of overlapping holes to rough out the mortise. Then clean up cheeks with a sharp chisel.

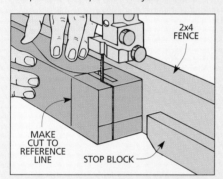

4 Set up band saw to make the face cuts on the corner post. Use a fence to guide the leg and clamp a stop block to the fence to stop the cut at reference line.

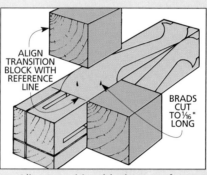

5 Align transition blocks on reference lines and glue and clamp in place. To keep block from shifting when clamped, drive in brads and cut off to 1/16" long.

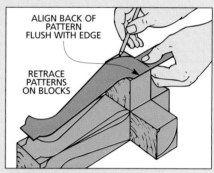

6 Trace the curve of the knee on the outer surfaces of the transition blocks. The reference line on the pattern should align with the top of the transition block.

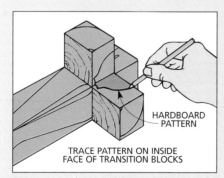

7 A second pattern is used to trace the profile on the inner surface of the transition blocks. Place the small pattern tight in the corner and mark outline.

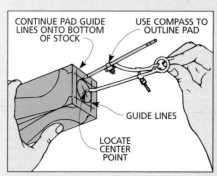

8 Use a square to draw lines across the bottom of the leg that continue the outline of the pad. Then use a compass to draw a circle that fits inside the square.

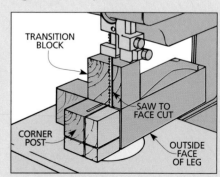

9 Start sawing at the corner post by aligning blade with top of transition block. Saw to the cut made in Step 4. Repeat the cut on the adjacent face.

transition blocks (Steps 6, 7) and the pad at the bottom of the leg (Step 8).

BANDSAW TO SHAPE. The cutting begins at the corner post (Step 9). After the corner post is sawed to shape, saw the profile of the knee (Step 10).

From this point on, save all the scraps that fall away while sawing. These are needed to cut the profile on the adjacent surface.

Now cut from the knee down to the foot (Step 11). Next, the bottom of the foot and the pad are sawn in two steps. First make a short, straight cut on the bottom end of the blank to define the front side of the pad. Then cut the curved part on the bottom of the foot by starting at the point of the toe and sawing down to the cut just made to define the pad.

Once the *front* face of the leg is cut, the whole process is repeated to cut the *back* face (Step 12).

Now all of the scraps can be put back in place (I use carpet tape or hot-melt glue), and the profiles cut on the adjacent face (Step 13). Finally remove the taped-on scraps (Step 14).

FLATTEN THE SURFACES. The band saw will leave some bumps, so the next step is to smooth these out with a spokeshave or rasp (Step 15). The section between the knee and the ankle should be worked until it's flat (Step 16). Then the curved sections can be smoothed with a plane and file (Steps 17, 18).

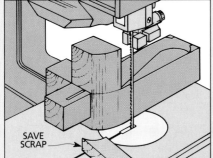

10 *Cut top of knee and transition block with blade guide raised. Saw from tip of knee back to corner post. Be careful not to nick corner post.*

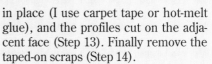
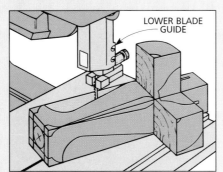

11 *Saw from knee to foot to remove waste on front of leg. Lower blade guide as soon as it clears transition block. Be sure to save waste pieces.*

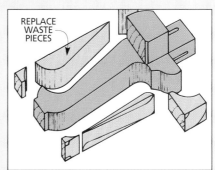

12 *The cut-away pieces are needed to support the leg blank in the next step. Use carpet tape to fasten cut-away pieces back in their original positions.*

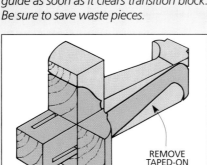

13 *After pieces are taped on, cut out the adjacent profile by flipping the workpiece and sawing along lines. Work in any direction that feels comfortable.*

14 *Remove the taped-on pieces to reveal basic shape of a cabriole leg. Complete each leg to this point before proceeding so scraps don't get mixed up.*

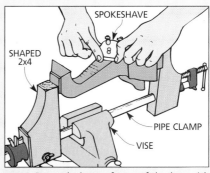

15 *Smooth the surfaces of the leg with a spokeshave or rasp. To hold the leg while working, mount it in a carver's cradle made from pipe clamp and 2x4's.*

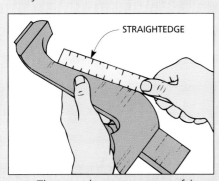

16 *The area between curve of knee and curve of ankle should be a straight line. Use a straightedge to check progress on all four sides of leg.*

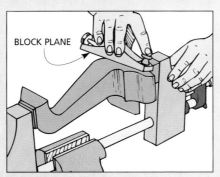

17 *To smooth the leg, use whatever tools seem to do the job best. With a sharp block plane, plane carefully across the grain to smooth outside of the knee.*

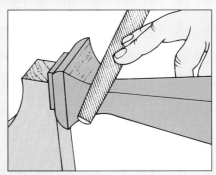

18 *Remove the marks left by the band saw and smooth the inside contour of the ankle with the rounded side of a rasp or wood file.*

Cabriole Legs . . . *Step-by-Step*

At this point the leg has been smoothed, but it's still square. The next step is to knock off all the corners at 45°.

LAYOUT LINES. To do this, first draw layout lines to mark the limits of how much is to be removed on each corner. Start by dividing the ankle into quarters (Step 19). Then draw centerpoint lines (Step 20) and quarterpoint lines (Step 21) up each leg.

CHANGE CROSS SECTION. The next step is to take the leg from a square leg to an eight-sided leg. This is simply a matter of removing the corners at 45° to create a flat surface down to the quarterpoint layout lines.

Start on the front of the leg, removing the corners of the straight "shin." I'm most comfortable using a spokeshave on these sections (Step 22), but I will switch to a rasp or file when working around the curved areas (Steps 23, 24). On these curved areas, taper the corners so they end in a point.

The back of the leg is shaped like the front and also comes to a point (Step 25). The sides are also similar, but stop the taper where the transition block begins (Step 26).

FOOT. Now you can switch your attention to the bottom of the foot. Start by marking each side of the foot into quarters. Then cut off the front and side corners between the marks (Step 27).

After the foot is shaped, the pad is also cut to an eight-sided shape. First

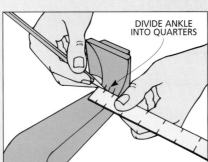

19 *Divide the narrowest part of the ankle into quarters. These marks position the layout lines used when shaping the square to its final contour.*

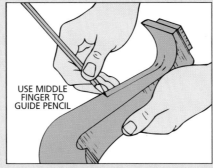

20 *Draw layout lines on both sides of each corner by marking lines from the centerpoints on the ankle. Use middle finger to maintain distance from edge.*

21 *Draw another set of layout lines extending from quarterpoint marks on the ankle. Again, draw two lines on each corner from knee to the ankle.*

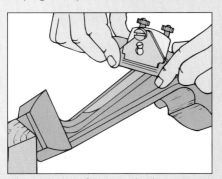

22 *To start forming the leg, remove the corners on the straight parts down to the quarterpoint layout lines. A spokeshave or flat side of a rasp works.*

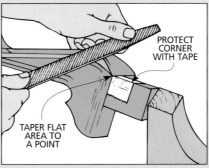

23 *Continue the flattened corner over the top of the knee so it forms a point at the corner post. Protect corner post with several layers of duct tape.*

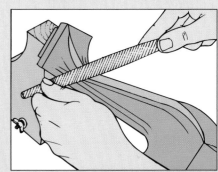

24 *Flatten corner of the front of the ankle with the rounded side of the rasp. Continue this surface over the top of the foot to form a point almost to the toe.*

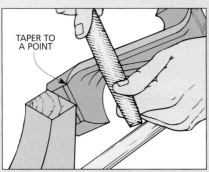

25 *Use a rasp or file to blend the flattened corner on the back of the leg down over the heel. This surface tapers to a point where the heel meets the pad.*

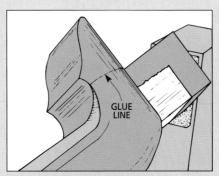

26 *At the top of the leg, shape the inside corners on the back of the knee to a tapered point that ends about where the transition block begins.*

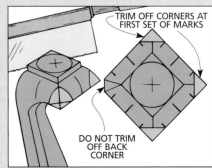

27 *Divide the bottom of the foot into quarters. Then use these marks to cut off the front corner and both side corners. Don't cut off the corner at the heel.*

undercut the four corners, then remove the corners by sawing down to the undercuts (Step 28).

FINAL SHAPING. Now that the entire leg has eight flat surfaces, the shaping can begin. This is just a process of rounding over all the corners.

Start by rounding over the pad until it's a circle (Step 29). Then move on to the foot using the edge of the pad as a visual guide (Step 30). The edge of the pad and the edge of the foot should be two concentric circles, but the foot doesn't get rounded at the heel.

Next rasp the high spots on the bottom of the foot (Step 31). Then finish off by contouring the heel (Step 32).

ROUND THE LEG. With the foot done, you can move back to the upper part of the leg. Rounding these areas is just a matter of filing from the center-point layout lines and blending the corner into a smooth arc (Step 33, 34).

Now the *top* of the foot can be brought to its final shape. To do this, file the ridge on the top of the foot to get a nice smooth curve from the ankle to the perimeter of the foot (Step 35).

The last rounding to do is to ease over the top of the transition block so it flows into the apron (Step 36).

SANDING. Once everything has been filed to final shape, it's just a matter of sanding the whole leg. The only way to make this easier is to talk someone else into doing it.

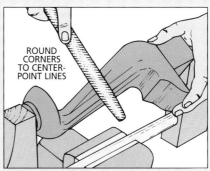

CUT OFF CORNERS OF PAD SQUARE TO FORM OCTAGON

28 To shape the pad, undercut the four corners first. Then, use the edge of the circle as a guide and cut down to the undercuts to remove corners.

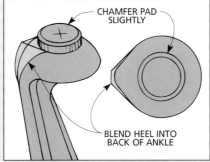

SHAPE PAD INTO CIRCLE

29 Use the flat side of a rasp or file to round the pad to the edge of the traced circle. Be careful not to score the bottom of the foot with the rasp edge.

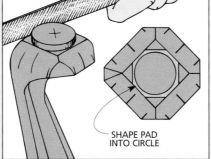

DO NOT ROUND OVER HEEL

ROUND PERIMETER FROM MARK TO MARK

30 Shape the perimeter of the foot from mid-point to mid-point to form a circle that's concentric with edge of pad. Do not round over area at heel.

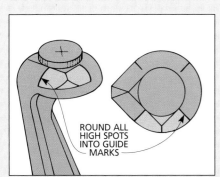

ROUND ALL HIGH SPOTS INTO GUIDE MARKS

31 Shape the bottom of the front so it curves from the pad up to the edge of the foot. Don't rasp over guide marks until the high spots have been smoothed.

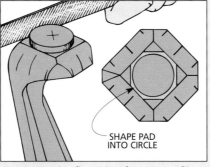

CHAMFER PAD SLIGHTLY

BLEND HEEL INTO BACK OF ANKLE

32 Shape back of the heel by continuing the curve on the foot bottom and blending it into the back of ankle. Also, chamfer pad to prevent chipping.

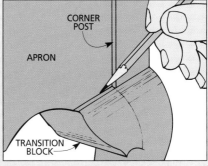

ROUND CORNERS TO CENTER-POINT LINES

33 Final shaping of the main part of the leg and the knee is just a matter of rounding over the corners. Use the centerpoint layout lines as a guide.

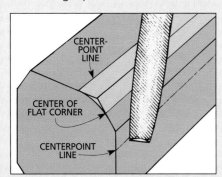

CENTER-POINT LINE

CENTER OF FLAT CORNER

CENTERPOINT LINE

34 To shape the corners, work from the centerpoint layout lines on one side to center of the flat area. Complete the arc by working from the other side.

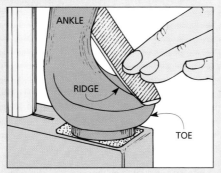

ANKLE

RIDGE

TOE

35 Complete the foot by standing the leg upright. Use a file to smooth the ridge that extends from the ankle, blending curve of the ankle into the foot.

CORNER POST

APRON

TRANSITION BLOCK

36 Temporarily put apron in place and trace edge on transition block. Then remove apron and use a chisel to round transition block to marked line.

DINING TABLE

Beneath the top of this table there are two extension wings. But wait a minute . . . how do those extensions actually work?

The biggest problem with this table is trying to explain how it works. I had such a hard time explaining the design to everyone, that I finally went to the shop and just built it.

When I finished, everyone said, "That's nice, but I thought you said this table had leaves?" I couldn't resist showing off a little; I simply lifted one end of the free floating top and pulled the leaf from *under* the table. I didn't even get a chance to pull out the other leaf before someone lifted the table top off to see how it worked.

HOW IT WORKS. On most extension tables the table top is cut in half and

each half is attached to some sort of runners. To extend the table you pull the halves apart and the leaves drop in — on top of the runners.

With this table the *leaves* are attached to the runners. When you want to extend the table, lift up one end of the top and pull out a leaf. When the leaf is fully extended the top drops down and rests on top of the runners.

WOOD. I built the legs and main parts of the table with solid red oak. The top and the leaves were cut from a single sheet of ³/₄" oak plywood. To make the grain of the top match up with the leaves, I laid out my cuts as if the

leaves were part of the top; see drawing to the left of the Exploded View.

Since the leaves fit under the table top (when stored), they are slightly smaller (narrower) than the top.

THE LEGS. One other interesting feature is the legs. They're mounted so they stand at a 45° angle to the aprons. They're held to the aprons with corner blocks and hanger bolts. This makes the legs removable and they can also be easily tightened up with a wrench if they loosen over time.

FINISH. To provide the table with extra protection I used two coats of polyurethane, sanding between coats.

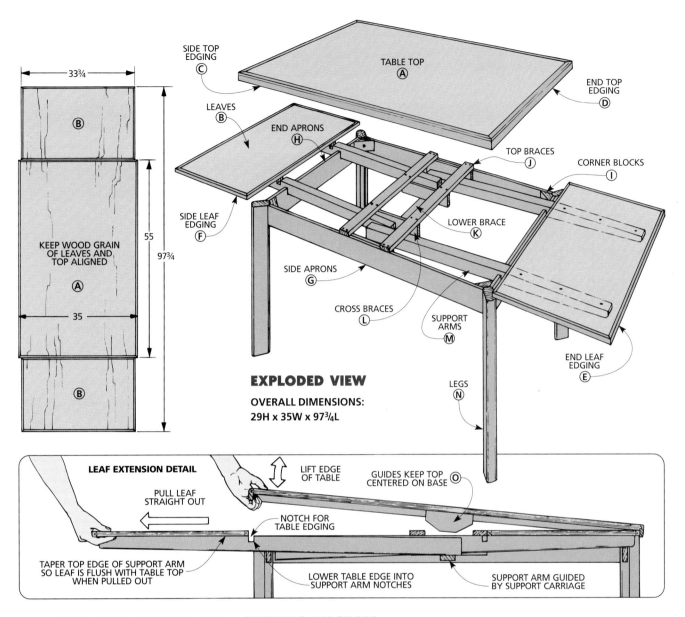

33¾

B

35

KEEP WOOD GRAIN OF LEAVES AND TOP ALIGNED

A

55

97¾

B

SIDE TOP EDGING
C

TABLE TOP
A

END TOP EDGING
D

LEAVES
B

END APRONS
H

TOP BRACES
J

CORNER BLOCKS
I

SIDE LEAF EDGING
F

LOWER BRACE
K

SIDE APRONS
G

CROSS BRACES
L

SUPPORT ARMS
M

END LEAF EDGING
E

LEGS
N

EXPLODED VIEW

OVERALL DIMENSIONS:
29H x 35W x 97¾L

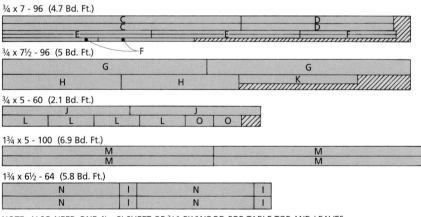

LEAF EXTENSION DETAIL

LIFT EDGE OF TABLE

GUIDES KEEP TOP CENTERED ON BASE **O**

PULL LEAF STRAIGHT OUT

NOTCH FOR TABLE EDGING

TAPER TOP EDGE OF SUPPORT ARM SO LEAF IS FLUSH WITH TABLE TOP WHEN PULLED OUT

LOWER TABLE EDGE INTO SUPPORT ARM NOTCHES

SUPPORT ARM GUIDED BY SUPPORT CARRIAGE

MATERIALS LIST

WOOD

A	Top (1)	¾ ply. - 34¼ x 54¼
B	Leaves (2)	¾ ply. - 33 x 20⅝
C	Side Top Edging (2)	½ x 1⅝ - 56 rough
D	End Top Edging (2)	½ x 1⅝ - 36 rough
E	End Lf. Edging (4)	½ x ⅞ - 35 rough
F	Side Lf. Edging (4)	½ x ⅞ - 22½ rough
G	Side Aprons (2)	¾ x 3½ - 47¾
H	End Aprons (2)	¾ x 3½ - 27¾
I	Corner Blocks (4)	1¾ x 3 - 4
J	Top Braces (2)	¾ x 2 - 29¾
K	Lower Brace (1)	¾ x 2 - 28¼
L	Cross Braces (4)	¾ x 2½ - 10¾
M	Support Arms (4)	1¾ x 2¼ - 49½
N	Legs (4)	1¾ x 3 - 27½
O	Guides (2)	¾ x 2½ - 6⅝

HARDWARE SUPPLIES

(32) No. 8 x 1¼" Fh woodscrews
(12) No. 8 x 1½" Fh woodscrews
(4) ⅜"-16 x 5" Hanger bolts
(4) ⅜" (I.D.) Washers
(4) ⅜" Nuts

CUTTING DIAGRAM

¾ x 7 - 96 (4.7 Bd. Ft.)

C   D
C   D
E   I   F
F

¾ x 7½ - 96 (5 Bd. Ft.)

G   G
H   H   K

¾ x 5 - 60 (2.1 Bd. Ft.)

J   J
L   L   L   L   O   O

1¾ x 5 - 100 (6.9 Bd. Ft.)

M   M
M   M

1¾ x 6½ - 64 (5.8 Bd. Ft.)

N   N
N   N
I   I   I   I

NOTE: ALSO NEED ONE 4' x 8' SHEET OF ¾" PLYWOOD FOR TABLE TOP AND LEAVES

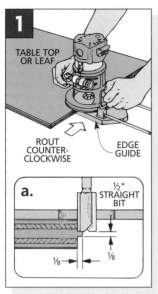

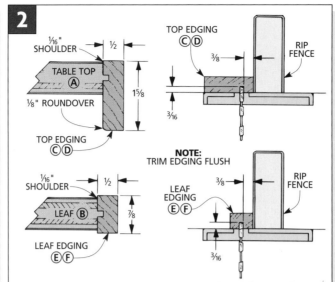

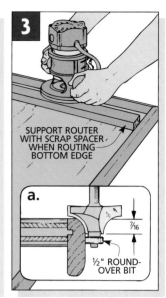

TOP AND LEAVES

The table begins by making the top and the two leaves. They're simply pieces of $3/4$" oak plywood framed with $1/2$"-thick solid stock.

LAY OUT PIECES. I started laying out the plywood by doing a little planning. Since I wanted the grain to flow from one end of the table to the other, the piece for the top (A) had to be cut from *between* the two pieces for the leaves (B); again, refer to the drawing to the left of the Exploded View on page 33.

CUT TO SIZE. So begin by ripping a $34 1/4$"-wide piece off the 4x8 sheet of plywood. (Note: The finished table top is 35" wide, but it's cut $3/4$" less to allow for the edging and joinery.)

Then cut a $54 1/4$"-long piece for the top (A) from the *exact middle* of the workpiece. And cut the two leftover end pieces $20 5/8$" long for the leaves (B).

Finally, trim $5/8$" off both edges of each leaf so the leaves will end up $1 1/4$" less in width (33") than the top. (Note: I trimmed some off *both* edges so the grain will stay aligned with the grain on the top when the leaves are extended.)

ROUT TONGUE. The edging pieces are attached to the plywood with tongue and groove joinery. So I routed a tongue on all the edges of each plywood piece. To do this, mount an edge guide and $1/2$" straight bit in the router; see Fig. 1. Then rout a rabbet on the top and bottom faces of the plywood to produce a $1/8$"-thick tongue; see Fig. la.

EDGING. After the tongue is routed, you can cut the four top edging pieces (C,D). These pieces are resawn to $1/2$"

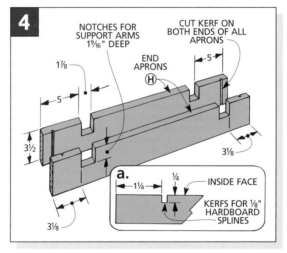

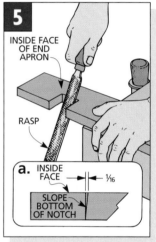

thick and then ripped to $1 5/8$" wide; see Fig. 2. They're cut to rough length about 2" longer than the sides and ends of the top. Also cut the eight $7/8$"-wide leaf edging pieces (E,F); see Fig. 2.

GROOVE IN EDGING. The edging is joined to the plywood pieces by cutting a $1/8$"-wide groove (to match the tongue) on the inside face of each piece; see Fig. 2. Position the groove so when the edging is mounted, the top edge sticks up about $1/16$" above the top face of the plywood. (It's trimmed flush later.)

ROUND INSIDE EDGE. Before mounting the top edging pieces (C,D), I also softened the *inside* bottom edge by rounding it over with a $1/8$" roundover bit; see Fig. 2.

APPLY EDGING. Now the edging can be glued and clamped to the plywood. Miter the ends of the top edging pieces (C,D) and glue them to the table top (A). (Shop Note: If you don't have long enough clamps, try taping the edging

tight while the glue dries. I used filament packaging tape that is strong and won't stretch.) Also miter and glue the leaf edging (E,F) to the leaves (B).

When the glue is dry, trim the edging flush with the plywood. (I used a flush trim bit in the router.) The edging on the leaves (B) is trimmed flush with both the top and the bottom faces.

ROUND OVER EDGING. To complete the edging on the top, use a $1/2$" roundover bit and rout the outside top and bottom edges; see Fig. 3. On the leaves, use a $1/8$" roundover bit.

APRONS

The next phase is to make the four aprons that hold the legs together. The side aprons (G) are very easy — just cut two pieces of $3/4$"-thick stock $3 1/2$" wide by $47 3/4$" long; refer to Fig. 11. The end aprons (H) are also $3 1/2$" wide, but only $27 3/4$" long.

NOTCH END APRONS. After the end aprons are cut to length, the next step is to lay out the location of two notches; see Fig. 4. These notches allow the leaf supports to be pulled out; refer to the Exploded View on page 33.

The notches in each end apron are in different positions so that the leaf supports will bypass each other under the table. To make the notches, raise the blade on the table saw to cut $1\frac{9}{16}$" deep. Then make repetitive passes to waste out the notches.

After the notches have been cut, use a rasp to form a slight bevel on the bottom of all four notches; see Fig. 5. This bevel should slope toward the *inside* face of the end aprons so the leaf support arms will smoothly pull out from under the table.

KERFS FOR SPLINES. To complete the aprons, kerfs are cut at both ends of *all four* aprons. These kerfs match up with kerfs in the corner blocks (I) so splines can be used to align the aprons to the corner blocks. Cut these kerfs $1\frac{1}{4}$" from the end of each apron, $\frac{1}{4}$" deep; see Fig. 4a.

CORNER BLOCKS

The table aprons are held together at each corner with a corner block (I); refer to Fig. 11.

CUT THE BLOCKS. Since the corner blocks are cut from the same $1\frac{3}{4}$"-thick stock as the legs (N), I made the leg blanks longer than needed and cut a corner block (I) off the end of each leg blank; refer to the Cutting Diagram on page 33. To do this, start by cutting four leg blanks from $1\frac{3}{4}$"-thick stock. Cut the blanks to a width of 3" and $31\frac{3}{4}$" long.

Then, to make the corner blocks, set the saw blade at 45° and cut a bevel off one end of each leg blank; see Fig. 6. Now turn the leg blank over and cut it again to form a triangular-shaped piece so one corner has a $\frac{1}{2}$"-wide flat face; see Fig. 6a.

KERF THE BLOCKS. The corner blocks are kerfed to accept $\frac{1}{8}$" hardboard splines. These splines align the corner blocks to the kerfs in the aprons.

Start by positioning the saw fence $1\frac{1}{2}$" from the blade, and setting the blade height to $\frac{1}{4}$"; see Fig. 7a. Then

cut a kerf in both beveled sides of the corner blocks; see Fig. 7. Note: The kerfs in the aprons are only $1\frac{1}{4}$" from the end of the apron so the corner block is set back a little from the ends of the aprons; refer to Fig. 8a.

SHANK HOLE. Later, the legs are mounted to the corner blocks with hanger bolts. To prepare for mounting these bolts, drill a $\frac{3}{8}$"-dia. shank hole through the corner block. I drilled the hole on my drill press, centering it on the inside face of the block; see Fig. 8.

ASSEMBLE THE APRONS. Now the aprons can be assembled by gluing the corner blocks in place (using $\frac{1}{8}$" hardboard splines) flush with the top edge of the aprons; see Figs. 8a and 11.

Shop Note: To keep the corners square, I made some special clamping blocks. The purpose of the blocks is to provide a surface that is parallel to the corner block so you can use a C-clamp; see Fig. 10. I made the clamping blocks from scrap 2x4 and cut them to shape with a band saw; see Fig. 9. The relief area directs the pressure directly over the splines; see Fig. 10a.

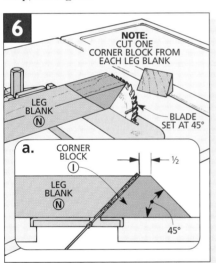

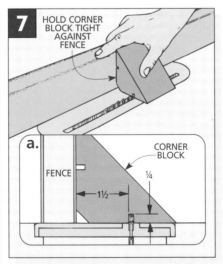

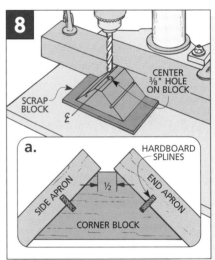

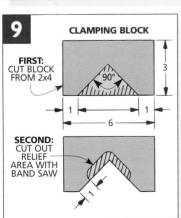

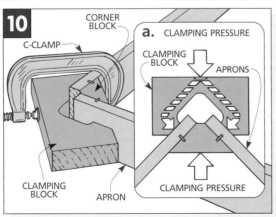

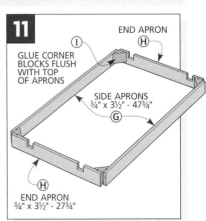

LEGS

The next step is to cut and shape the legs (N). First, cut them to a finished length of 27½".

CHAMFER THE LEGS. The inside edges of each leg (N) are chamfered so the leg can butt up against the aprons at a 45° angle.

Begin by setting the saw blade to 45° and positioning the rip fence 1" from the blade; see Fig. 12a. Now, cut a chamfer on one edge, then turn the piece around and chamfer the other edge. This should leave a ¼"-wide flat on the inside face of the leg; see the Cross Section in Fig. 12.

ROUND THE EDGES. After the legs are chamfered, I routed both *outside* edges with a ½" roundover bit in the router table; see Fig. 12b.

DRILL PILOT HOLES. The legs are joined to the corner blocks with ⅜"-dia. hanger bolts. To do this, drill a pilot hole 1½" down from the top and centered on the ¼" flat on the inside face of the leg; see Fig. 13.

ASSEMBLY. Now, the table base can be assembled. First, screw a hanger bolt into each leg; see tip box below. Then fit the hanger bolt through the hole in the corner block and tighten on a washer and nut; see Fig. 14.

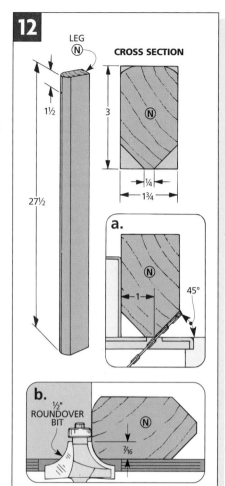

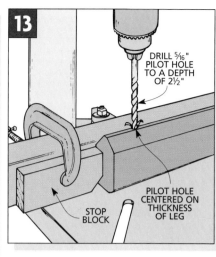

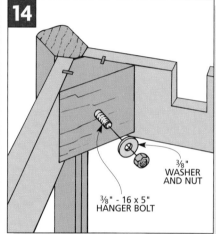

Hanger Bolts

The dining table uses virtually no hardware. In fact, the only metal pieces in the table are a few wood-screws and four hanger bolts. A hanger bolt has threads like a lag screw on one end and machine threads on the other end; see Fig. 1.

Hanger bolts come in a variety of sizes, and for the dining table I used one of the largest (⅜"-16 x 5").

You could use a lag screw to attach the leg to the corner block on the table, but I used a hanger bolt for two reasons. First, the machine thread end of the bolt allows you to easily remove the nut, and

then remove the leg. That's handy if you're moving or have to replace or repair the leg.

The other benefit to a hanger bolt is that if the leg becomes loose you can tighten up the nut.

To screw in a hanger bolt I start by turning two nuts onto the bolt until the top nut is flush with the end.

After the nuts are tight against each other, place a socket wrench over the top nut only and tighten the

hanger bolt into the leg; see Fig. 2.

Then remove the nuts and fit the hanger bolt through the corner block and tighten a washer and nut up tight against the block; see Fig. 14 above.

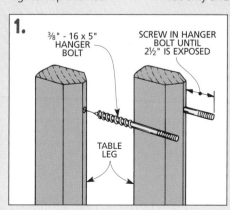

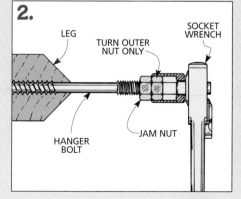

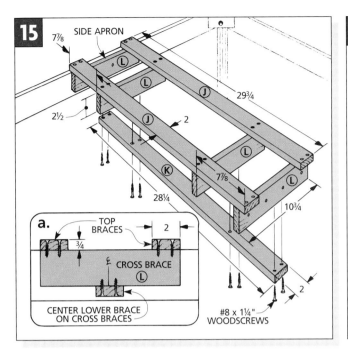

15 SIDE APRON
7⅞
2½
L
L
J
J
2
29¾
K
7⅞
28¼
L
L
10¾
2
2
#8 x 1¼"
WOODSCREWS

a. TOP BRACES
2
¾
CROSS BRACE
L
CENTER LOWER BRACE
ON CROSS BRACES

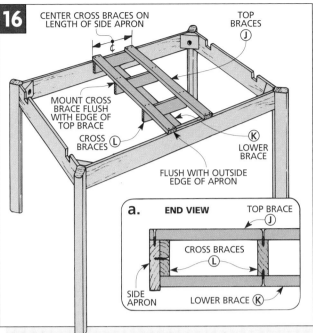

16 CENTER CROSS BRACES ON LENGTH OF SIDE APRON
TOP BRACES
J
MOUNT CROSS BRACE FLUSH WITH EDGE OF TOP BRACE
CROSS BRACES
L
K
LOWER BRACE
FLUSH WITH OUTSIDE EDGE OF APRON

a. END VIEW
TOP BRACE
J
CROSS BRACES
L
SIDE APRON
LOWER BRACE
K

SUPPORT ARM CARRIAGE

With the legs attached to the aprons, I started working on the support carriage that guides the support arms.

CUT PIECES TO SIZE. All the pieces for the carriage are made from ¾"-thick stock. Start by cutting four cross braces (L) 2½" wide by 10¾" long; see Fig. 15. Next, cut two top braces (J) 2" wide by 29¾" long. Then cut a lower brace (K) 2" wide by 28¼" long.

ATTACH CROSS BRACES. When all the pieces are cut to size, screw two of the cross braces (L) to the inside faces of the side aprons; see Fig. 15. Center the brace on the length of the apron and screw it to the apron so the top edges are flush; see Fig. 16a.

LOWER BRACE. With the cross braces attached, turn the table over and

screw the lower brace (K) to the center of the cross braces (L); see Fig. 15a.

TOP BRACES. Now turn the table back upright and screw the two top braces (J) to the top of the aprons. They should be flush with the outside of the aprons and their edges flush with the ends of the cross braces (L); see Fig. 16.

Next, slide the remaining two cross braces between the top braces and the lower brace and screw them in place.

SUPPORT ARMS

The four support arms (M) are the key to making this table work. Since I wanted the leaves to slide up to be level with the main top, I tapered the top edge of each arm so that the leaves are level with the top when extended.

CUT THE BLANKS. To make the sup-

port arms (M) begin by cutting 1¾"-thick stock, 2¼" wide by 49½" long; see Fig. 17.

CUT NOTCHES. The top edge of each arm is notched so the edging (D) on the table top can fit into it. Locate the 1"-deep notches 20½" in from the end of the support arms; see Fig. 17. To cut the notch, use the same method as on the aprons, but leave the bottom flat.

TAPER SUPPORT ARMS. After cutting the notch, lay out the taper on the *top* edge of each support arm; see Fig. 17. I cut it slightly oversize on the band saw (Fig. 18) and then planed it smooth with a hand plane.

SOFTEN THE END. Next, file the bottom corner of each arm to a ¾" radius; see Fig. 17. Then finish the supports by routing a ⅛" roundover on both bottom edges.

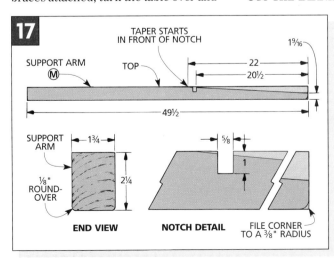

17 TAPER STARTS IN FRONT OF NOTCH
1⁹⁄₁₆
SUPPORT ARM
M
TOP
22
20½
49½
SUPPORT ARM
1¾
⅛" ROUND-OVER
2¼
⅝
1
END VIEW
NOTCH DETAIL
FILE CORNER TO A ⅜" RADIUS

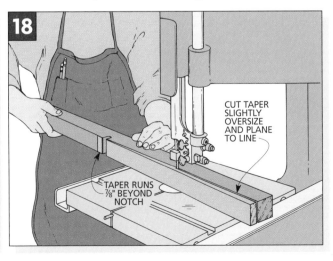

18 CUT TAPER SLIGHTLY OVERSIZE AND PLANE TO LINE
TAPER RUNS ⅞" BEYOND NOTCH

ATTACHING THE LEAVES

Once the tapers have been cut on the four support arms, screw holes are drilled on the bottom side of each arm so the support arm can be screwed to the leaves.

DRILLING THE ARMS. Begin by locating three shank holes on the bottom side of each support arm. The first hole is $2\frac{1}{2}$" from the narrow end, and then two more holes are $8\frac{1}{2}$" apart; see Fig. 19.

With the hole locations marked, place the tapered side of the support arm face *down* on the drill press table. Now, at the marked locations, drill $\frac{3}{8}$" holes centered on the thickness of each arm for the counterbore so the screws can reach up into the leaf.

Shop Note: To get the correct counterbore depth, set the depth stop on the drill press so the bottom of the bit stops 1" from the table; see Fig. 19.

Once the counterbores are complete drill the rest of the way through with a $\frac{3}{16}$" bit for the shank holes.

POSITION THE LEAVES. After the holes are counterbored, the leaves are positioned on the support arms. Begin by putting the arms in place in the table, so that the inside of the notches in the arms are flush with the outside edge of the apron; see Fig. 20a.

Next place a leaf on top of the arms so the inside edge of the leaf is flush with the outside edge of the notches.

ATTACH THE LEAVES. Now, adjust the leaf so it's centered on the support arms. Using No. 8 x $1\frac{1}{2}$" woodscrews, attach the leaf to the support arm at the deepest counterbores only. This allows for adjusting the arm.

With the leaf in place, slide it all the way into the table. Now, adjust the tapered end of the arm so it's centered in the apron notch; see Fig. 20b. With the arm centered, reach under the table and screw in the rest of the screws through the arms and into the leaves.

TOP GUIDES

Now that the leaves have been attached to the support arms, the last step on the table is to attach two guides (0) to the bottom of the table top. These guides are what keep the table top from moving around.

CUT TO SIZE. Beginning with $\frac{3}{4}$"-thick stock, cut two pieces $2\frac{1}{2}$" wide by $6\frac{5}{8}$" long; see Fig. 23. With the guides cut to length and width, cut a tapered notch off each end. The taper is cut so there's a 2"-long flat left on the bottom of the guide; see Fig. 20.

Now rout a $\frac{1}{8}$" roundover on the bottom and end edges of both guides.

POSITION GUIDES. With the guides completed, I located their position on the bottom side of the table top. First locate the guides so they're centered on the length of the table top; see Fig. 21.

Then, measuring from the inside of the side top edging, mark lines $3\frac{7}{8}$" in from either side; see Fig. 22.

Since the guides *must* fit between the top braces, I tested their location before I glued them in place by sticking them on with double-sided carpet tape. Once everything fit, I marked their location and glued them in place.

Now the leaves should slide out when the top is lifted up.

That brings up one final point that may still be a bit confusing. The table top is *not* fastened down to the aprons. It's held down simply by gravity, but won't move around because of the way the guides and top edging fit over the table base. ∎

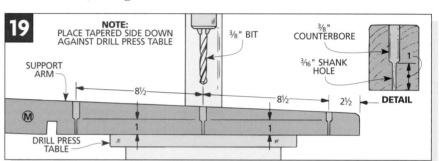

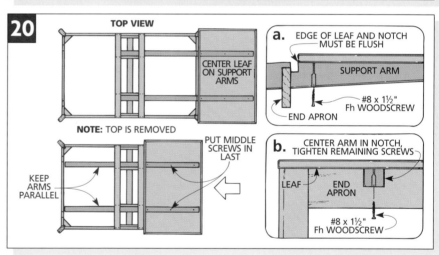

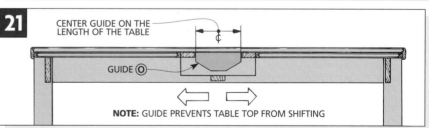

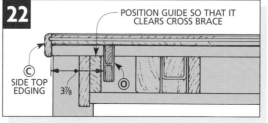

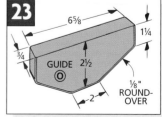

LADDER-BACK CHAIR

Chairs aren't as difficult to build as you might think. The trick on the curved parts is to use a template with a band saw and router table.

Building chairs: just the thought of it brings out a certain uneasiness in many woodworkers. Okay, I'll admit this chair isn't the easiest project I've ever built. But it isn't the most difficult either.

At first, the curved back leg and back slats may seem a little intimidating. But they're fairly easy to cut by using a template to rough out the shape on a band saw. Then you can use the same template to smooth them on a router table.

JOINERY. I found the process of building the chairs to be more time-consuming than it was difficult. It took me about 100 hours to complete a set of six

chairs. There are 22 mortise and tenon joints on each chair.

It may appear as though you have to cut angled tenons on the back slats; see the Exploded View on page 40. That's not the case. All of the tenons are cut straight, on square stock. Then, after the tenons are cut, the stock is cut on a curve with the band saw.

DESIGN. The thing I like most about this chair is sitting in it. The curved back allows the slats to fit the shape of my body. And it's a comfortable angle — straight enough for eating, yet comfortable for sitting.

WOOD. The chairs are simple and

contemporary. Using oak enhances the contemporary feel. However, by using mahogany or walnut, the chairs would take on a more formal, traditional appearance. (For a similar, but more formal chair, see the one on page 47.)

UPHOLSTERY. Woodworking is not the only challenge when building a chair, you also have to upholster the seat. On page 45 we show how to upholster the seat (without bunching at the corners).

FINISH. To provide a durable finish, I applied two coats of satin polyurethane to each chair, sanding lightly between coats with 220-grit sandpaper.

EXPLODED VIEW... LADDER-BACK CHAIR

OVERALL DIMENSIONS:
17³/₁₆W x 38H x 18³/₄D

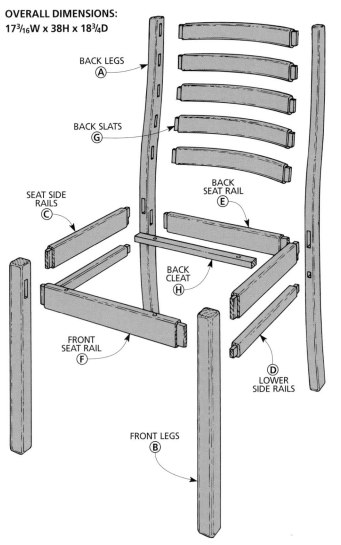

BACK LEGS (A)

BACK SLATS (G)

SEAT SIDE RAILS (C)

BACK SEAT RAIL (E)

BACK CLEAT (H)

FRONT SEAT RAIL (F)

LOWER SIDE RAILS (D)

FRONT LEGS (B)

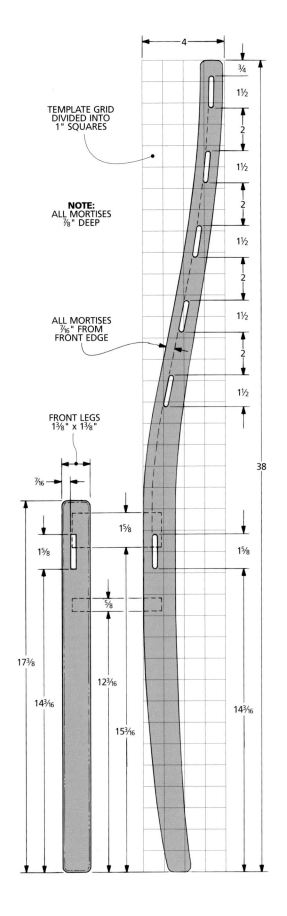

TEMPLATE GRID DIVIDED INTO 1" SQUARES

NOTE:
ALL MORTISES ⅞" DEEP

ALL MORTISES ⁷/₁₆" FROM FRONT EDGE

FRONT LEGS 1³/₈" x 1³/₈"

4

³/₄
1½
2
1½
2
1½
2
1½
2
1½

38

⁷/₁₆

1⁵/₈
1⁵/₈
5/8
1⁵/₈

17³/₈
14³/₁₆
12³/₁₆
15³/₁₆
14³/₁₆

MATERIALS LIST & CUTTING DIAGRAM
FOR ONE CHAIR

WOOD

A	Back Legs (2)	1¹/₁₆ x 4 - 39 rough
B	Front Legs (2)	1³/₈ x 1³/₈ - 17³/₈
C	Seat Side Rails (2)	⁵/₈ x 2 - 14½
D	Lwr. Side Rails (2)	⁵/₈ x 1 - 14½
E	Back Seat Rail (1)	⁵/₈ x 2 - 16½
F	Front Seat Rail (1)	⁵/₈ x 2 - 15¹⁵/₁₆
G	Back Slats (5)	1½ x 1³/₄ - 16½
H	Back Cleat (1)	³/₄ x 1 - 15
I	Seat (1)	³/₄ ply - 15¼ x 15¼

HARDWARE AND UPHOLSTERY SUPPLIES

(4) No. 8 x 1½" Fh woodscrews
(1) 2" x 17¼" x 17¼" Foam
(1) 24" x 24" Piece of fabric
(20) ³/₈" Staples and staple gun

1¹/₁₆ x 6¼ - 39 (2.1 Bd. Ft.)

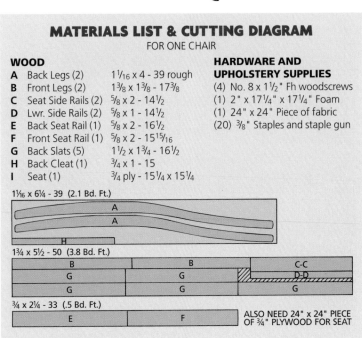

1³/₄ x 5½ - 50 (3.8 Bd. Ft.)

³/₄ x 2¼ - 33 (.5 Bd. Ft.)

ALSO NEED 24" x 24" PIECE OF ³/₄" PLYWOOD FOR SEAT

BACK LEGS

I began work on the chairs by making a back leg template. The template is used as a guide to cut both back legs to the same shape, and to lay out the mortises.

TEMPLATE. To make the template, I laid out the shape of the leg on a piece of $1/4$" hardboard 4" x 38". (Follow the grid drawing on the opposite page.)

Also lay out the mortises for the back slats and back seat rail; see Fig. 1.

After the mortises were laid out, I cut the template a little oversize on the band saw; see Fig. 2. Then I carefully filed and sanded down to the line.

MORTISES. Since the template is used as a guide for the mortises, I drilled out the mortises on the template. To keep the mortises a consistent distance from the front edge of the template, I used a special jig; see Fig. 3.

To make this jig, drill a $3/8$" hole in a piece of plywood and insert a short length of $3/8$"-dia. dowel. Then mark a reference line on the plywood straight out from the center of the dowel.

Now position the plywood on the drill press table so the dowel is $7/16$" behind the bit and the center of the bit is aligned with the reference line; see Fig. 3a. Once everything is in place, clamp the plywood to the drill press table.

Now the mortises can be roughed out on the drill press. As each hole is drilled, keep the front edge of the template against the dowel stop pin, and the back edge 90° to the reference line on the plywood base; see Figs. 3 and 3a.

CUT OUT LEG. When the template is completed, you can begin work on the back legs (A). I was able to get two back legs out of one $1^{1}/16$"-thick blank that measured $6^{1}/4$" by 39" (see the Cutting Diagram on the opposite page).

Start by fastening the template to the blank with double-sided carpet tape.

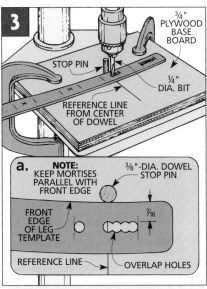

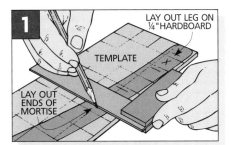

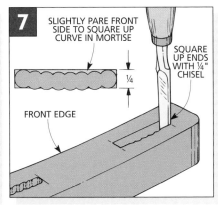

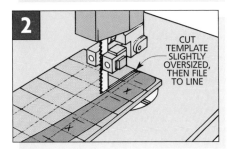

Then roughly cut out the first leg about $1/4$" oversize; see Fig. 4.

Next, I cut out the leg exactly $1/16$" oversize by using a guide block on the band saw. Then it's cut to final size with a flush trim bit on a router table. (For a detailed explanation of these steps; see the article on page 46.)

MARK MORTISES. Before removing the template, draw through the mortises in the template to mark the mortises on the leg; see Fig. 5.

MIRRORED SET. To make one chair, you need a mirrored set of back legs. Since both legs are exactly the same shape, you can use the same template — but the mortises have to be cut into opposite faces. To do this, I stuck the template on the *back* side of the blank. Then cut out the second leg following the same procedure as the first leg.

MORTISES. After both legs are cut out and the mortises outlined, you can drill them out using the same stop jig and procedure used on the template. The only difference is these mortises are $7/8$" deep; see Fig. 6.

These mortises will be slightly curved because they follow the curve of the leg (sort of a cooked hot dog shape). To get the tenon to fit, use a chisel to square the front edge of the mortise to a straight line. Also square up the ends of the mortise; see Fig. 7.

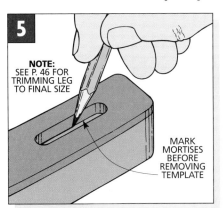

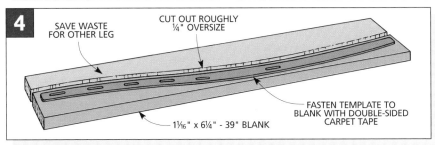

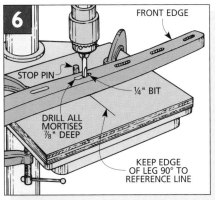

After drilling out five mortises for the slats and one for the back rail, you can begin laying out the mortises on the *front* edge of each back leg. These mortises will hold the seat side rail (C) and lower side rail (D).

MORTISE LAYOUT. The trick is to lay out the mortises so they will be at the exact same location on both of the legs. Begin by laying one leg down on its side at the end of a bench; see Fig. 8. Then lay down a framing square so one arm of the square is flush with the end of the bench (and the bottom of the leg) and the other arm rests against the flat section on the front of the leg.

Now measure up $12^3/_{16}$" and $15^3/_{16}$" from the end of the framing square to mark the bottom of the mortises. The lower mortise is $5/_8$" long and the upper one $1^5/_8$" long.

DRILL OUT MORTISES. To drill out these mortises, start by clamping a straight piece of 2x4 to the drill press table as a fence; see Fig. 9. Position the fence so the $1/_4$" bit is centered on the thickness of the leg.

Since the back of the leg is curved, there isn't a long enough flat spot on it to allow the leg to sit down flat on the drill press table. I solved this problem by putting a 5"-long scrap block under the mortise locations to raise the leg up

off the drill press table, see Fig. 9. (Stick the block to the leg with double-sided carpet tape.)

Now, drill $7/_8$"-deep mortises, moving the spacer block along with the leg as you drill. Complete the mortises by squaring up the ends with a chisel.

ROUND OVER EDGES. When all the mortises are cut in the back leg, the only step left is to round over the edges and ends with a $1/_4$" roundover bit set $3/_{16}$" high in the router table; see Fig. 10.

FRONT LEGS

At this point, the back legs are complete. Now you can begin work on the front legs (B). It's critical that the mortises in the front legs align with those in the back legs.

CUT OUT LEGS. Start making the front legs by cutting out two blocks $1^3/_8$" square by $17^3/_8$" long.

MORTISE LAYOUT. Once the blocks are cut to size, lay out two $1/_4$"-wide mortises on the back face of each leg to join to the side rails (C, D); see Fig. 11. These mortises are located the same distances ($12^3/_{16}$" and $15^3/_{16}$") from the bottom end of the front leg (B) as the two mortises on the back leg (A).

Note that the mortises are *not* centered on the thickness, but $7/_{16}$" from

the *outside* edge of each leg. (Here's where you have to start thinking of the two front legs as a mirrored set.)

After the mortises are laid out on the back face of each leg, lay out a $1^5/_8$"-long mortise on the *inside* face of each leg to join to the front seat rail; see Fig. 11. Locate these mortises $14^3/_{16}$" up from the bottom end of the legs, $7/_{16}$" from the outside edge; refer to page 40. And be sure they face each other. (Again, so you end up with a mirrored set of legs.)

CUT MORTISES. Now you can drill out all the $7/_8$"-deep mortises on the drill press. (As before, clamp a fence to the top of the drill press table.)

When you drill out the mortises on adjacent sides, the bottoms will break through very slightly into each other; see Fig. 11. That's okay, the tenons will be cut back later where they meet.

ROUND EDGES. After squaring up the mortises with a chisel, I rounded over the edges and ends of the front legs on the router table. First, round over the two edges nearest the mortises with a $1/_4$" roundover bit set $3/_{16}$" high; see Steps 1 and 2 in Fig. 12.

Then raise the bit to rout a full $1/_4$" roundover on the inside edge (Step 3) and both top and bottom ends. Finally, switch to a $1/_2$" roundover bit and rout the outside edge; see Step 4.

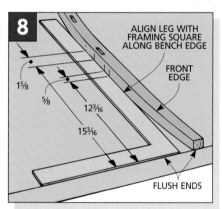

8 ALIGN LEG WITH FRAMING SQUARE ALONG BENCH EDGE
FRONT EDGE
$1^5/_8$
$5/_8$
$12^3/_{16}$
$15^3/_{16}$
FLUSH ENDS

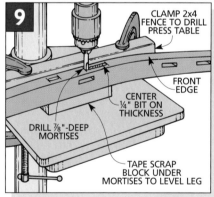

9 CLAMP 2x4 FENCE TO DRILL PRESS TABLE
FRONT EDGE
CENTER $1/_4$" BIT ON THICKNESS
DRILL $7/_8$"-DEEP MORTISES
TAPE SCRAP BLOCK UNDER MORTISES TO LEVEL LEG

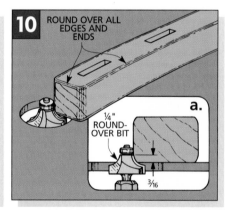

10 ROUND OVER ALL EDGES AND ENDS
a.
$1/_4$" ROUND-OVER BIT
$3/_{16}$

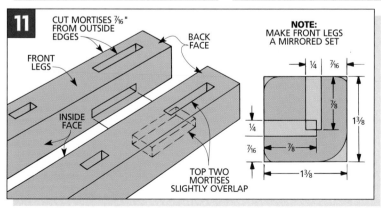

11 CUT MORTISES $7/_{16}$" FROM OUTSIDE EDGES
BACK FACE
FRONT LEGS
INSIDE FACE
TOP TWO MORTISES SLIGHTLY OVERLAP
NOTE: MAKE FRONT LEGS A MIRRORED SET
$1/_4$ $7/_{16}$
$1/_4$
$7/_8$
$1^3/_8$
$7/_{16}$ $7/_8$
$1^3/_8$

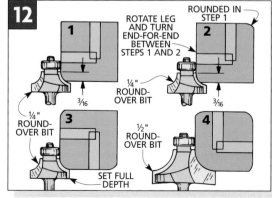

12 ROTATE LEG AND TURN END-FOR-END BETWEEN STEPS 1 AND 2
ROUNDED IN STEP 1
1 $1/_4$" ROUND-OVER BIT $3/_{16}$
2 $3/_{16}$
3 $1/_4$" ROUND-OVER BIT SET FULL DEPTH
4 $1/_2$" ROUND-OVER BIT

BACK SLATS

After the legs are complete you can begin working on the back slats (G).

CUT TO SIZE. Start by cutting five blanks of $1^3/_4$"-thick stock to a width of $1^1/_2$" and length of $16^1/_2$"; see Fig. 13.

CUT TENONS. It's easiest to cut the $3/_4$"-long offset tenons on the ends of the back slats *before* cutting the slats to shape. To do this, first raise a $13/_{16}$" dado blade $1/_8$" high and cut rabbets on the ends of the blank. (Shop Note: To do this, I "buried" the dado blade $1/_{16}$" into an auxiliary fence; see Fig. 14a). Cut the rabbets on the front face and top and bottom (but not the back) of the blank.

To complete the offset tenon, I cut a deeper rabbet into the back face of the block. Since it's a heavy cut, make it in a series of passes sneaking up on the finished height; see Fig. 14. Check the fit of the tenon in one of the mortises cut in the back legs as you work.

MAKE A TEMPLATE. After all the tenons are cut to fit the mortises, you can cut the back slats to shape. I started by making a template out of $1/_4$" hardboard; see Fig. 15. Cut the template 15" long and about 3" wide.

To get the curve, strike and cut a 36" radius arc on the template. Shop Note: To strike the radius, I made a trammel from a strip of hardboard; see Fig. 15.

CUT ARC ON BLANK. After the arc on the template has been filed smooth, attach the template to the top of the slat blank with double-sided carpet tape. Be sure to face the arc on the template to the *front* of the blank. (That's the face nearest the tenon that's offset by $1/_8$".)

Now, cut out the curved front face of the slat $1/_{16}$" from the template; see Fig. 16. (Use the same technique used to cut out the back legs.) Then mark the front edge of the template on the blank and remove the template.

To remove the last $1/_{16}$", I used a rasp and a drum sander; see Fig. 17.

CUT BACK FACE. Then, to form the back face, make a guide block with a pointed end and clamp the guide so the pointed end is $9/_{16}$" away from the blade; see Fig. 18. Next, cut the back slat to shape by running it between the pointed block and the blade. Now file (or plane) the back edge smooth so it ends up about $1/_2$" thick.

ROUND OVER EDGES. The last step is to round over the four edges with a $1/_4$" roundover bit; see Fig. 19.

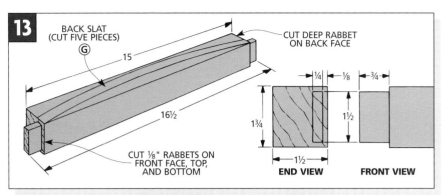

13 BACK SLAT (CUT FIVE PIECES) G — 15 — CUT DEEP RABBET ON BACK FACE — 16½ — CUT ⅛" RABBETS ON FRONT FACE, TOP, AND BOTTOM — ¼ ⅛ ¾ — 1¾ — 1½ — 1½ — END VIEW — FRONT VIEW

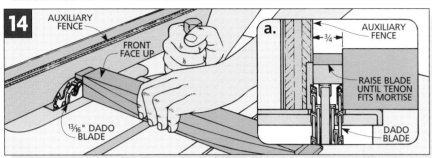

14 AUXILIARY FENCE — FRONT FACE UP — 13/16" DADO BLADE — a. AUXILIARY FENCE — ¾ — RAISE BLADE UNTIL TENON FITS MORTISE — DADO BLADE

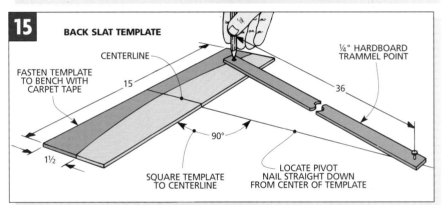

15 BACK SLAT TEMPLATE — CENTERLINE — FASTEN TEMPLATE TO BENCH WITH CARPET TAPE — 15 — 1½ — 90° — ¼" HARDBOARD TRAMMEL POINT — 36 — SQUARE TEMPLATE TO CENTERLINE — LOCATE PIVOT NAIL STRAIGHT DOWN FROM CENTER OF TEMPLATE

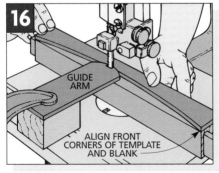

16 GUIDE ARM — ALIGN FRONT CORNERS OF TEMPLATE AND BLANK

17 FILE FRONT FACE UP TO LINE WITH RASP AND DRUM SANDER

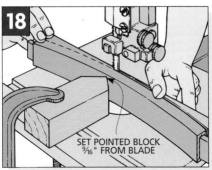

18 SET POINTED BLOCK 9/16" FROM BLADE

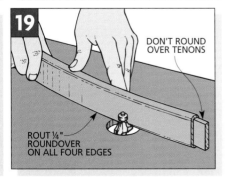

19 DON'T ROUND OVER TENONS — ROUT ¼" ROUNDOVER ON ALL FOUR EDGES

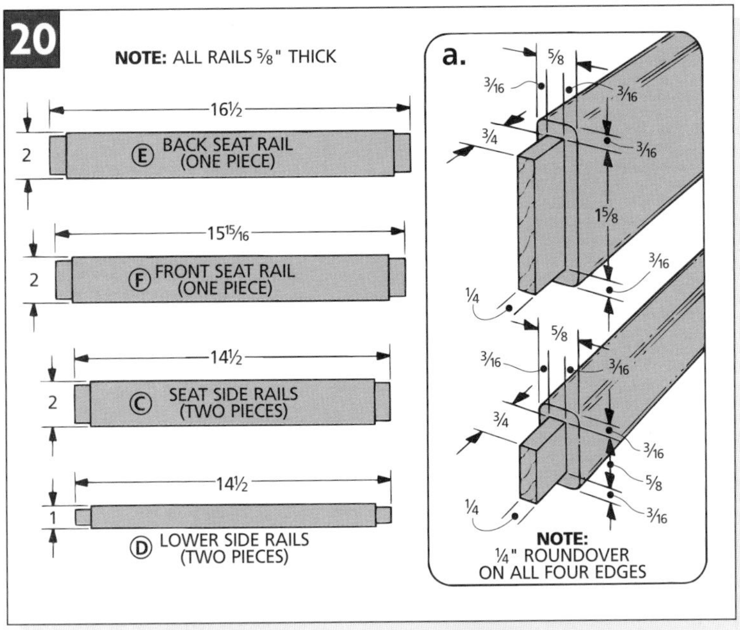
20
NOTE: ALL RAILS 5/8" THICK
16½
2
E BACK SEAT RAIL (ONE PIECE)
15 15/16
2
F FRONT SEAT RAIL (ONE PIECE)
14½
2
C SEAT SIDE RAILS (TWO PIECES)
14½
1
D LOWER SIDE RAILS (TWO PIECES)
a.
5/8
3/16
3/16
3/4
3/16
1 5/8
3/16
1/4
5/8
3/16
3/16
3/4
3/16
5/8
3/16
1/4
NOTE: 1/4" ROUNDOVER ON ALL FOUR EDGES

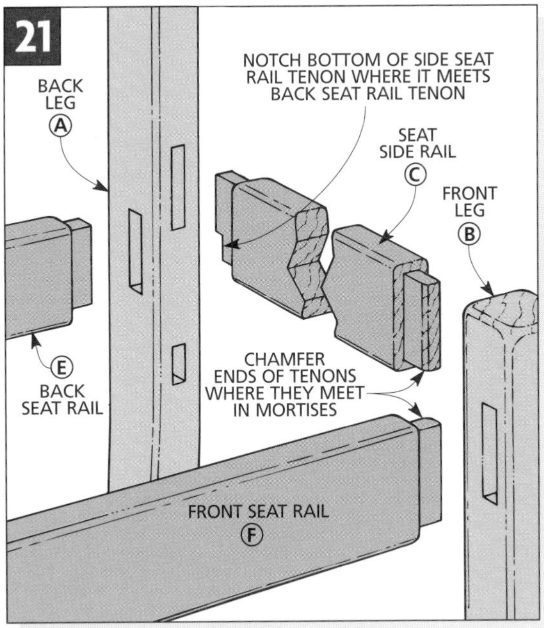
21
BACK LEG A
NOTCH BOTTOM OF SIDE SEAT RAIL TENON WHERE IT MEETS BACK SEAT RAIL TENON
SEAT SIDE RAIL C
FRONT LEG B
E BACK SEAT RAIL
CHAMFER ENDS OF TENONS WHERE THEY MEET IN MORTISES
FRONT SEAT RAIL F

SEAT RAILS

Next, you can make the seat rails and side rails. I started by resawing enough wood for the four seat rails and two lower side rails to $\frac{5}{8}$" thick.

CUT TO SIZE. Now, cut all of the seat rails 2" wide and the lower side rails 1" wide; see Fig. 20. As for length, the seat side rails (C) and the lower side rails (D) are both cut $14\frac{1}{2}$" long.

The back seat rail (E) is cut the same length as the back slats ($16\frac{1}{2}$"). Since the front legs are thicker than the back legs, the front seat rail (F) is $\frac{9}{16}$" shorter ($15\frac{15}{16}$").

CUT TENONS. After all of the pieces are cut to length, next cut $\frac{3}{4}$"-long tenons centered on the ends of all the rails; see Fig. 20a. Cut the tenons to thickness and width to fit the mortises in the legs.

ROUND OVER EDGES. Next, round over all four edges of each rail (but not the tenons) with a $\frac{1}{4}$" roundover bit on the router table; refer back to Fig. 19.

NOTCH AND CHAMFER TENONS. There are a couple more things that have to be done before assembly. When the rails are mounted into the legs, the tenons of the seat side rails (C) will run into the back and front seat rails (E,F); see Fig. 21.

To solve this problem at the back leg, I notched the bottom of the tenons on the seat side rails. Since the overlap at the front is very slight, you only need to chamfer the tenons of the side and front seat rails.

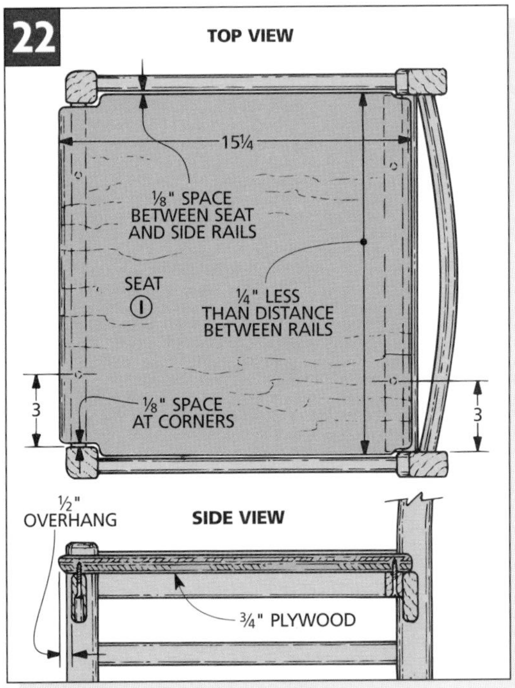
22
TOP VIEW
15¼
1/8" SPACE BETWEEN SEAT AND SIDE RAILS
SEAT I
1/4" LESS THAN DISTANCE BETWEEN RAILS
3
1/8" SPACE AT CORNERS
3
1/2" OVERHANG
SIDE VIEW
3/4" PLYWOOD

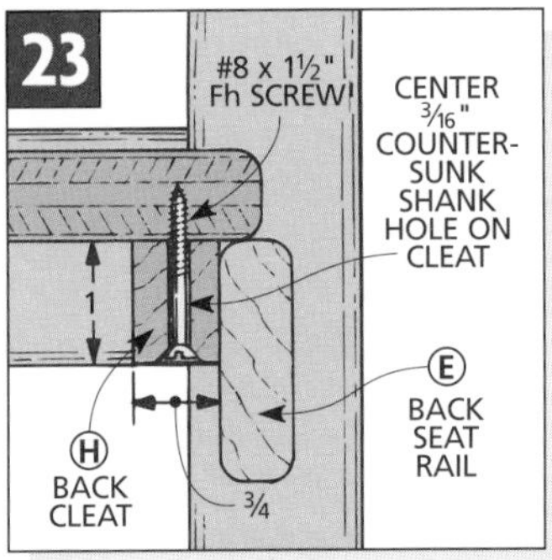
23
#8 x 1½" Fh SCREW
CENTER 3/16" COUNTER-SUNK SHANK HOLE ON CLEAT
1
E BACK SEAT RAIL
H BACK CLEAT
3/4

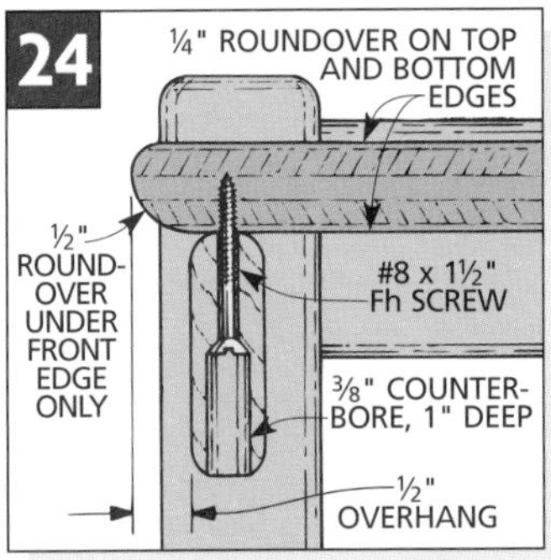
24
1/4" ROUNDOVER ON TOP AND BOTTOM EDGES
1/2" ROUND-OVER UNDER FRONT EDGE ONLY
#8 x 1½" Fh SCREW
3/8" COUNTER-BORE, 1" DEEP
1/2" OVERHANG

ASSEMBLY AND SEAT

I started assembling the chair by gluing and clamping each side independently. Connect the front and back legs with the side rails checking that the assembly is square.

After the side units are dry, glue the front and back rails and the back slats between the side units to complete the chair. (Shop Note: I assembled the chair on top of my table saw since it's the flattest surface in my shop.)

CLEAT. The plywood seat is mounted to a back cleat (H) that's glued to the front face of the back seat rail (E); see Fig. 23. To attach the seat, drill screw holes through the back cleat and the front seat rail (F).

SEAT. The last piece to make is the $\frac{3}{4}$" plywood seat (I); see Fig. 22. It's cut to overhang $\frac{1}{2}$" on the front, but leave $\frac{1}{8}$" space between the sides and corners of the seat for the upholstery.

Before upholstering the seat, rout a $\frac{1}{4}$" roundover on the top and bottom edges and $\frac{1}{2}$" roundover under the front edge; see Fig. 24. Finally, after finishing the chair, screw the upholstered seat in place. ■

I know very little about fabric and foam. So when it came time to upholster the chairs, I went to a local upholstery supplier for information and materials. As usual, there was more to learn than I thought.

The foam I used on the chairs is not foam rubber. Foam rubber is latex rubber, which is made from the sap of the rubber tree. The foam I used on the chairs is polyurethane foam which is a synthetic product.

There are three different densities of polyurethane foam; low, medium, and high. The higher the density, the less likely you are to "bottom out" when you sit on it and it will last longer.

The fabric I used on the seats also has some special features. First, the back of the fabric has a surface coating on it. This surface coating keeps the weave of the fabric from being distorted when it's stretched tight.

Second, I wanted a fabric that would stand up well to everyday use but, would look appropriate in a dining room. The fabric I used is a nylon/polyester blend. The thread size is fairly large and the weave of the fabric is rather loose, which gives the seat a soft texture and allows the air to escape from the foam when you sit down.

To get professional quality results, I suggest you go to a upholstery shop or a fabric store and ask for materials that are intended specifically for upholstery.

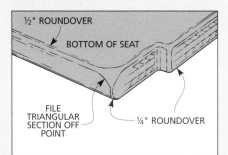

1 Before upholstering plywood, round over edges with a $\frac{1}{4}$" roundover and front bottom edge with a $\frac{1}{2}$" roundover. Then file point off bottom front corner.

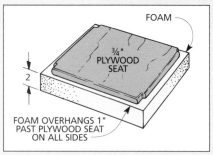

2 Cut 2"-thick foam 2" wider and longer than plywood seat. This leaves a 1" overhang on each side. You can cut the foam easily on the band saw.

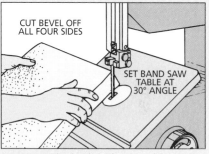

3 Next, tilt the band saw table to 30° and bevel each edge of the foam. Start the bevel right on the extreme outside edge of the foam.

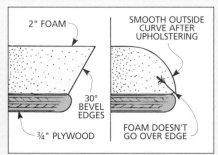

4 Foam is placed on top of the seat with the bevel facing down. Undercutting the foam allows it to be pulled down to a smooth outside curve.

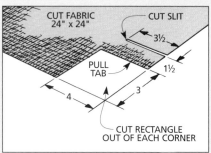

5 Cut a piece of fabric to a 24" x 24" square. To keep the fabric from bunching in the corner, cut a rectangle from each corner, then slit a pull tab.

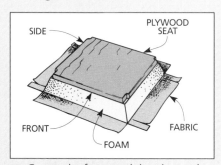

6 Center the foam and the plywood on the back side of the fabric. Align sides of the plywood seat with the sides of the fabric that have the $3\frac{1}{2}$" slits.

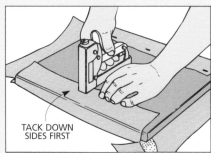

7 Beginning with the sides, push down on plywood and pull fabric up and over the plywood. Use a staple gun to tack the fabric in place every 2" or 3".

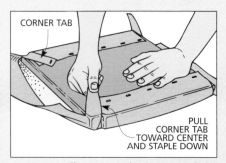

8 Now pull corner tabs in toward the center of the plywood. Lap corner tabs over the stapled-down fabric, so the fold is in the notch. Staple tab down.

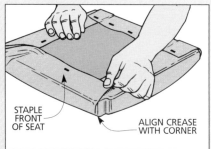

9 With the tabs stapled down, stretch the remaining fabric around the front and back of the plywood. Staple down fabric to form a crease at corner.

The trick to making uniform curved-back legs for the chairs is to use a template. The template makes cutting out the pieces a simple two-step operation on a band saw and router table — a process that produces all the pieces you want with the exact same shape.

TEMPLATE. You can use either ¼" hardboard or plywood to make the template. The important thing is that the edge of the material doesn't have any knots or voids in it.

LAY OUT PATTERN. Start by laying out the pattern of the chair leg right on the template material; see grid drawing on page 40. Or cut a full-size pattern out of paper and glue it to the hardboard or plywood. Then cut out the shape slightly oversize, and file up to the line.

Shop Note: Any gouges on the edge of the template will show up later on the finished pieces, so it's important to take the time to work the edges smooth.

It's not critical your template is exactly the same as the pattern. If the curve is slightly different, that's okay. All *your* legs will be identical — they will match *your* template.

CUTTING TO SHAPE. After the template is made, attach it to the leg blank with double-sided carpet tape. Then,

roughly saw the leg out of the blank so it's about ¼" larger than the template.

Next, cut the shape again, but this time carefully so it's ¹⁄₁₆" oversize. (Since the next step is to rout the leg to *exact* size, there's less chipout when only routing off ¹⁄₁₆".) Although you can make this cut freehand, I clamped a "guide arm" to the band saw to make a more precise cut; see Fig. 1.

The arm is made from a piece of ¼" hardboard glued to the top of a 1⅛"-thick block. The arm is mounted to the

block so it's raised up high enough to rub against the *template*, not the rough edge of the workpiece. The trick to this arm is to round the end, and then cut a notch for your blade to fit in. (I cut a ³⁄₈" notch for the ¼" band saw blade I used.) Now clamp the guide arm to the table so the blade is ¹⁄₁₆" from the outside edge of the curved end; see Fig. 1a.

To cut out the leg, push the blank so the template rubs against the guide arm; see Fig. 2. As you're cutting, move the tail end of the blank right or left to keep the template parallel to the blade.

ROUTING TO FINAL SHAPE. Now you can rout off the last ¹⁄₁₆" with a flush trim bit on the router table.

With the template still taped to the workpiece, raise the bit up until the bearing rides on the template; see Step 1 in Fig. 4. Then to cut the leg the exact shape of the template, rout in a clockwise direction around the bit; see Fig. 3.

Shop Note: Since the bit I used only has a 1"-long cutting edge and the leg is 1¹⁄₁₆" thick, I had to lower the bit to make a second cut; see Step 2 in Fig. 4. (Note: You have to use a ¼"-shank flush trim bit when routing a piece this thick. The shank of a ½"-shank bit would rub against the workpiece on the first cut.)

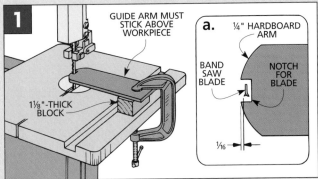

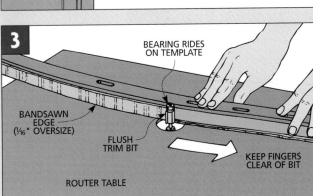

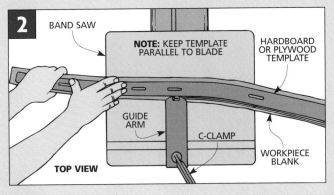

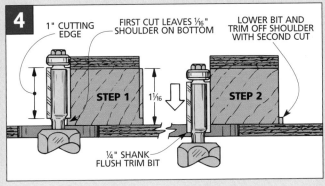

FORMAL DINING CHAIR

Built from mahogany, this chair could be used with a desk or formal dining set. It's built using the same techniques as the ladder-back chair.

After building the set of oak ladder-back chairs shown on page 39, I decided to make a slight change to the design and was surprised how it changed the whole "look" of the chair.

What I did was use *vertical* back slats instead of the horizontal "ladder-back" slats. And, at the same time, I made the slats narrower, and so a little more ele-

gant. Immediately the chair took on a more traditional or formal look. A look that might work with a desk or formal dining set. (Though I still think this design would look fine with the modern dining table on page 32.)

WOOD. A more formal design called for a more formal wood. So this time I built the chairs from Honduras mahogany. It has a light reddish color

when first cut but over time takes on a beautiful deep reddish-brown patina.

Mahogany is a medium-textured wood with fairly straight, consistent grain. Straight-grained walnut or cherry would also be a good choice for this formal chair.

FINISH. To finish the chairs, I hand rubbed in four coats of tung oil and then buffed it to a soft shine with paste wax.

EXPLODED VIEW... FORMAL DINING CHAIR

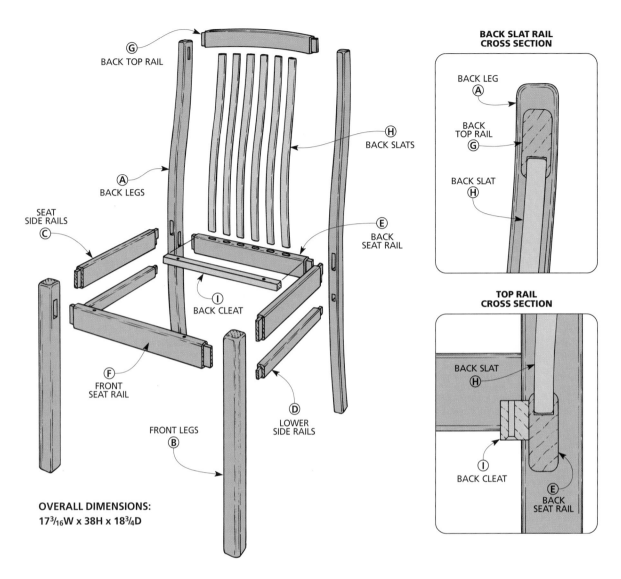

BACK TOP RAIL Ⓖ

BACK SLATS Ⓗ

BACK LEGS Ⓐ

SEAT SIDE RAILS Ⓒ

BACK SEAT RAIL Ⓔ

BACK CLEAT Ⓘ

FRONT SEAT RAIL Ⓕ

LOWER SIDE RAILS Ⓓ

FRONT LEGS Ⓑ

OVERALL DIMENSIONS:
17³/₁₆W x 38H x 18³/₄D

BACK SLAT RAIL CROSS SECTION

BACK LEG Ⓐ

BACK TOP RAIL Ⓖ

BACK SLAT Ⓗ

TOP RAIL CROSS SECTION

BACK SLAT Ⓗ

BACK CLEAT Ⓘ

BACK SEAT RAIL Ⓔ

MATERIALS LIST & CUTTING DIAGRAM
FOR ONE CHAIR

WOOD

A	Back Legs (2)	1¹/₁₆ x 4 - 39 rough
B	Front Legs (2)	1³/₈ x 1³/₈ - 17⁷/₈
C	Seat Side Rails (2)	⁵/₈ x 2 - 14¹/₂
D	Lwr. Side Rails (2)	⁵/₈ x 1 - 14¹/₂
E	Back Seat Rail (1)	³/₄ x 2 - 16¹/₂
F	Front Seat Rail (1)	⁵/₈ x 2 - 15¹⁵/₁₆
G	Back Top Rail (1)	1¹/₂ x 1³/₄ - 16¹/₂
H	Back Slats (6)	¹/₂ x 1¹/₁₆ -20³/₄
I	Back Cleat (1)	³/₄ x 1 - 15
J	Seat (1)	³/₄ ply - 14⁷/₈ x 15¹/₄

HARDWARE AND UPHOLSTERY SUPPLIES

(4) No. 8 x 1¹/₂" Fh woodscrews   (1) 24" x 24" Piece of fabric
(1) 2" x 16⁷/₈" x 17¹/₄" Foam   (20) ³/₈" Staples and staple gun

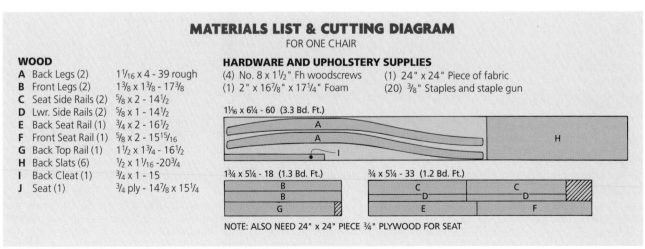

1¹/₁₆ x 6¹/₄ - 60 (3.3 Bd. Ft.)

1³/₄ x 5¹/₄ - 18 (1.3 Bd. Ft.)   ³/₄ x 5¹/₄ - 33 (1.2 Bd. Ft.)

NOTE: ALSO NEED 24" x 24" PIECE ³/₄" PLYWOOD FOR SEAT

CONSTRUCTION STEPS

The steps to building this chair are almost identical to the ladder-back chair — until it's time to work on the back slats. I started by following all of the same steps for making the legs as on the ladder-back chair (pages 41 to 42) with one exception. Since the slats are vertical rather than horizontal, you don't need four of the mortises (the middle four) on the back legs.

The top and bottom mortises, though, are still needed in exactly the same locations to hold the back top rail (G) and the back seat rail (E) in place.

BACK SLATS

All six back slats (H) are cut out of one blank of $1^1/_{16}$"-thick stock that measures $6^1/_4$" wide by $20^3/_4$" long; see Fig. 1. The trick is following the correct cutting sequence to get all six slats out of the blank so each slat ends up the exact same thickness and shape.

USE BACK LEG TEMPLATE. Since the six slats follow the same contour as the back legs, you can use the back leg template to set up the first cut on the slat blank.

Start by attaching the template along one edge of the blank with double-sided carpet tape so the top end of the template sticks out $1^7/_8$" beyond the end of the blank; see Fig. 1.

MAKE FIRST CUT. Next, I clamped the guide arm to the band saw to make the initial cut $^1/_{16}$" away from the template; see Step 2. (This is the same guide arm used to cut out the back legs; see page 46.)

Once the oversize cut was made along the front edge of the template, I switched to the router table to clean up the bandsawn edge. This is done with a flush trim bit mounted so the pilot bearing rides along the edge of the template; see Fig. 3 and page 46.

CUT TO THICKNESS. Now that you have established the front contour of the first slat, the trick is cutting the back face to the same shape so the slat will be a uniform thickness. To do this, make a guide block with a pointed end; see Fig. 4. Clamp this guide block to the band saw table so it's $^9/_{16}$" away from the blade. Now, you can cut the back edge of the slat by pushing the front (routed) edge against the guide block. The slat will end up a uniform $^9/_{16}$" thickness.

REPEAT THE STEPS. To get another slat out of the blank, just repeat these steps. First, reattach the template so it's inside the cut edge of the blank and trim it flush on the router table (Fig. 3).

Then remove the template and cut off another $^9/_{16}$"-thick slat (Fig. 4). Continue this process until all six slats have been cut from the blank.

SMOOTH BACK FACE. At this point, the slats should be fairly uniform in thickness, but the back faces will be rough from the band saw cuts. I smoothed the back faces with a sanding drum on the drill press; see Fig. 5.

To do this, clamp the guide block (with the pointed end) to the drill press table $^1/_2$" away from the outside of the sanding drum. Then feed the slats at a steady rate between the drum and the guide block.

The goal here is not only to remove the band saw marks, but to be sure the slats are sanded to a uniform $^1/_2$" thick (especially at the ends). Later, the ends fit into $^1/_2$" mortises. If the slats are too thick, they won't fit in, and if too thin, the fit will be sloppy.

ROUND OVER EDGES. After all the slats are sanded smooth, round over all four edges with a $^1/_4$" roundover bit on the router table; see Fig. 6.

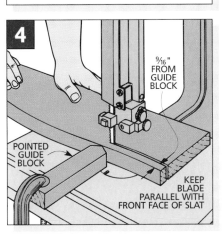

1 BACK SLAT BLANK (H)

6¼
20¾
1⅞

NOTE: ATTACH TEMPLATE TO BLANK WITH DOUBLE-SIDED CARPET TAPE

BACK LEG TEMPLATE

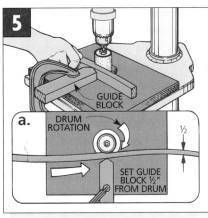

2 KEEP TEMPLATE PARALLEL WITH BLADE — BLADE CUTS ¹⁄₁₆" OUTSIDE TEMPLATE

GUIDE ARM
SPACER BLOCK

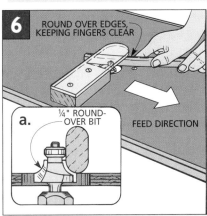

3 ROUTER TABLE

FLUSH TRIM BIT

KEEP BEARING AGAINST TEMPLATE ON FIRST PASS

BAND SAWN EDGE

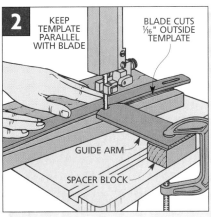

4 ⁹⁄₁₆" FROM GUIDE BLOCK

POINTED GUIDE BLOCK

KEEP BLADE PARALLEL WITH FRONT FACE OF SLAT

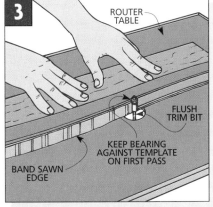

5

GUIDE BLOCK

a. DRUM ROTATION
½
SET GUIDE BLOCK ½" FROM DRUM

6 ROUND OVER EDGES, KEEPING FINGERS CLEAR

a. ¼" ROUND-OVER BIT
FEED DIRECTION

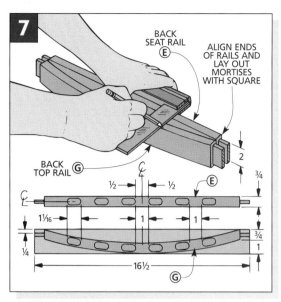

7

BACK SEAT RAIL (E)

ALIGN ENDS OF RAILS AND LAY OUT MORTISES WITH SQUARE

BACK TOP RAIL (G)

½ ½

¾

1¹⁄₁₆

1 1

¾

¼

1

16½

(E)

(G)

2

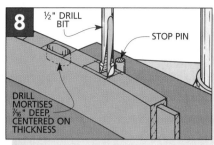

8

½" DRILL BIT

STOP PIN

DRILL MORTISES ⁷⁄₁₆" DEEP, CENTERED ON THICKNESS

10

SHAPE ENDS OF BACK SLATS FOR GOOD FIT IN MORTISES

NOTE: DO NOT SQUARE UP ENDS OF MORTISES

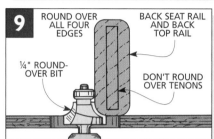

9

ROUND OVER ALL FOUR EDGES

BACK SEAT RAIL AND BACK TOP RAIL

¼" ROUND-OVER BIT

DON'T ROUND OVER TENONS

BACK RAILS

The back slats are held between a top rail and a seat rail.

SEAT RAIL. Start by cutting the back seat rail (E) from ¾" stock, 2" wide and 16½" long; see Fig. 7. Then cut ¾"-long centered tenons on the ends of the rail.

TOP RAIL. The basic procedure for cutting the curved back top rail (G) is the same as used on the back slats on the ladder-back chair (refer to page 43), but the rail is thicker. This means there are two changes to the procedure.

First, set the tenon *back* farther (¼") from the front face; see Fig. 7. Second, when cutting out the piece on the band saw, set the pointed block ¹³⁄₁₆" from the band saw blade. After filing, this will make the back top rail about ¾" thick.

LAY OUT MORTISES. After these two rails are cut, lay out 1¹⁄₁₆"-long mortises (with 1" between them) for the vertical slats. To do this, align the two rails and use a square to mark the mortises across from each other; see Fig. 7.

DRILL MORTISES. Now drill out ⁷⁄₁₆"-deep mortises with a ½" bit on the drill press. Since the seat rail (E) is straight, clamp a straightedge to the drill press table to keep the mortises centered on the workpiece. But on the curved top rail (G) you will have to run the workpiece against a stop pin; see Fig. 8.

ROUND OVER EDGES. After the mortises are drilled (don't square them up), round over the edges of both rails with a ¼" roundover bit; see Fig. 9. Then fit the slats into the mortises. If they're too tight, you may have to slightly shave the ends; see Fig. 10.

ASSEMBLY AND SEAT

When all the back slats fit into the mortises, the chair can be assembled.

ASSEMBLY. Start by gluing a front leg, side rails, and back leg to form a side unit. After assembling the other side unit, set both units aside to dry.

Next, dry assemble the vertical back slats (H) into the back rails (G,E). The slats aren't glued in since there isn't anywhere they can go once the chair is assembled.

Now fit the back assembly and front seat rail (F) between the side units; see Fig. 11. To keep the chair sitting flat, I

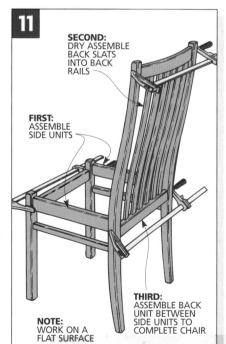

11

SECOND: DRY ASSEMBLE BACK SLATS INTO BACK RAILS

FIRST: ASSEMBLE SIDE UNITS

THIRD: ASSEMBLE BACK UNIT BETWEEN SIDE UNITS TO COMPLETE CHAIR

NOTE: WORK ON A FLAT SURFACE

placed the chair on top of my table saw.

BACK CLEAT. After the chair is assembled, glue a back cleat (I) to the front face of the back seat rail (E); see Fig. 13. Position the cleat so it's located ¼" down from the top edge of the back seat rail.

SEAT. Since the plywood seat (J) on this chair has to fit *inside* the back slats, it's cut shorter (14⁷⁄₈") than the ladder-back chair and rests on the cleat; see Figs. 12 and 13.

After the chair is finished and the seat upholstered, the seat can be screwed down to the back cleat and front rail. ∎

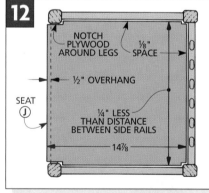

12

NOTCH PLYWOOD AROUND LEGS

⅛" SPACE

½" OVERHANG

SEAT (J)

¼" LESS THAN DISTANCE BETWEEN SIDE RAILS

14⁷⁄₈

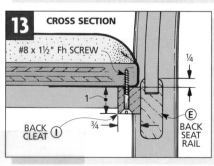

13

CROSS SECTION

#8 x 1½" Fh SCREW

¼

1

¾

BACK CLEAT (I)

(E)

BACK SEAT RAIL

COMPUTER DESK

A modular design and knock-down hardware allow you to tailor the components of this computer desk to suit your needs.

Somehow, a computer sitting on a traditional writing desk has always seemed a bit out of place to me. Maybe it's the contrast between old and new. But I think it also has something to do with size and proportion. Most writing desks are just too small and shallow for a computer and all the equipment that goes along with it.

So when designing this computer desk, I wanted it to be large enough for a computer monitor and other desk accessories. But I didn't want to make it so big that it took over the whole room. The answer came in two parts. First, I designed the desk to fit in a corner. This allows you to make the desk deep enough for the monitor. But since it sits

in a corner, it won't take up much more space than an ordinary writing desk.

MODULAR DESIGN. The second thing I did was design the desk to be modular. You can build just the basic corner unit (see photo at right), or if you need more space, you can expand the desk by adding an extension wing (or two) as shown above. And because the extension wings can be added to either end of the desk, you can configure it to conform to your own size and space requirements. (More on this on page 60.)

MODERN MATERIALS. To go along with the modern design of the com-

puter desk, we used some modern materials as well. Like plastic laminate and MDF (medium-density fiberboard) for the top. And instead of traditional woodworking joinery methods, we used knock-down hardware to assemble most of the components of the desk.

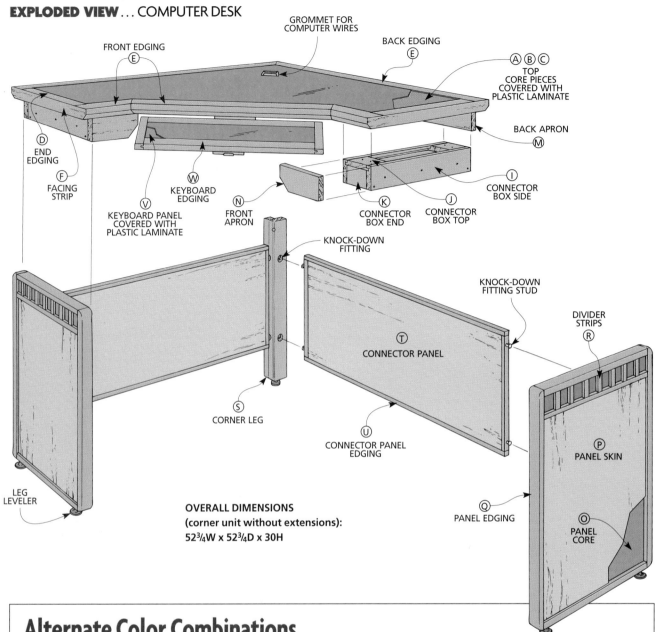

GROMMET FOR
COMPUTER WIRES

BACK EDGING
E

Ⓐ Ⓑ Ⓒ
TOP
CORE PIECES
COVERED WITH
PLASTIC LAMINATE

FRONT EDGING
E

BACK APRON
Ⓜ

Ⓓ
END
EDGING

CONNECTOR
BOX SIDE
Ⓘ

Ⓕ
FACING
STRIP

Ⓦ
KEYBOARD
EDGING

CONNECTOR
BOX TOP
Ⓙ

Ⓥ
KEYBOARD PANEL
COVERED WITH
PLASTIC LAMINATE

Ⓝ
FRONT
APRON

CONNECTOR
BOX END
Ⓚ

KNOCK-DOWN
FITTING

KNOCK-DOWN
FITTING STUD

DIVIDER
STRIPS
Ⓡ

Ⓣ
CONNECTOR PANEL

Ⓢ
CORNER LEG

Ⓤ
CONNECTOR PANEL
EDGING

Ⓟ
PANEL SKIN

LEG
LEVELER

OVERALL DIMENSIONS
(corner unit without extensions):
52¾W x 52¾D x 30H

Ⓠ
PANEL EDGING

Ⓞ
PANEL
CORE

Alternate Color Combinations

I used black plastic laminate, solid cherry, and cherry plywood to build the computer desk shown on page 51. The contrast between the warm look of the cherry and the black laminate gives the desk a classy and formal appearance. It was exactly the look I wanted for my office.

For a different look, you may want to try changing the combination of wood and laminate. By choosing a different type of wood and a different color of laminate, the desk can be tailored to blend in with its surroundings. In the photos at right you will see two more alternatives.

For a less formal look, this desk was made with a combination of solid red oak and oak plywood, along with a dark laminate.

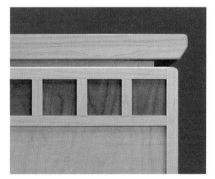

This desk was made using maple and maple plywood, with cherry-colored plastic laminate. It's hard to tell the laminate is not solid wood.

MATERIALS LIST

TOP

A	Core Piece (1)	¾ MDF - 19 x 47¾
B	Core Piece (1)	¾ MDF - 19 x 28¾
C	Core Piece (1)	¾ MDF - 21¼ x 21¼
D	End Edging (2)	1½ x 2⅜ - 19
E	Frt./Back Edging	1½ x 2½ - 14 ft. rough
F	Facing Strips (2)	⅛ x 1½ - 24
G	Corner Block (1)	2½ x 5 - 5
H	Block Filler (1)	¾ x 5 - 5
I	Conn. Box Sides (4)	¾ x 3⅜ - 20
J	Conn. Box Tops (4)	¾ x 2⅝ - 5
K	Conn. Box Ends (4)	¾ x 2⅝ - 4½
L	Box Fillers (2)	¾ x 5 - 19
M	Back Aprons (2)	¾ x 3⅜ - 47¹¹⁄₁₆
N	Front Aprons (2)	¾ x 3⅜ - 8½

*Also 22 lin. ft. of ¼ x ¹⁵⁄₁₆ hardboard splines

END PANELS/CORNER LEG

O	Panel Cores (2)	¾ MDF - 21⅜ x 26½
P	Panel Skins (4)	¼ ply. - 21⅜ x 26½
Q	Panel Edging	¾ x 1½ - 18 ft. rough
R	Divider Strips	¼ x ⅝ - 7 ft. rough
S	Corner Leg (1)	3 x 3 - 28

*Also 16 lin. ft. of ¼ x ¹¹⁄₁₆ hardboard splines

CONNECTOR PANELS/KEYBOARD TRAY

T	Panels (2)	¾ ply. - 46³⁄₁₆ x 16½
U	Edging	¾ x ¾ - 22 ft. rough
V	Keyboard Panel (1)	¾ ply. - 7½ x 24½
W	Keyboard Edging	¹³⁄₁₆ x 1½ - 6 ft. rough

HARDWARE SUPPLIES

- (7) ¼"-20 ID Threaded inserts
- (8) No. 8 x 1¼" Fh woodscrews
- (10) No. 8 x 2" Fh woodscrews
- (2) No. 8 x 3½" Fh woodscrews
- (6) ¼" x 1¼" Hex bolts
- (1) ¼" x 2" Hex bolt
- (7) ¼" Washers
- (8) Knock-down fittings
- (1) 4" x 2" Rectangular grommet
- (1) Keyboard tray slide
- (5) Leg levelers, 1⅝"-dia. with ⅜"-dia. shaft

CUTTING DIAGRAM

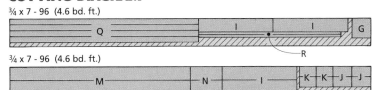

¾ x 7 - 96 (4.6 bd. ft.)

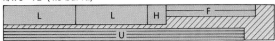

¾ x 7 - 96 (4.6 bd. ft.)

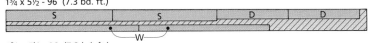

¾ x 9 - 72 (4.5 bd. ft.)

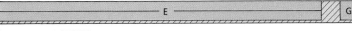

1¾ x 5½ - 96 (7.3 bd. ft.)

1¾ x 5½ - 96 (7.3 bd. ft.)

¾" MEDIUM DENSITY FIBERBOARD (MDF) 48 x 96

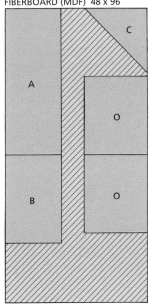

¼" PLYWOOD 48 x 72

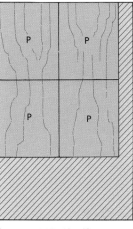

¾" PLYWOOD 48 x 48

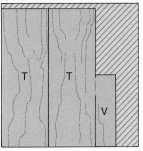

PLASTIC LAMINATE 48 x 48

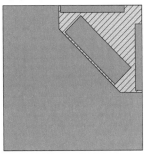

NOTE: ALSO NEED SMALL PIECE OF ¼" HARDBOARD FOR SPLINES

MDF

When building the computer desk I wanted a solid, flat, top surface that I could cover with plastic laminate and edge with solid wood. MDF (medium-density fiberboard) was the perfect material.

MDF is a man-made product that has been around since the 1960's. It's smooth, flat, and uniform and can be worked and glued like any other wood product. Since it can quickly dull standard bits and blades, I'd recommend using carbide cutters when cutting or routing it.

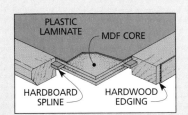

MDF is made from a mixture of wood fibers and shavings held together with resin similar to particleboard. But the fibers in MDF are *much* finer and this makes it denser, stronger, and heavier than particleboard.

To find the nearest MDF distributor, call the National Particleboard Association at (301) 670–0604.

DESK TOP CORE

Whether you're building the entire computer desk or just the corner unit, it's best to start by building the corner unit top. That's because most of the other components of the desk are fastened to it in some way.

CORE PIECES. The top consists of a 3/4"-thick MDF core covered with plastic laminate. Instead of trying to wrestle with a heavy, single sheet of MDF, I made the top out of three separate core pieces (A, B, and C); see Fig. 1. This also solves the problem of trying to cut the inside miters for the front of the desk.

The two rectangular pieces can be easily cut on the table saw. But when it came to the triangular piece, I used a little different approach.

I started with a 21 1/4" square blank, and laid out a diagonal line across two corners. But instead of cutting the piece on a table saw, I used a hand-held sabre (jig) saw, staying on the waste side of the line.

The sabre saw leaves a rough edge, but this can be cleaned up with a router and a flush-trim bit. Just screw the MDF down to a straight piece of scrap and trim the edge; see Figs. 2 and 2a.

CORE ASSEMBLY. When it comes to gluing the core pieces together, there are a couple of things to consider. First, the pieces need to be kept aligned. The solution to this is simple. I used 1/4" hardboard splines inserted into grooves along the edges of the pieces.

I cut the grooves for the splines with a router and a slot-cutting bit; see Fig. 1a. And since splines will also be used later to attach edging, I cut grooves on all the edges of the core pieces.

CLAMPING ANGLED PIECES. The other challenge I faced when gluing up the top was trying to clamp the triangular piece to the two rectangular pieces. Because of the angles involved, there wasn't a convenient place to apply clamping pressure.

The answer here was to build a simple clamping block; see Fig. 3. The clamping block has a notch cut in it to fit over the back corner of the desk.

PLASTIC LAMINATE

Once the core pieces are glued up, they can be covered with plastic laminate. I used a single, oversize piece of laminate because I didn't want any seams in the finished top.

The laminate is glued to the core with contact cement. Then I trimmed the edges of the laminate with a router and a special, solid-carbide bit; see Fig. 4. The tight radius of this bit allows it to trim all the way up to the inside corners of the desk top. (For sources of this special bit, see page 95.)

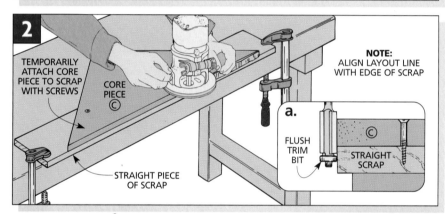

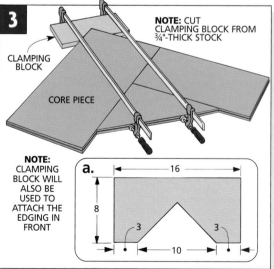

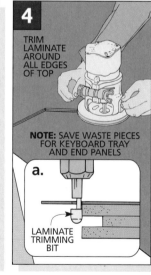

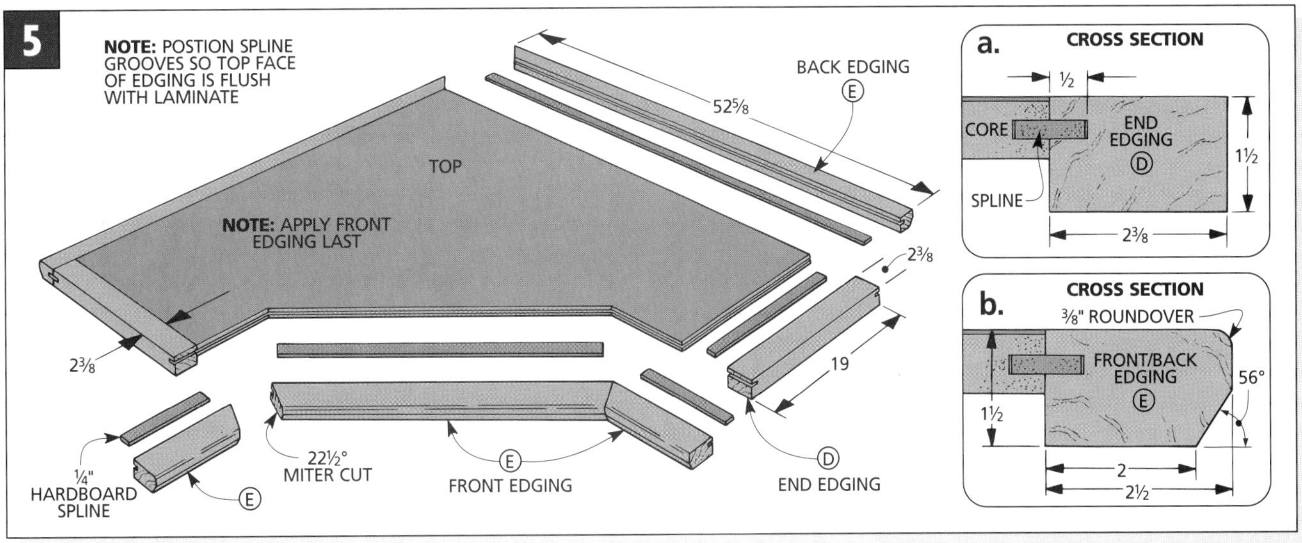
5
NOTE: POSTION SPLINE GROOVES SO TOP FACE OF EDGING IS FLUSH WITH LAMINATE
TOP
NOTE: APPLY FRONT EDGING LAST
BACK EDGING
E
52⅝
2⅜
19
2⅜
1/4" HARDBOARD SPLINE
E
22½° MITER CUT
E
FRONT EDGING
D
END EDGING
a.
CROSS SECTION
½
CORE
END EDGING
D
1½
SPLINE
2⅜
b.
CROSS SECTION
⅜" ROUNDOVER
FRONT/BACK EDGING
E
56°
1½
2
2½

EDGING

To finish off the top, I added hardwood edging; see Fig. 5.

End Edging. The end edging (D) is a piece of $1\frac{1}{2}$" stock cut to align with the front and back edges of the top. Grooves are cut on the ends and one edge of each piece for splines; see Fig. 5a. (Note: I used the laminate-covered top as a gauge to set the depth of the bit.) Then the edging can be glued on.

Front and Back Edging. The front and back edging (E) are also made from $1\frac{1}{2}$"-thick stock, but their profiles are different; see Fig. 5b. I cut the grooves for the splines first. Then I rounded over the top edge and ripped a bevel on the bottom; see Fig. 6.

To cut the edging to length, miter the ends of the two back pieces at the back corner; see Fig. 5. The front ends are cut flush with the end edging.

To fit the three front pieces, start with the center piece and miter the ends at $22\frac{1}{2}°$. The length should equal the diagonal edge of the front of the desk.

The other two front pieces are also mitered at $22\frac{1}{2}°$, but only on one end. The other end is square; refer to Fig. 8.

Gluing On Edging. To help align the edging when gluing, again I used splines. And here there was another challenging clamping problem.

This time, the solution was to screw a block to the front edge; see Fig. 7. (The screw holes will be covered by edging later.) This block has two triangles attached to it; see Fig. 7a.

Facing Strips. To conceal the splines and the exposed end grain at the ends of the top, I added a couple of $\frac{1}{8}$"-thick facing strips (F) to the ends; see Fig. 8. These facing strips are simply glued and clamped in place.

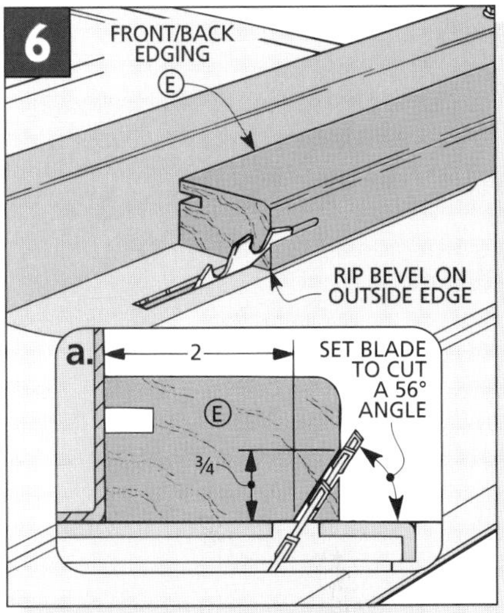
6
FRONT/BACK EDGING
E
RIP BEVEL ON OUTSIDE EDGE
a.
2
E
¾
SET BLADE TO CUT A 56° ANGLE

I removed the overlapping material at the lower corners of the facing strips with a small hand saw, followed by some light sanding; see Fig. 8a. Then I rounded over the edges with a router and a $\frac{1}{8}$" roundover bit; see Fig. 8b.

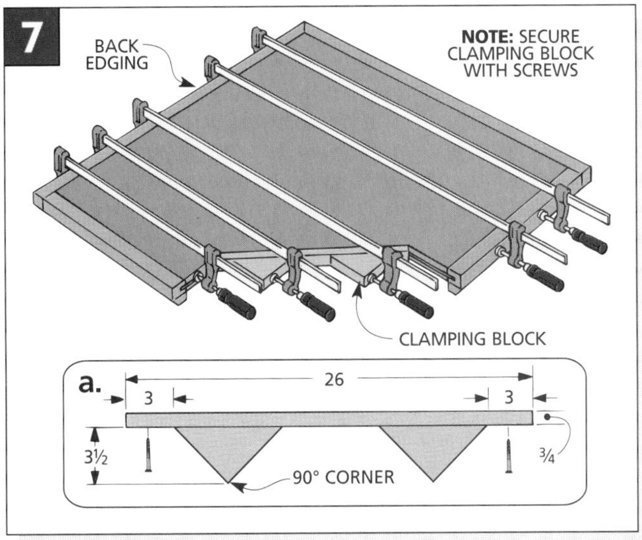
7
BACK EDGING
NOTE: SECURE CLAMPING BLOCK WITH SCREWS
CLAMPING BLOCK
a.
26
3
3
3½
¾
90° CORNER

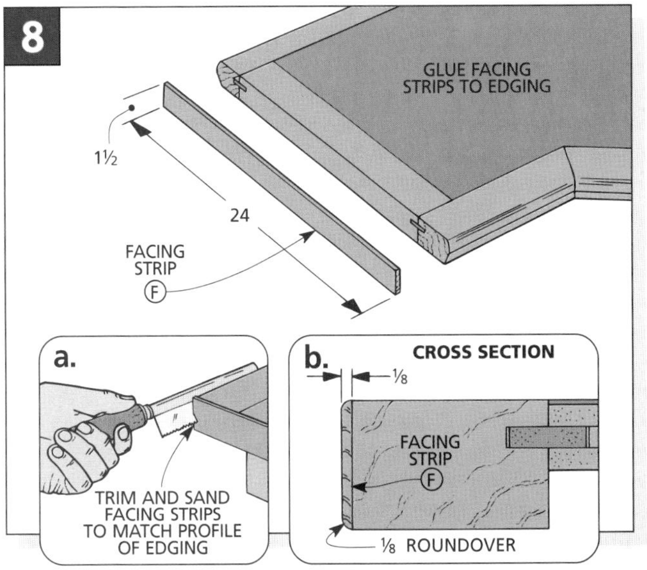
8
GLUE FACING STRIPS TO EDGING
1½
24
FACING STRIP
F
a.
TRIM AND SAND FACING STRIPS TO MATCH PROFILE OF EDGING
b.
CROSS SECTION
⅛
FACING STRIP
F
⅛ ROUNDOVER

SUPPORT SYSTEM

The top of the desk is supported by a corner leg at the back and two end panels on the sides. But the top isn't fastened directly to these pieces. Instead, there's a support "system" comprised of a corner block and a pair of connector boxes; refer to Fig. 11. Then the leg and panels are attached to these pieces with bolts and threaded inserts.

CORNER BLOCK. To attach the back corner leg to the top, I built a triangular-shaped corner block (G); see Fig. 9. This $2\frac{1}{2}$"-thick block is made by laminating two pieces of wood ($1\frac{3}{4}$" and $\frac{3}{4}$"-thick) together to form a 5" x 5" square. Then the square is cut diagonally to leave a 7"-long front edge.

Next, drill five holes through the edges and the face to screw the block under the desk; see Fig. 9. Finally, cut a notch out of the back corner of the block for the leg to fit into.

Since the top edging is thicker than the core, I made a block filler (H) to create a level surface for mounting the corner block; see Fig. 11. This filler is simply glued to the top core. Then the corner block can be screwed in place.

CONNECTOR BOXES. In addition to the corner block, a pair of connector boxes are mounted under the top; refer to Fig. 11. These are used to join the end panels with the top.

Each connector box has two sides (I), two tops (J), and two ends (K); see Fig. 10. The tops are attached to the sides with $\frac{1}{4}$" x $\frac{1}{4}$" tongue and groove joints. But the ends are simply cut to fit between the sides and then glued and screwed in place.

As with the corner block, I glued a couple box fillers (L) to the underside of the top before attaching the connector boxes; see Fig. 11.

APRONS. To conceal the corner block and connector boxes, I added $\frac{3}{4}$"-thick aprons to the front and back of the desk; see Fig. 12.

Note that there's a $\frac{3}{8}$" roundover on the front aprons (N), but only a $\frac{1}{8}$"

roundover on the back aprons (M). Also, the lower corners of the front aprons are lopped off so you don't hit your knees on them; see Fig. 12a.

The front aprons are simply glued to the connector boxes and the top. But with the back aprons, I also drove a couple of screws through the corner block into the aprons; see Fig. 12b.

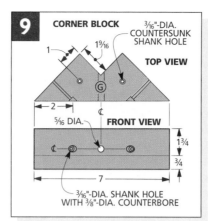

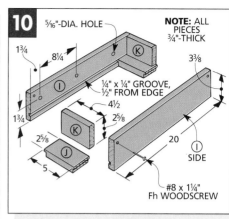

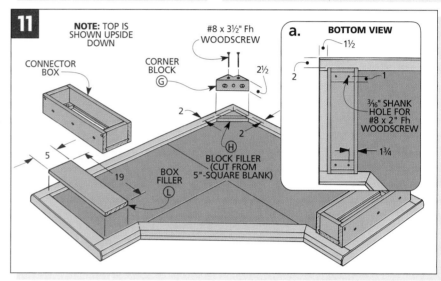

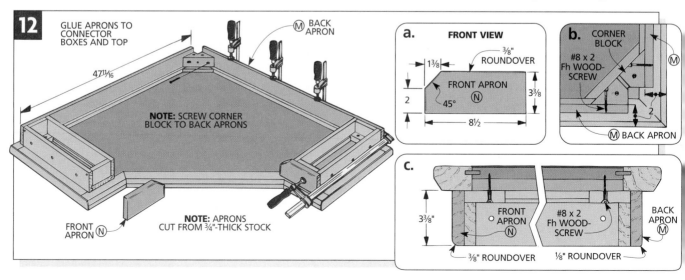

END PANELS

With the top of the desk completed, you can begin work on the two end panels.

BASIC PANEL. Like the top, each end panel starts off as a $3/4$"-thick MDF core (O) ($21^3/8$" x $26^1/2$"); see Fig. 13. But this time, I laminated both sides with $1/4$"-thick plywood. These plywood skins (P) are cut oversize and flush-trimmed after they're glued on with contact cement.

PLASTIC LAMINATE. The outside face of each panel has a narrow band of plastic laminate at the top to match the top of the desk; see Fig. 13. To position this laminate, I drew a layout line on one side of each panel $2^1/8$" down from the top. Using contact cement, I glued down an oversize piece of laminate flush with the line and then flush-trimmed the other three sides.

EDGING. Next, I applied some $3/4$"-thick edging (Q) to the panel; see Fig. 14. This edging is wider than the thickness of the panel to create an overhang around the outside face; see Fig. 15b. To attach the edging, I cut grooves in both the panels ($1/2$" deep) and the edging ($1/4$" deep), and inserted hardboard splines; see Figs. 13a and 15.

DIVIDER STRIPS. After the edging was glued in place, I added wood divider strips (R) to the plastic laminate on the outside of each panel to create a row of "windows;" see Fig. 14.

The trick to making these strips is getting them to the correct thickness. They should end up flush with the edging. But because the horizontal strip is glued to the plywood instead of the laminate, it needs to be a little thicker than the vertical strips.

Gluing the strips down is easy. The horizontal strip is glued to the plywood, just below the laminate. Then the vertical strips are glued onto the laminate, using a "super glue" adhesive; see Fig. 14a. I found that a gel glue was the easiest to apply in this situation.

To soften the look of the panels, I routed a $3/8$" radius on all four corners; see Fig. 14a. Then a $1/8$" roundover is routed on the edges.

HARDWARE. Next, holes for the hardware can be drilled on the inside face of each panel; see Figs. 15a and 15b. First, drill two 25mm holes and install the knock-down cams. (Note: They're installed with the line on them in the vertical position and the "screw" toward the *inside* of the desk; see an example of this in Fig. 20a on page 59.)

Then, drill a double row of $1/4$"-dia. holes, $3/8$"-deep for shelf support pins. Note: If you don't intend to build the extension wings, you can omit these.

Finally, holes are drilled for threaded inserts and they're installed near the top of each panel.

To complete the end panels, I added leg levelers to the bottom of each panel; see Fig. 15a. (I painted my leg levelers black to match the laminate.)

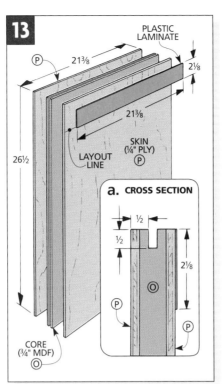

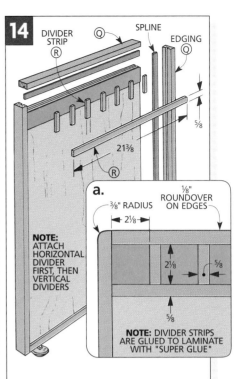

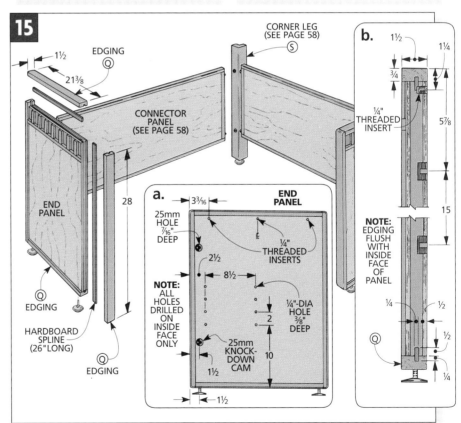

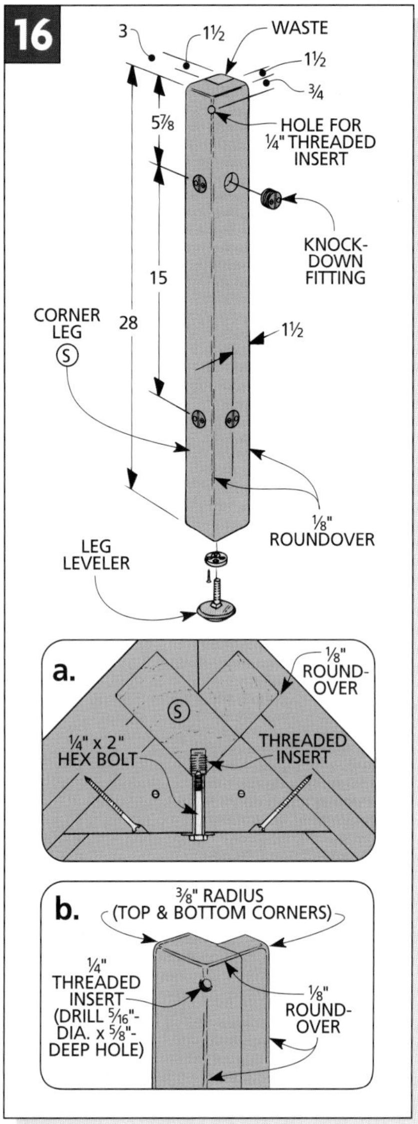
16
3
1½
WASTE
1½
¾
5⅞
HOLE FOR ¼" THREADED INSERT
KNOCK-DOWN FITTING
15
CORNER LEG (S)
28
1½
⅛" ROUNDOVER
LEG LEVELER
a.
⅛" ROUND-OVER
(S)
¼" x 2" HEX BOLT
THREADED INSERT
b.
⅜" RADIUS (TOP & BOTTOM CORNERS)
¼" THREADED INSERT (DRILL 5/16"-DIA. x ⅝"-DEEP HOLE)
⅛" ROUND-OVER

CORNER LEG

The end panels alone are not enough to support the top. To support the back of the desk, I added a V-shaped corner leg (S). This leg starts out as 3" x 3" post glued up from 1½" stock; see Fig. 16.

Next, I drilled the holes for the knock-down fittings. Once these are drilled, the back corner of the leg can be cut away on the table saw to create the "V" shape; refer to Fig. 16b.

To get the corner leg to match the profile of the end panels, I rounded over the corners and edges of the leg; see Figs. 16a and 16b. Then to complete the leg, I added a threaded insert and a leg leveler; see Figs. 16 and 16b.

CONNECTOR PANELS

The connector panels serve an important purpose in the design. They join the end panels with the leg, bracing the desk to prevent it from racking.

There's not much to these connector panels. Each one starts as a ¾"-thick plywood panel (T); see Fig. 17. Then the panels are framed with hardwood edging (U). I found it easiest to rip the edging a little wider than the thickness of the panels. Then after gluing it on, I routed it flush with a flush trim bit.

After trimming the edging flush, I rounded over the top and bottom edges only with a ⅛" roundover bit; see Fig. 17a. Then I added the knock-down fitting studs; see Fig. 17b.

KEYBOARD TRAY

The next step is to add the keyboard tray. To make this tray, I started by cutting a keyboard panel (V) to size from ¾" plywood; see Fig. 18. Then I glued an oversized piece of laminate to the panel and flush-trimmed the edges.

EDGING. To complete the tray, I cut ¼" x ¼" tongues for edging (W) on all four edges; see Figs. 18 and 18a.

The keyboard edging is made from 1¾"-thick stock that has been planed to match the thickness of the laminated panel (in my case, 13/16"). After cutting the pieces to size, the grooves and stub tenons can be cut.

Once the edging is glued to the panel, a ⅜" radius can be rounded off each corner, as well as a ⅛" roundover on all the edges; see Figs. 18 and 18a.

HARDWARE. Now the panel can be mounted to the desk with some special hardware. This hardware allows the keyboard to be hidden under the desk.

I mounted the bottom plate first. It's simply centered underneath the desk, butted up to the edging, and screwed to the core; see Fig. 19.

Next, place the tray holder in the grooves on the plate, slide the holder forward, and lock it in a "working position." Then center the keyboard tray on the holder and screw it in place.

Finally, to prevent the tray holder from sliding out the back, screw the stop into the bottom plate; see Fig. 19.

GROMMET. The other piece of "com-

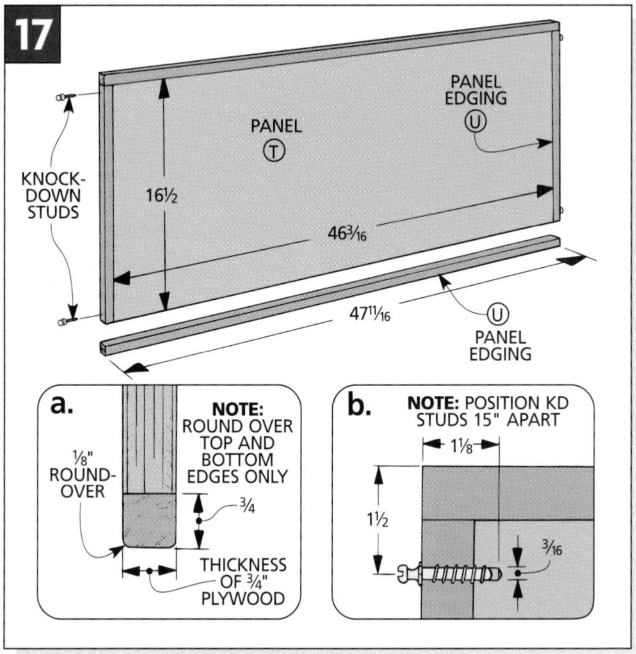
17
KNOCK-DOWN STUDS
PANEL (T)
PANEL EDGING (U)
16½
46 3/16
47 11/16
(U) PANEL EDGING
a.
NOTE: ROUND OVER TOP AND BOTTOM EDGES ONLY
⅛" ROUND-OVER
¾
THICKNESS OF ¾" PLYWOOD
b.
NOTE: POSITION KD STUDS 15" APART
1⅛
1½
3/16

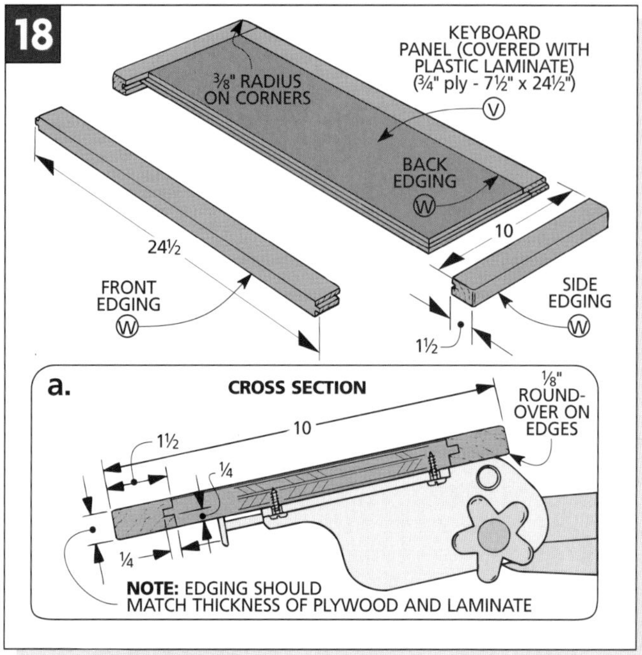
18
KEYBOARD PANEL (COVERED WITH PLASTIC LAMINATE) (¾" ply - 7½" x 24½")
(V)
⅜" RADIUS ON CORNERS
BACK EDGING (W)
24½
10
FRONT EDGING (W)
SIDE EDGING (W)
1½
a.
CROSS SECTION
⅛" ROUND-OVER ON EDGES
10
1½
¼
¼
NOTE: EDGING SHOULD MATCH THICKNESS OF PLYWOOD AND LAMINATE

puter" hardware to install is a plastic grommet for the wires to run through; see the tip box below.

FINAL ASSEMBLY

With all the parts made, the corner unit can be assembled with knock-down hardware; see Fig. 20. Start by joining the connector panels to the end panels and the corner leg; see Fig. 20a. Then add the top using bolts through the connector boxes into the threaded inserts in the end panels; see Fig. 20b.

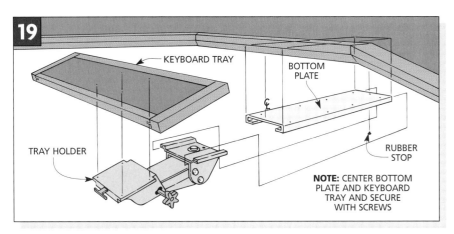

19

KEYBOARD TRAY

BOTTOM PLATE

TRAY HOLDER

RUBBER STOP

NOTE: CENTER BOTTOM PLATE AND KEYBOARD TRAY AND SECURE WITH SCREWS

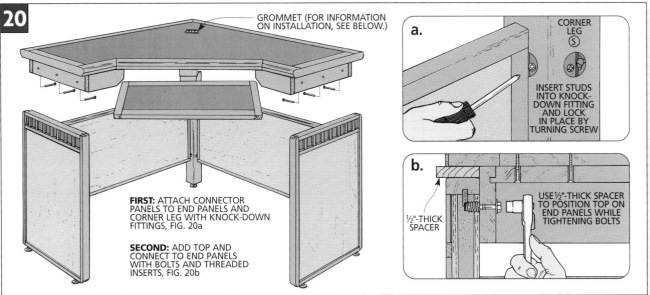

20

GROMMET (FOR INFORMATION ON INSTALLATION, SEE BELOW.)

FIRST: ATTACH CONNECTOR PANELS TO END PANELS AND CORNER LEG WITH KNOCK-DOWN FITTINGS, FIG. 20a

SECOND: ADD TOP AND CONNECT TO END PANELS WITH BOLTS AND THREADED INSERTS, FIG. 20b

a.

CORNER LEG Ⓢ

INSERT STUDS INTO KNOCK-DOWN FITTING AND LOCK IN PLACE BY TURNING SCREW

b.

½"-THICK SPACER

USE ½"-THICK SPACER TO POSITION TOP ON END PANELS WHILE TIGHTENING BOLTS

Installing Computer Grommets

One thing you have to consider when building a computer desk is what to do with all the wires. On the desk shown I used two styles of plastic grommets. (For sources, see page 95.)

The easiest grommet to install is a round one. I used these on the extension wings; see Fig. 7, page 64. All you need to install them is a hole saw.

On the corner unit I used a rectangular grommet.

To lay out the grommet, first tape over the area so you can see your layout lines. Then draw on the layout lines with a combination square; see Fig. 1.

Now, to create the opening, drill a hole in each corner and cut out the waste with a sabre saw (jig saw). To prevent chipout, I used a special reverse cut sabre saw blade; see Fig. 2.

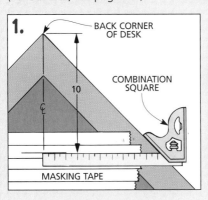

1.

BACK CORNER OF DESK

COMBINATION SQUARE

10

MASKING TAPE

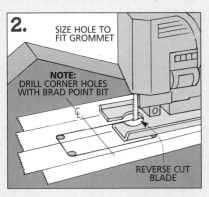

2.

SIZE HOLE TO FIT GROMMET

NOTE: DRILL CORNER HOLES WITH BRAD POINT BIT

REVERSE CUT BLADE

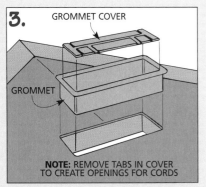

3.

GROMMET COVER

GROMMET

NOTE: REMOVE TABS IN COVER TO CREATE OPENINGS FOR CORDS

EXTENSION WING

The corner unit of the computer desk is designed so that it can be used alone. But for more space and storage, you might want to consider building one or two extension wings to fit on the ends of the corner unit. The wings are designed so that they can fit on either side of the corner unit as shown in the top photo below. Or they can be placed alongside each other to fit against a long wall; see bottom photo below.

The number of extension wings you build and how you arrange them will not only effect the look, but also the usefulness of the desk. Maybe you want one wing to hold a printer or scanner, and another on the other side to use as a writing surface.

DRAWER AND SHELF. There are a couple of additional features on the extension wings that aren't on the basic corner unit. First of all, each extension wing has a convenient drawer that pulls out on full extension slides.

Each wing also has an adjustable storage shelf underneath for storing books and extra paper.

CONSTRUCTION. After building the corner unit, the extension wing is a snap. That's because the construction is almost identical. Note: The cutting diagram and materials list on the opposite page are for a single extension wing. If you plan on making two wings, be sure to purchase enough material.

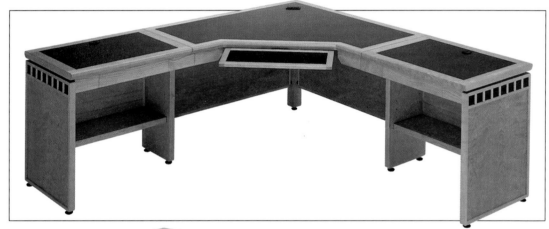

Extension wings can be added to each side of the corner unit.

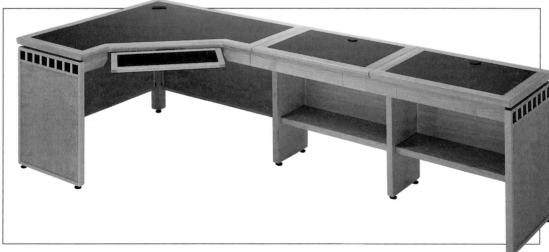

Two extension wings can be placed side-by-side.

EXPLODED VIEW

OVERALL DIMENSIONS:
31³⁄₄W x 24D x 30H

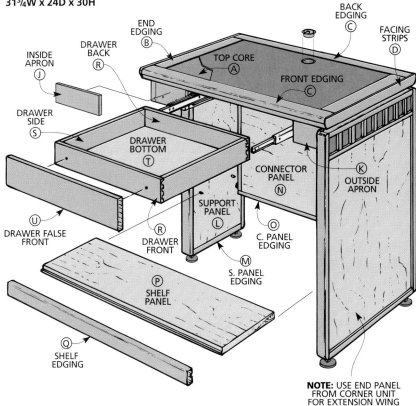

INSIDE
APRON
J

DRAWER BACK
R

END EDGING
B

BACK EDGING
C

FACING STRIPS
D

TOP CORE
A

FRONT EDGING
C

DRAWER SIDE
S

DRAWER BOTTOM
T

CONNECTOR PANEL
N

OUTSIDE APRON
K

DRAWER FALSE FRONT
U

SUPPORT PANEL
L

C. PANEL EDGING
O

DRAWER FRONT
R

S. PANEL EDGING
M

SHELF PANEL
P

SHELF EDGING
Q

NOTE: USE END PANEL FROM CORNER UNIT FOR EXTENSION WING

MATERIALS LIST
FOR ONE EXTENSION WING

WING TOP
A	Top Core (1)	³⁄₄ MDF - 19 x 27
B	End Edging (2)	1¹⁄₂ x 2¹⁄₂ - 19
C	Frt./Bk. Edging (2)	1¹⁄₂ x 2¹⁄₂ - 31³⁄₄
D	Facing Strips (2)	¹⁄₈ x 1¹⁄₂ - 24
E	Conn. Box Sides (4)	³⁄₄ x 3³⁄₈ - 20
F	Conn. Box Tops (4)	³⁄₄ x 2⁵⁄₈ - 5
G	Conn. Box Ends (4)	³⁄₄ x 2⁵⁄₈ - 4¹⁄₂
H	Box Fillers (2)	³⁄₄ x 5 -19
I	Back Apron (1)	³⁄₄ x 3³⁄₈ - 30¹⁄₂
J	Inside Apron (1)	³⁄₄ x 3³⁄₈ - 7¹⁄₂
K	Outside Apron (1)	³⁄₄ x 3³⁄₈ - 6

*Also need 8 lin. ft. of ¹⁄₄ x ¹⁵⁄₁₆ hardboard for splines

SUPPORT PANEL/CONNECTOR PANEL
L	Support Panel (2)	³⁄₄ ply. - 12 x 26¹⁄₂
M	Supp. Panel Edging	³⁄₄ x 1¹⁄₂ - 7 ft. rough
N	Conn. Panel (1)	³⁄₄ ply. - 16¹⁄₂ x 29
O	Conn. Panel Edging	³⁄₄ x ³⁄₄ - 8 ft. rough

DRAWER/SHELF
P	Shelf Panel (1)	³⁄₄ ply. - 10 x 30³⁄₈
Q	Shelf Edging (1)	³⁄₄ x 1¹⁄₂ - 30³⁄₈
R	Drw. Frt/Back (2)	¹⁄₂ x 2⁵⁄₈ - 17¹⁄₂
S	Drw. Sides (2)	¹⁄₂ x 2⁵⁄₈ - 15⁵⁄₈
T	Drw. Bottom (1)	¹⁄₄ ply. - 15¹⁄₂ x 17
U	Drw. False Front (1)	³⁄₄ x 3⁵⁄₁₆ - 18¹⁄₂

HARDWARE SUPPLIES
(6) ¹⁄₄"-20 ID Threaded inserts
(12) #8 x 1¹⁄₄ Fh Woodscrews
(8) #8 x 2" Fh Woodscrews
(4) ¹⁄₄" Brass shelf pins
(6) ¹⁄₄" x 1¹⁄₄" Hex bolts
(6) ¹⁄₄" Washers
(2) #8 x 1" Washerhead screws
(4) Knock-down fittings
(1) 2"-Dia. grommet
(1pr.) 16" Drawer glides
(2) Leg levelers, 1⁵⁄₈"-dia. with ³⁄₈"-dia. shaft

CUTTING DIAGRAM

1³⁄₄ x 5¹⁄₂ - 60 (4.6 bd. ft.)

C | B

³⁄₄ x 7 - 72 (3.5 bd. ft.)
E | E | G | G | F | F

³⁄₄ x 7 - 72 (3.5 bd. ft.)

I | K | U | J
M

³⁄₄ x 7 - 72 (3.5 bd. ft.)

O | Q
H | H | D

¹⁄₂ x 5¹⁄₂ - 36 (1.4 Sq. ft.)
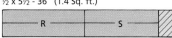
R | S

NOTE: ALSO NEED 24" x 48" SHEET OF PLASTIC LAMINATE AND ¹⁄₄"HARDBOARD FOR SPLINES

³⁄₄" PLYWOOD 24 x 48
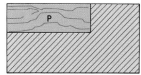
P

³⁄₄" PLYWOOD 48 x 48
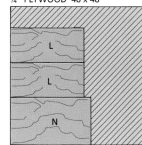
L
L
N

³⁄₄" MDF 24 x 48
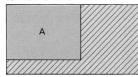
A

¹⁄₄" PLYWOOD 24 x 48

T

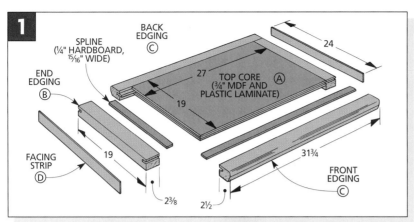

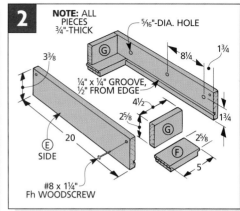

TOP

I started building the extension wing by working on the top. It's built the same as the corner unit top, but it's smaller and there are no angles; see Fig. 1.

CONSTRUCTION. The top consists of a rectangular MDF core (A) covered with plastic laminate. Splines are used to attach the end edging (B) and front and back edging (C). (Refer to page 55 for spline locations.) Then facing strips (D) are applied to both ends.

SUPPORT SYSTEM

Under the top of the extension wings is a support system similar to the one on the basic corner unit. There are a pair of connector boxes and front and back aprons; see Fig. 3. By shifting the connector boxes to the left or right and switching the two front aprons, the extension wing can be used on either side of the corner unit; see Fig. 4.

CONNECTOR BOXES. The connector boxes are identical to the ones used on the corner unit. They consist of two box sides (E) that are grooved to accept the box tops (F); see Fig. 2. Then the two box ends (G) are added.

Once the boxes are complete, you can make a couple of box fillers (H) to fit between the boxes and the top; see Fig. 3. Then the boxes can be screwed to the underside of the top; see Fig. 4.

APRONS. When it comes to making the back, inside, and outside aprons (I, J, K), the profiles are identical to those used on the aprons of the corner unit, but the lengths are different; see Fig. 3. And, when cutting the *front* aprons to finished size, it's important to note they're different lengths — one is longer to span the gap between the corner unit and the extension wing.

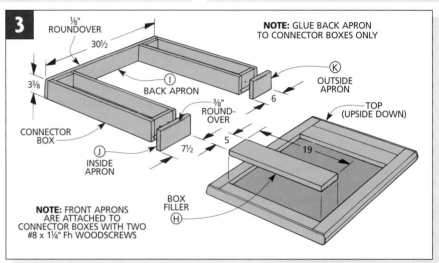

The back apron is simply glued to the connector boxes. But be careful not to glue it to the top itself, since it will have to be shifted along with the connector boxes if you move the extension wing from one side of the desk to the other. And since the front aprons have to be switched in order to move the wing, I attached them to the connector boxes with screws rather than glue; see Fig. 3.

SUPPORT PANEL

With the top assembled, you can begin working on the other elements of the extension wing. One end of the extension wing will be supported by the end panel of the corner unit. (The end panel is removed from the corner unit and attached to the end of the wing.)

To support the other end of the extension wing and to connect the wing

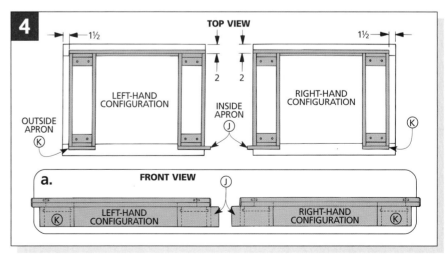

with the corner unit, I built a support panel. This support panel is narrower than the end panel to allow for leg room underneath the desk.

PANEL CONSTRUCTION. I used two ³⁄₄" plywood panels (L) to make up the support panel. This creates a slight problem. The support panel needs to be the same thickness as the end panel (1¹⁄₂") in order to fit between the wing and corner unit. But most ³⁄₄" plywood is a little less than ³⁄₄" thick. So I cut several *very* thin spacers to place between the two pieces of plywood to make their combined thickness 1¹⁄₂"; see Fig. 5. (You'll have to experiment a little. Mine were a little more than ¹⁄₁₆" thick.)

PANEL EDGING. To conceal the edges of the plywood, I added hardwood edging (M) all around the support panel; see Fig. 5. Unlike the edging on the corner unit end panels, the edging on the support panels is flush with both sides; see Fig. 5c. And this time, I didn't use any splines to attach the edging — it's simply glued in place.

Once the edging is attached, the corners can be rounded to a ³⁄₈" radius and a ¹⁄₈" roundover can be routed on all the edges; see Fig. 5b.

ADD HARDWARE. I used threaded inserts to attach the support panel to the connector boxes; see Fig. 5a. But since there will be a connector box on both sides of the support panel (one for the wing and one for the corner unit), I installed inserts on each side.

I also installed knock-down fittings on both sides of the support panel to attach the connector panels. Finally, I drilled holes on both sides of the panel for some shelf support pins and added a couple of leg levelers to the bottom of the panel; see Fig. 5a.

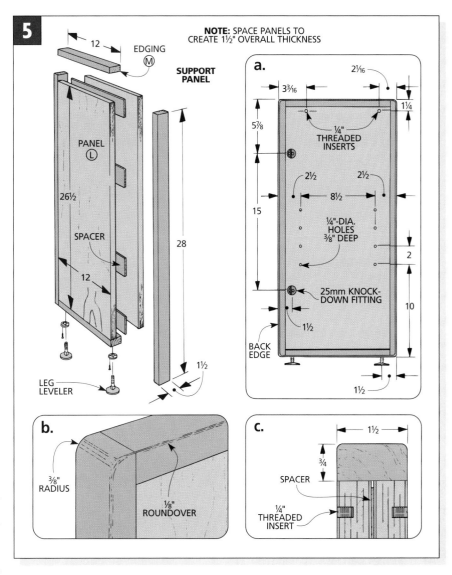

CONNECTOR PANEL

The extension wing connector panel is identical to the ones used on the corner unit except for its length (30¹⁄₂"); see Fig. 6. To build the panel, I just cut out a plywood panel (N) and added some hardwood edging (O); see Figs. 6 and 6a. After rounding over the corners and edges of the panel, I added the studs for the knock-down fittings to both ends, see Fig. 6b.

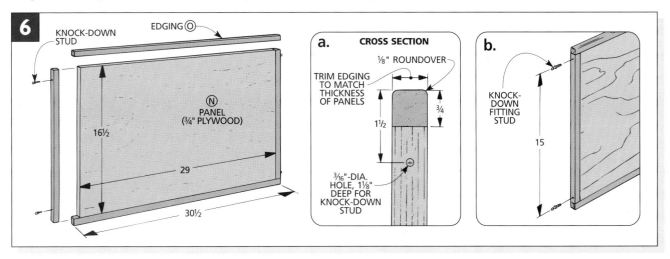

SHELF & DRAWER

To complete the extension wing, I added a shelf and a drawer. The shelf provides a convenient area to store all those software manuals. And the drawer makes a handy storage space for some old-fashioned "word processors" — pens and pencils.

SHELF. The shelf (P) fits between the end panel and the support panel and sits on brass shelf pins. It's nothing more than a piece of $3/4$"-thick plywood cut to size; see Fig. 7a.

To help strengthen the shelf and conceal the plywood edge, I added a strip of hardwood edging (Q) to the front of the shelf. The edging is attached with a tongue and groove joint; see Fig. 7a. Note: I positioned the groove so the edging was just a hair proud of the top surface of the shelf. Then I sanded the edging flush.

DRAWER. The drawer fits in the opening between the two front aprons. I made it out of $1/2$"-thick poplar stock, with a $3/4$"-thick cherry false front to match the aprons; see Fig. 8.

The drawer sides (S) are joined to the front and back (R) with machine-cut dovetails. (I used a router and a dovetail jig to make these.) Then I cut a $1/4$"-deep groove on the inside face of all four pieces for a bottom (T); see Fig. 8a.

DRAWER HARDWARE. Once the drawer is glued up, it can be mounted to the desk. To do this, I used full-extension drawer glides; see Fig. 8. Mount the glides to the drawer first, centering them on the sides; see Fig. 8b.

Then the drawer can be positioned in the opening and the glides attached to the connector boxes; see Fig. 7b. Note: The drawer should be positioned so that it hangs $1/4$" below the front edging of the top.

After the drawer is mounted and adjusted to fit, the $3/4$"-thick false front (U) can be added. Before mounting the front to the drawer, round over the two bottom edges and the inside top edge; see Fig. 8b. (The outside top edge is left square to match the aprons on either side of the drawer.) Then the false front is attached to the drawer with a couple of screws from the inside; see Fig. 8a.

ATTACH THE WING

To attach the wing to the desk, simply unbolt the end panel from the corner unit (you'll have to prop up the end of the desk) and fasten it to the end of the extension wing. Now attach the support panel to the desk. Finally, connect the wing to the support panel.　■

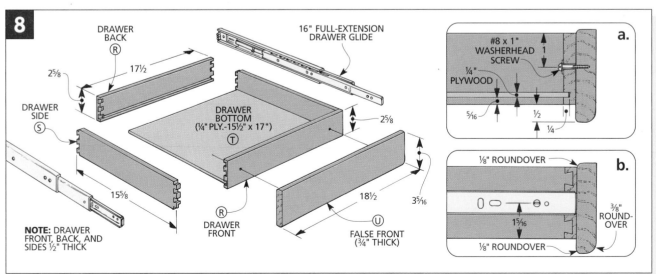

ROLL-TOP DESK

A tambour door is only part of what makes this desk special. It also features a simple, classic shape and pigeonhole organizer.

Sometimes the more obvious things tend to hide the important ones. Take this roll-top desk. Your eye is automatically drawn to the tambour door. There's just something about a door that opens and closes without swinging on a hinge. But you really need to look past the door to see what makes this desk special.

For one thing, there's the desk organizer with pigeonholes hidden behind the door. Normally, an organizer is built as an integral part of the desk. But this one is designed as a totally separate pro-

ject that can fit on any desk. (For more on building the organizer; see page 78.)

Another example is the desk hardware. Or more accurately, the lack of it. The only hardware you need for this whole desk is a few woodscrews.

Also, take a look at the design features. Sure the decorative cutout on the bottom edge of the front rail is appealing. But at the same time, it provides additional clearance when sitting down to write at the desk. And the tapered legs give the desk a light, graceful appearance.

WOOD. I built this project from solid cherry. Not only does it look great, but it has a fairly tight grain. This provides a good writing surface, even if you don't want to use a desk blotter.

All of the pieces are cut from $^3/_4$" stock except for the legs. For these I used 8/4 ($1^3/_4$"-thick) stock.

FINISH. When finishing a project that has a lot of crevices like the tambour on this roll-top desk, I like to use an oil finish. On this project I used General Finishes' Royal Finish, a tung oil and urethane combination.

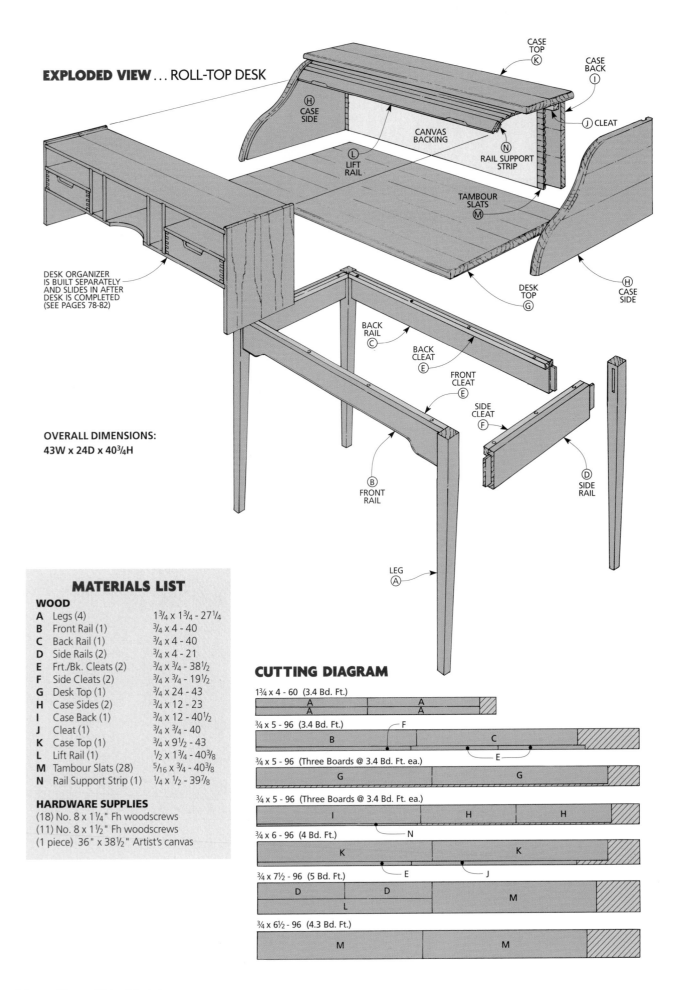

EXPLODED VIEW ... ROLL-TOP DESK

CASE TOP (K)

CASE BACK (I)

(H) CASE SIDE

CANVAS BACKING

(J) CLEAT

(L) LIFT RAIL

(N) RAIL SUPPORT STRIP

TAMBOUR SLATS (M)

DESK ORGANIZER IS BUILT SEPARATELY AND SLIDES IN AFTER DESK IS COMPLETED (SEE PAGES 78-82)

DESK TOP (G)

(H) CASE SIDE

BACK RAIL (C)

BACK CLEAT (E)

FRONT CLEAT (E)

SIDE CLEAT (F)

OVERALL DIMENSIONS:
43W x 24D x 40³⁄₄H

(B) FRONT RAIL

(D) SIDE RAIL

LEG (A)

MATERIALS LIST

WOOD

A	Legs (4)	$1^3/4 \times 1^3/4 - 27^1/4$
B	Front Rail (1)	$3/4 \times 4 - 40$
C	Back Rail (1)	$3/4 \times 4 - 40$
D	Side Rails (2)	$3/4 \times 4 - 21$
E	Frt./Bk. Cleats (2)	$3/4 \times 3/4 - 38^1/2$
F	Side Cleats (2)	$3/4 \times 3/4 - 19^1/2$
G	Desk Top (1)	$3/4 \times 24 - 43$
H	Case Sides (2)	$3/4 \times 12 - 23$
I	Case Back (1)	$3/4 \times 12 - 40^1/2$
J	Cleat (1)	$3/4 \times 3/4 - 40$
K	Case Top (1)	$3/4 \times 9^1/2 - 43$
L	Lift Rail (1)	$1/2 \times 1^3/4 - 40^3/8$
M	Tambour Slats (28)	$5/16 \times 3/4 - 40^3/8$
N	Rail Support Strip (1)	$1/4 \times 1/2 - 39^7/8$

HARDWARE SUPPLIES

(18) No. 8 x 1¼" Fh woodscrews
(11) No. 8 x 1½" Fh woodscrews
(1 piece) 36" x 38½" Artist's canvas

CUTTING DIAGRAM

$1^3/4 \times 4 - 60$ (3.4 Bd. Ft.)

A	A
A	A

$3/4 \times 5 - 96$ (3.4 Bd. Ft.)

F

B	C

E

$3/4 \times 5 - 96$ (Three Boards @ 3.4 Bd. Ft. ea.)

G	G

$3/4 \times 5 - 96$ (Three Boards @ 3.4 Bd. Ft. ea.)

N

I	H	H

$3/4 \times 6 - 96$ (4 Bd. Ft.)

K	K

E   J

$3/4 \times 7^1/2 - 96$ (5 Bd. Ft.)

D	D	M

L

$3/4 \times 6^1/2 - 96$ (4.3 Bd. Ft.)

M	M

BASE

The base for this roll-top desk is built like a simple table. There are four legs and a top joined by rails. I started work on the base by making the legs.

LEGS. These legs (A) start out as $1^3/_4$"-square pieces of 8/4 stock cut to a finished length of $27^1/_4$"; see Fig. 1. Near one end, I marked the location for a pair of $^1/_4$"-wide mortises to hold the tenons cut later on the rails. These mortises are drilled on adjacent faces; see Fig. 1a. But they aren't centered on the leg. Instead, they're positioned $^1/_2$" from the outside edge; see Fig. 2a.

To cut the mortises, I used a $^1/_4$" Forstner bit and drilled overlapping holes $^{13}/_{16}$"-deep to remove most of the waste; see Fig. 2. This depth provides a little extra clearance for the $^3/_4$"-long tenons on the ends of the rails. Since the bit cuts a clean, flat-bottom hole, it only takes a few minutes to square up the ends and clean up the sides of the mortise with a chisel.

TAPER. Now to make the legs look more graceful, I cut a taper on all four sides; see Fig. 3. (See page 73 for more on making and using the taper jig.)

RAILS. After tapering the legs, set them aside until the rails are completed. The rails that hold the legs together are identical in width (4"). But their lengths are different. The front rail (B) and back rail (C) are 40" long, while the side rails (D) are only 21" long; see Fig. 1.

Next, I cut a $^3/_4$"-long tenon on both ends of each rail; see Fig. 4. This tenon is centered on the thickness, but there's really no trick to cutting a centered tenon on the table saw. Just flip the rail over between passes to remove stock from both sides. But to make sure the tenon fits snug in the mortise, you'll want to sneak up on the final thickness.

To complete each tenon on the rails, all that's left is to create a shoulder on the top and bottom so the tenon matches the length of the mortise in the legs. To do that, stand the workpiece up on edge, and remove $^1/_2$" of the tenon from each edge; see Fig. 4a.

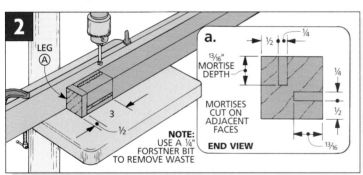

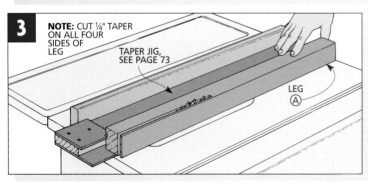

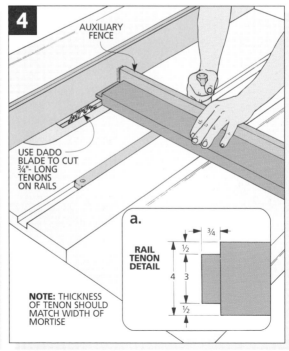

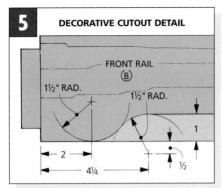

5 DECORATIVE CUTOUT DETAIL

FRONT RAIL (B)

1½" RAD.

1½" RAD.

1

2

4¼

½

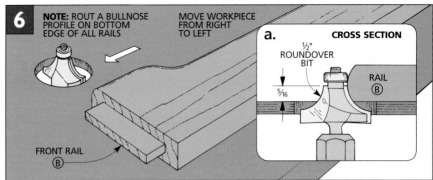

6 NOTE: ROUT A BULLNOSE PROFILE ON BOTTOM EDGE OF ALL RAILS

MOVE WORKPIECE FROM RIGHT TO LEFT

FRONT RAIL (B)

a. CROSS SECTION

½" ROUNDOVER BIT

5⁄16

RAIL (B)

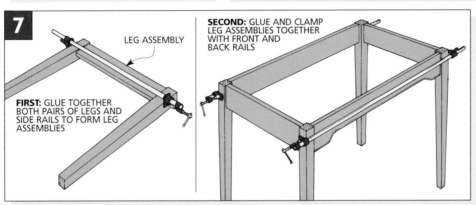

7

LEG ASSEMBLY

SECOND: GLUE AND CLAMP LEG ASSEMBLIES TOGETHER WITH FRONT AND BACK RAILS

FIRST: GLUE TOGETHER BOTH PAIRS OF LEGS AND SIDE RAILS TO FORM LEG ASSEMBLIES

DECORATIVE CUTOUT. Up to this point the front and back rails are identical. But to provide extra clearance for sitting at the desk, I cut away part of the front rail; see Fig. 5. To do this, simply lay out the curves at the ends of the rail and connect them with a straight line. Then remove the waste with a band saw and finish by sanding to the line.

BULLNOSE PROFILE. The legs and rails could now be assembled, but I wanted to break the sharp corners on the rails and create a smooth edge. So I routed a bullnose profile on the bottom edge of *all* the rails; see Fig. 6. To do this, I used a ½" roundover bit raised 5⁄16" above the router table; see Fig. 6a.

With the bullnose complete, the base can now be glued together. To make this easier, I glued the legs and side rails first; see Fig. 7. Then I clamped the front and back rails between the side assemblies.

CLEATS. Next, I worked on making the cleats that hold the desk top in position. These are ¾"-square pieces of stock with oversized shank holes drilled in them; see Fig. 8a. The front and back cleats (E) are the same length (38½"), while the side cleats (F) are shorter (19½").

These cleats are simply glued to the desk rails. But to make sure the desk top is pulled down tight against the top

of the rails, the cleats aren't flush with the top edge; see Figs. 8 and 8a. Instead, they're glued on just a little bit below the edge to create a small clearance gap.

DESK TOP

Next, I edge-glued six ¾"-thick boards to create a solid wood blank for the desk top (G); see Fig. 9. After the glue dried, I planed and sanded the top down flat and smooth.

Then after cutting the top to finished size (24" x 43"), rout a bullnose profile on all four edges. Here again this required a ½" roundover bit, but since the top is too big to easily rout on my router table, this time I used a hand-held router.

Finally, it's a good idea to *temporarily* attach the table top to the base; see Fig. 9. It will help strengthen the base as you move it around in the shop. You can go ahead and drill the holes, but don't put in all the screws just yet. Later, you'll have to remove the desk top before the roll-top case and tambour door can be installed.

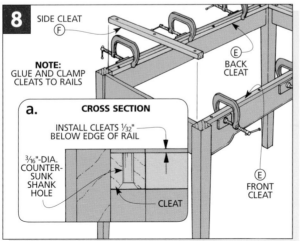

8 SIDE CLEAT (F)

BACK CLEAT (E)

NOTE: GLUE AND CLAMP CLEATS TO RAILS

a. CROSS SECTION

INSTALL CLEATS 1⁄32" BELOW EDGE OF RAIL

3⁄16"-DIA. COUNTER-SUNK SHANK HOLE

CLEAT

FRONT CLEAT (E)

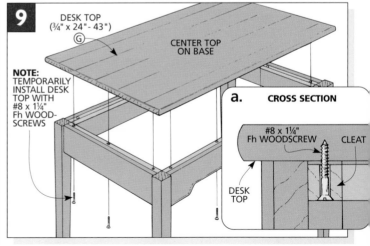

9 DESK TOP (¾" x 24" - 43") (G)

CENTER TOP ON BASE

NOTE: TEMPORARILY INSTALL DESK TOP WITH #8 x 1¼" Fh WOOD-SCREWS

a. CROSS SECTION

#8 x 1¼" Fh WOODSCREW

CLEAT

DESK TOP

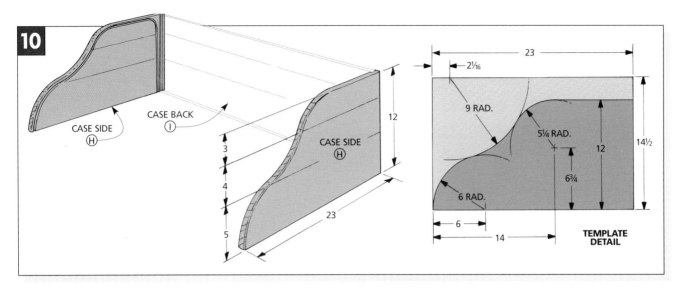

10

CASE SIDE (H)

CASE BACK (I)

CASE SIDE (H)

12

3

4

5

23

23

2¹⁄₁₆

9 RAD.

5¼ RAD.

12

14½

6 RAD.

6¾

6

14

TEMPLATE DETAIL

ROLL-TOP CASE

After completing the base I turned my attention to building the roll-top case. It consists of two case sides (H) held together by a back panel (I); see Fig. 10.

BLANKS. I started by working on the sides. They're glued-up blanks that are cut oversize (mine were 12¹⁄₂" x 24").

SIDE TEMPLATE. Once the glue dries, the "S-shape" for the side pieces can be drawn on the blanks. An easy way to do this is by making a template; see Template Detail in Fig. 10. Draw the shape on a piece of ¹⁄₄" hardboard, cut it out, and sand the edges smooth.

Now the template can be used to transfer the profile to the glued-up blanks. Just trace around it and cut out the case sides (H). To make sure these pieces are identical, I stuck them

together with double-sided carpet tape and sanded them smooth.

GROOVE TEMPLATE. Once the side pieces are sanded, the next step is to rout identical grooves on the *inside* face of each piece. This ¹⁄₄"-deep groove follows the shape of the case side and provides a channel for the tambour door to slide in. To make the door slide smoothly, the grooves have to be positioned in the exact same location on both pieces.

So I used a template again, but this time to guide my router so the grooves will be positioned in the same location. But I didn't make a new template, I just downsized the old one. This smaller template is used with a ⁵⁄₈"-dia. guide bushing in the router; see box below.

How much smaller is the template? To determine this, add up the distance

from the edge of the workpiece to the groove (³⁄₈"), the groove width (³⁄₈"), and the distance from the edge of the router bit to the outer edge of the guide bushing (¹⁄₈"). This adds up to ⁷⁄₈".

Now use a compass set at ⁷⁄₈" and follow the existing shape of the template along the front edge and across the top; see Figs. 11 and 11a. But the back edge is a little unusual.

Here you need a 1¹⁄₂" radius so the door can slide around the corner. And for clearance between the door and case back, the distance changes to 1³⁄₄"; see Fig. 11a. Once the lines are drawn, cut the template to size and sand the edges smooth.

Now stick the template to the case side with double-sided carpet tape so the bottom edge is flush and the front edge is set back ⁷⁄₈"; see Fig. 12.

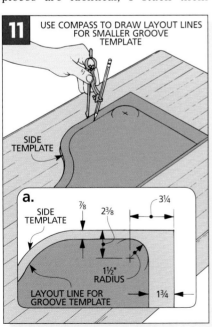

11 USE COMPASS TO DRAW LAYOUT LINES FOR SMALLER GROOVE TEMPLATE

SIDE TEMPLATE

a.

SIDE TEMPLATE

⁷⁄₈

2³⁄₈

3¼

1½" RADIUS

LAYOUT LINE FOR GROOVE TEMPLATE

1³⁄₄

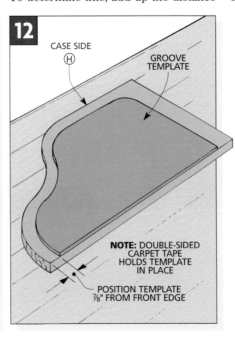

12

CASE SIDE (H)

GROOVE TEMPLATE

NOTE: DOUBLE-SIDED CARPET TAPE HOLDS TEMPLATE IN PLACE

POSITION TEMPLATE ⁷⁄₈" FROM FRONT EDGE

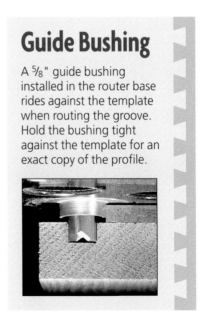

Guide Bushing

A ⁵⁄₈" guide bushing installed in the router base rides against the template when routing the groove. Hold the bushing tight against the template for an exact copy of the profile.

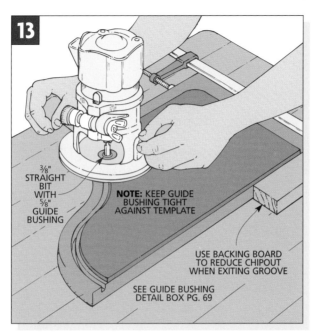

13

³⁄₈" STRAIGHT BIT WITH ⁵⁄₈" GUIDE BUSHING

NOTE: KEEP GUIDE BUSHING TIGHT AGAINST TEMPLATE

USE BACKING BOARD TO REDUCE CHIPOUT WHEN EXITING GROOVE

SEE GUIDE BUSHING DETAIL BOX PG. 69

ROUTING THE GROOVE. Before routing the groove, I did one more thing. I clamped a backing board to the workpiece where the bit exits the groove; see Fig. 13. This keeps the edge of the board from chipping out.

Now the groove can be routed with a ³⁄₈" straight bit and ⁵⁄₈" outside diam-eter guide bushing. I made two passes to reach the full (¹⁄₄") depth. You could do it in one pass. But a light cut makes it easier to keep the bushing tight against the template.

Note: Be sure to rout the groove on the the *inside* face of each case side. That way you will end up with a mirrored set of sides.

BULLNOSE. After routing the grooves, I switched to the router table to rout a bullnose profile on all the edges except the top; see Fig. 14. I didn't want a radius here so the case top would sit nice and flat. To do that, just measure out about 9" from the back edge and make a mark where you want to stop the profile.

BACK DADO. To complete the side pieces, a dado is cut along the back edge to hold the case back (I) see Fig. 15. This ¹⁄₄"-deep dado is cut to match the thickness of the back panel.

CASE BACK. With the dado cut, the case back (I) is added next to join the sides. This glued-up panel matches the height of the sides (12") and is glued in the dadoes; see Fig. 16.

But before the glue dries, it's impor-tant to check that the sides are perpen-dicular to the back. If not, the tambour door may "rack" in the opening.

CLEAT. One more thing to add to the case that's needed to attach the case top is a cleat (J); see Fig. 16. It fits between the sides and is glued and clamped to the back. Just like the cleat on the base, it isn't glued flush with the top edge; see Fig. 16b.

CASE TOP. All that's left to complete the case is building the case top (K). Like the side pieces it's also a solid wood panel with a bullnose profile routed on the edges.

The case top is screwed and glued to the case. The screws secure the back edge of the top to the cleats; see Fig. 16b. But the front edge is glued in place in just a couple spots; see Fig. 16a. If you glued the whole edge, it would prevent the solid top from expanding and con-tracting when the humidity changes.

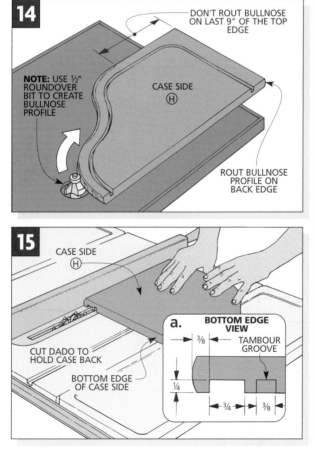

14

DON'T ROUT BULLNOSE ON LAST 9" OF THE TOP EDGE

NOTE: USE ¹⁄₂" ROUNDOVER BIT TO CREATE BULLNOSE PROFILE

CASE SIDE (H)

ROUT BULLNOSE PROFILE ON BACK EDGE

15

CASE SIDE (H)

CUT DADO TO HOLD CASE BACK

BOTTOM EDGE OF CASE SIDE

a. BOTTOM EDGE VIEW

³⁄₈
TAMBOUR GROOVE
¹⁄₄
³⁄₄   ³⁄₈

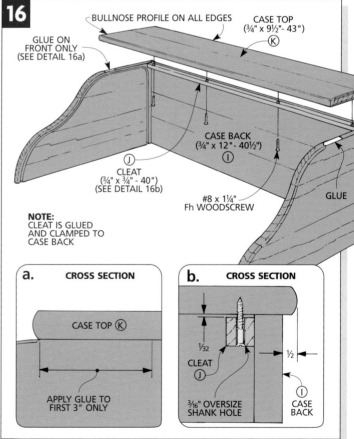

16

BULLNOSE PROFILE ON ALL EDGES

CASE TOP (³⁄₄ x 9½"- 43") (K)

GLUE ON FRONT ONLY (SEE DETAIL 16a)

CASE BACK (³⁄₄" x 12"- 40½") (I)

CLEAT (³⁄₄" x ³⁄₄" - 40") (SEE DETAIL 16b)

J

#8 x 1¼" Fh WOODSCREW

GLUE

NOTE: CLEAT IS GLUED AND CLAMPED TO CASE BACK

a. CROSS SECTION

CASE TOP (K)

APPLY GLUE TO FIRST 3" ONLY

b. CROSS SECTION

¹⁄₃₂

CLEAT (J)

½

³⁄₁₆" OVERSIZE SHANK HOLE

CASE BACK (I)

LIFT RAIL

After putting the case together, the next step is building the tambour door that fits inside. Tambour doors are basically all the same. There's a lift rail to open and close the door, slats that make up the body, and a fabric "hinge" on the backside that holds everything together; see Fig. 17. (For more on making tambours, see pages 74–77.)

CUT BLANK. Begin work on the door by making the lift rail (L). I started with an extra-wide (3") blank of $\frac{1}{2}$"-thick stock. (You'll see the reason for the extra width in a minute.) Though it's extra wide, cut the blank to finished length. To determine the length, measure the distance between the grooves in the case sides and subtract $\frac{1}{8}$" for clearance. (My rail was $40\frac{3}{8}$" long.)

CUTOUTS. Next, a pair of cutouts are routed in the front face of the lift rail that will become hand grips; see Fig. 17.

Just draw a couple stop lines on the front face to mark the location for the cutouts; see Fig. 18. Then use a hand-held router and a $\frac{1}{2}$" cove bit to create each recess; see Fig. 18a. (Here's why you need an extra-wide workpiece. The extra width helps to keep the router steady during the cut.)

Shop Note: This is a fairly deep cut so I didn't make it in one pass. I set the router for full depth, but didn't push the router bearing all the way to the workpiece on the first pass.

BEVEL. Next, I ripped a 7° bevel on the *bottom* edge of the lift rail so it would sit flush on the desk top; see Fig. 17a. Then rip the lift rail to final width ($1\frac{3}{4}$").

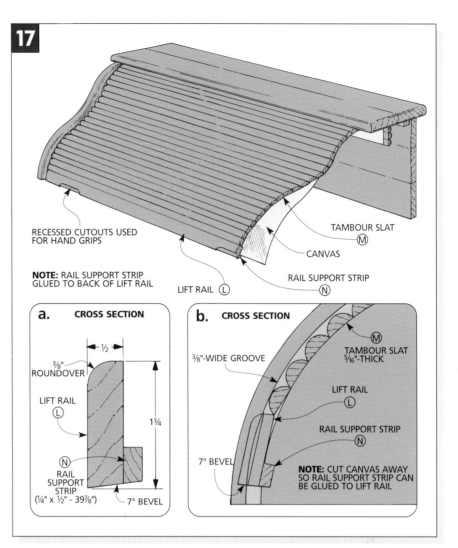

RECESSED CUTOUTS USED FOR HAND GRIPS

TAMBOUR SLAT Ⓜ

CANVAS

RAIL SUPPORT STRIP

LIFT RAIL Ⓛ

RAIL SUPPORT STRIP Ⓝ

NOTE: RAIL SUPPORT STRIP GLUED TO BACK OF LIFT RAIL

a. CROSS SECTION

$\frac{1}{2}$

$\frac{3}{8}$ ROUNDOVER

LIFT RAIL Ⓛ

$1\frac{3}{4}$

Ⓝ RAIL SUPPORT STRIP ($\frac{1}{4}$" x $\frac{1}{2}$" - $39\frac{7}{8}$")

7° BEVEL

b. CROSS SECTION

$\frac{3}{8}$"-WIDE GROOVE

TAMBOUR SLAT $\frac{5}{16}$"-THICK Ⓜ

LIFT RAIL Ⓛ

RAIL SUPPORT STRIP Ⓝ

7° BEVEL

NOTE: CUT CANVAS AWAY SO RAIL SUPPORT STRIP CAN BE GLUED TO LIFT RAIL

RABBET AND ROUNDOVER. Now to complete the lift rail there are two more steps. First, the ends need to be thinner so they'll slide in the grooves in the case sides. I did this by rabbetting each end to create a $\frac{1}{4}$" x $\frac{1}{4}$" tongue; see Figs. 15 and 15a.

Also, to match the profile of the slats, I used a $\frac{3}{8}$" roundover bit to rout the top outside corner; see Fig. 17a.

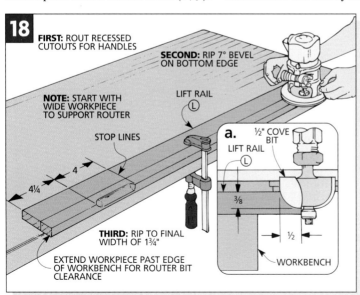

FIRST: ROUT RECESSED CUTOUTS FOR HANDLES

SECOND: RIP 7° BEVEL ON BOTTOM EDGE

LIFT RAIL Ⓛ

NOTE: START WITH WIDE WORKPIECE TO SUPPORT ROUTER

STOP LINES

4

$4\frac{1}{4}$

THIRD: RIP TO FINAL WIDTH OF $1\frac{3}{4}$"

EXTEND WORKPIECE PAST EDGE OF WORKBENCH FOR ROUTER BIT CLEARANCE

a. $\frac{1}{2}$" COVE BIT

LIFT RAIL Ⓛ

$\frac{3}{8}$

$\frac{1}{2}$

WORKBENCH

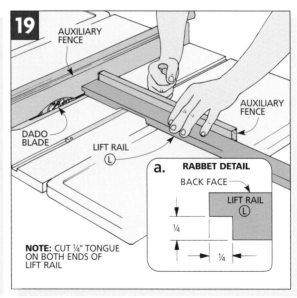

AUXILIARY FENCE

AUXILIARY FENCE

DADO BLADE

LIFT RAIL Ⓛ

NOTE: CUT $\frac{1}{4}$" TONGUE ON BOTH ENDS OF LIFT RAIL

a. RABBET DETAIL

BACK FACE

LIFT RAIL Ⓛ

$\frac{1}{4}$

$\frac{1}{4}$

SLATS

With the lift rail complete, I concentrated on the tambour slats (M). For the roll-top desk, 28 slats the same length as the lift rail are needed to complete the door. But I made a few extra so I wouldn't come up short if any twisted out of shape.

Making the slats is a two-step process. First, I used a roundover bit to create a rounded profile on the edge of the workpiece; see Fig. 20a. Then using a carrier board, it's quick and easy to rip a thin slat off the edge; see Fig. 17 and refer to page 76.

The important thing is that all the slats end up ⁵⁄₁₆" thick. Then the door will slide freely in the ³⁄₈" groove.

GLUE-UP. Once you have your slats cut, both the lift rail and slats can be glued to a canvas backing; see page 77.

DRY ASSEMBLY. After the slats are glued to the canvas, it's a good time to check the fit of the door. I wanted to see if it would slide freely in the grooves. If there's a problem, refer to the troubleshooting tips on page 77.

Also, since I planned on adding the desk organizer later (refer to page 78), I checked the height of the opening (mine was 10").

RAIL SUPPORT STRIP. To complete the door, a rail support strip (N) is glued to the back of the lift rail; refer back to

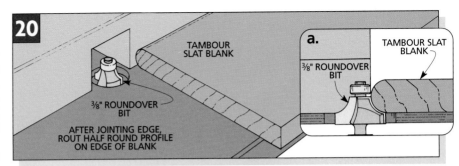

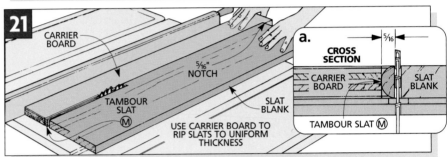

Figs. 17a and 17b. This strip gives you something to grip to close the tambour door. There's a 7° angle ripped on one edge and it's sized to fit easily between the case sides (39⁷⁄₈"). (Note: Cut away a strip of canvas to get a wood-to-wood joint between the lift rail and the strip.)

FINAL ASSEMBLY

Once the tambour door is complete the desk can be assembled. The first step is to install the case on the desk top. This meant drilling mounting holes through the top and into the case sides and back.

To locate the holes, I centered the case on the desk top and placed tape around the outside edges; see Fig. 22. When the case is removed, just measure in from the edge of the tape ³⁄₈" and drill the oversize shank holes.

Now the door can be installed into the case, and the case screwed to the desk top; see Fig. 22a. Finally, set the desk top on the base and screw it in place; see Fig. 23. ■

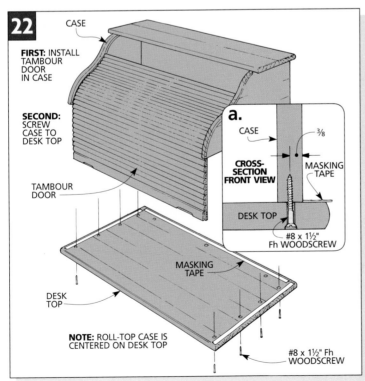

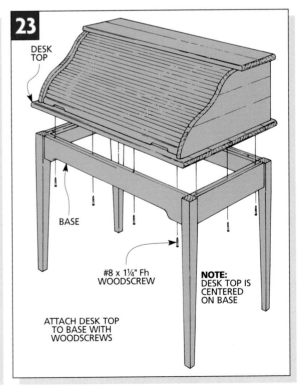

Tapering all four sides of a leg requires an "adjustable" jig. That's because after two faces of are tapered, there aren't any more straight faces to work from.

To cut the tapers on the legs of the roll-top desk, I made a special jig with a piece of 3/4" plywood and a stop block; see Fig. 1. These pieces are screwed to a 1/4" hardboard sled that carries the leg past the blade.

STOP BLOCK. The stop block is the key to the jig. It's made from 1/4" hardboard and has two notches in it to offset the leg and set the angle of the taper; see Fig. 1a.

One of the nice things about using this jig is that you don't have to worry about any angles. Just determine how much stock needs to be cut from each side of the leg (1/4" for the legs on the roll-top desk). This is how far the first notch needs to be offset from the edge of the plywood; see Fig. 1a. Then the second one is offset 1/4" from the first.

To determine the length of the taper, the stop block also needs to be positioned on the length of the plywood; see Fig. 1b. (The tapers on the desk legs are 22 1/4" long.)

Note: I attached the stop block to the *front* of the jig. This means you push the workpiece, not just the jig. I find it safer to use this way.

USING THE JIG. To use the taper jig, first lock down the rip fence so the distance from the fence to the blade is equal to the width of the plywood on the jig *plus* the width of the leg. (It's okay if you trim off a little bit of the sled on the very first pass.)

Now simply place the leg in the first notch and then make two passes, rotating the leg 90° between passes; see Fig. 2. (Note: For safety, I stuck the leg to the sled with double-sided carpet tape.)

For the last two faces, place the leg in the other notch, and make two more passes, rotating 90° between passes.

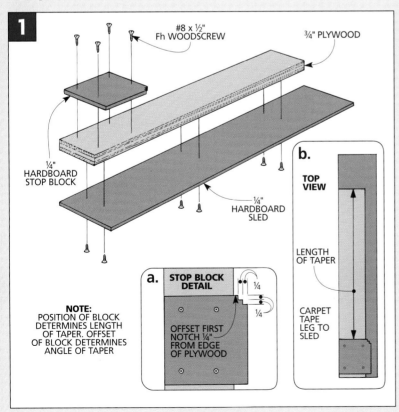

1

#8 x 1/2" Fh WOODSCREW

3/4" PLYWOOD

1/4" HARDBOARD STOP BLOCK

1/4" HARDBOARD SLED

NOTE: POSITION OF BLOCK DETERMINES LENGTH OF TAPER. OFFSET OF BLOCK DETERMINES ANGLE OF TAPER

a. **STOP BLOCK DETAIL**

1/4

1/4

OFFSET FIRST NOTCH 1/4" FROM EDGE OF PLYWOOD

b. **TOP VIEW**

LENGTH OF TAPER

CARPET TAPE LEG TO SLED

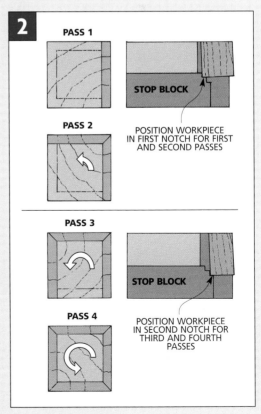

2

PASS 1

STOP BLOCK

PASS 2

POSITION WORKPIECE IN FIRST NOTCH FOR FIRST AND SECOND PASSES

PASS 3

STOP BLOCK

PASS 4

POSITION WORKPIECE IN SECOND NOTCH FOR THIRD AND FOURTH PASSES

One of the things I enjoy about wood-working is there's usually more than one way to solve a problem. And maybe that's how tambour doors were invented. Someone needed a door that would store out of the way when open.

The "solution," a slatted tambour or roll-top door, seems fairly obvious now. Make it flexible by gluing a bunch of thin slats to a piece of fabric. Then cut a groove for the pieces to follow so the door can slide out of sight inside its own cabinet. That's it. Nothing complicated about it.

A lot of people think tambour doors are a mystery. After all, there must be some trick in getting all those pieces to work together as a sliding door. But all you really need is a good design to follow and a little patience cutting and assembling the parts.

DESIGN SHAPE

So when building a tambour door, I find it's easiest to stick to a couple tried-and-true designs. These designs are straightforward and give me consistent results. They incorporate what I refer to as an "S-shaped" (double curve) or "C-shaped" (single curve) tambour; see drawings at right.

Each design has some advantages over the other. For example, I like to use an S-shaped tambour when the project calls for a wide door (like the roll-top desk in this book). This shape looks less bulky and more graceful for a large tambour. Plus, adding the extra curve helps the thin slats to resist sagging in the middle. And having a door with less sag means it will slide that much more smoothly.

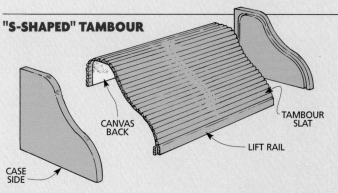

"S-SHAPED" TAMBOUR

CANVAS BACK

TAMBOUR SLAT

LIFT RAIL

CASE SIDE

"C-SHAPED" TAMBOUR

CANVAS BACK

TAMBOUR SLAT

LIFT RAIL

CASE SIDE

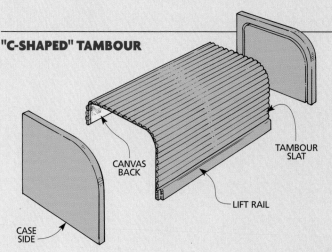

On the other hand, when a project needs to provide the maximum amount of storage space, a C-shaped tambour may be a better choice. It provides the largest amount of usable space behind and under the door. This comes in handy when you need to store a large mixer or blender in an "appliance garage" in the kitchen.

TAMBOUR ANATOMY

Deciding which shape to use is the first step to building a tambour door. Once that's taken care of, the parts of the tambour are the next thing to consider. What this means is figuring out how the actual pieces of the door will be cut and put together.

All tambour or roll-top doors consist of the same three parts; see drawing on the next page. There's usually a thick, heavier piece at the front (a lift rail), followed by a quantity of thinner pieces (tambour slats), all held together with a piece of fabric. The roll-top desk on page 65, for example, has a lift rail and 28 slats glued to a piece of canvas.

CANVAS. If there's one thing that's similar about all the tambour doors that I build, it's the fabric. I always use canvas. Usually this is a light to medium-weight artist's canvas available at art supply stores. Some people like using a dark denim backing because it doesn't show between the slats. But whatever the material, it not only holds the pieces together, it also acts as the hinge. The canvas allows all the individual pieces to flex as the door slides through the groove.

But it takes more than a piece of canvas to allow a door to flex in more than one direction (like it has to for an S-shaped tambour). The real "secret" is the style (or profile) of the tambour lift rail and slats.

SLAT PROFILE. The key to creating this flex is building in enough *clearance* between the slats. This can be easily accomplished by changing the slat profile. I wanted the door on the roll-top

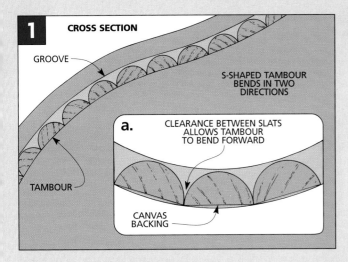

1 CROSS SECTION

GROOVE

S-SHAPED TAMBOUR BENDS IN TWO DIRECTIONS

a. CLEARANCE BETWEEN SLATS ALLOWS TAMBOUR TO BEND FORWARD

TAMBOUR

CANVAS BACKING

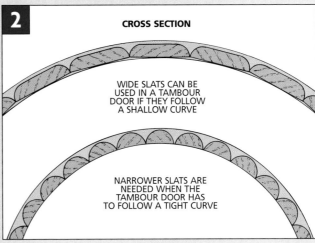

2 CROSS SECTION

WIDE SLATS CAN BE USED IN A TAMBOUR DOOR IF THEY FOLLOW A SHALLOW CURVE

NARROWER SLATS ARE NEEDED WHEN THE TAMBOUR DOOR HAS TO FOLLOW A TIGHT CURVE

desk to move through some pretty tight curves. By rounding over the slats, they can flex or move back and forth as the door moves through the curved groove; see Figs. 1 and 1a. The greater the clearance between the slats, the tighter the curve the door can follow.

SLAT WIDTH. But there are a couple of other things that come into play to allow the door to slide smoothly through the groove. One is adjusting the width of the slat; see Fig. 2. A wider slat makes a sturdier door. But a wide slat can't slide through a tight curve. It's physically impossible. That's why you typically don't find slats wider than 1" on most tambour doors.

There is one exception to this: the lift

rail located at the front of the door. Here you want a wide piece to take all the wear and tear of being pushed and pulled as the door is opened and closed. It's traditionally cut wider and thicker to make it stronger. The lift rail on the roll-top desk is $1^{3}/_{4}$" wide.

Getting a wide piece like this to work in a groove doesn't require any wood-working magic. Simply reduce the thickness on the ends of the rail by cutting a rabbet to create a tongue; see Fig. 3. For the desk, this tongue was only $1/_{4}$"-thick so it could slide smoothly in the $3/_{8}$"-wide groove.

THICKNESS. When you reduce the thickness of a lift rail or slat, you can make it wider and still have it slide

smoothly. This is because you've created more clearance around it. Of course you can go too far and make them too thin. Then on a wide door the slats could start to sag and even fall out of the grooves.

CLEARANCE. Finally, there's one other consideration for making tambour doors slide smoothly. You need to allow for clearance between the slat and the groove. You can't expect a $3/_{8}$"-thick slat to slide very well in a $3/_{8}$"-wide groove. The tambour door in the roll-top desk used $5/_{16}$"-thick slats in a $3/_{8}$" groove; see Fig. 3. This provided just enough clearance so the tambour door would slide smoothly but without rattling around when it moves.

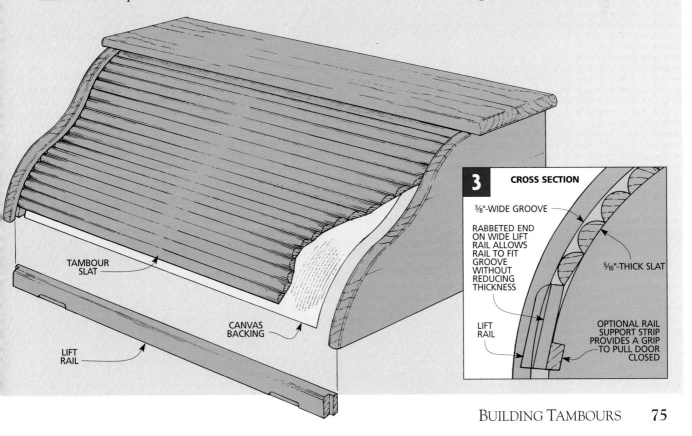

TAMBOUR SLAT

CANVAS BACKING

LIFT RAIL

3 CROSS SECTION

$3/_{8}$"-WIDE GROOVE

RABBETED END ON WIDE LIFT RAIL ALLOWS RAIL TO FIT GROOVE WITHOUT REDUCING THICKNESS

$5/_{16}$"-THICK SLAT

LIFT RAIL

OPTIONAL RAIL SUPPORT STRIP PROVIDES A GRIP TO PULL DOOR CLOSED

CONSTRUCTION

Okay, so now you know there's more to designing a tambour door than gluing some sticks to a piece of canvas. The next step is to put this information to use. For me this means starting on the case sides that hold the door.

TAMBOUR CASE. The first step is to make the grooves on the sides that guide the door. They're exact mirror images of each other.

The easiest way to keep these grooves aligned is by making a template; see Fig. 4. This way a guide bushing in a hand-held router can follow the template and rout the groove; see Fig. 5. If the template is installed in the same spot on both pieces and the guide bushing stays tight against the template, the grooves will be identical.

LIFT RAIL. After routing the grooves, the lift rail can be built for the door. Just cut it to length to fit between the grooves and rabbet the ends so it slides easily in the grooves.

SLATS. Next I turn my attention to the tambour slats. The safest and most accurate way to make these is to start with a wide piece of stock and cut several slats off it like strips of bacon.

To do this, first rout the profile on one edge; see Figs. 6 and 6a. Then switch to the table saw to rip the slats from the edge of the board.

Here I use a carrier board with a notch cut at one end that matches the thickness of the slats; see Figs. 7 and 7a. As the slat is cut from the blank, the carrier pushes it safely past the blade.

I also like to number the slats as

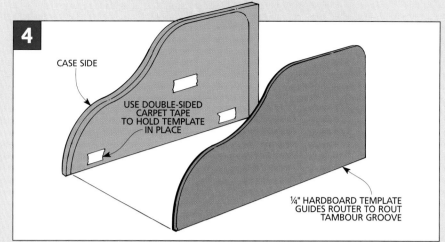

CASE SIDE

USE DOUBLE-SIDED CARPET TAPE TO HOLD TEMPLATE IN PLACE

¼" HARDBOARD TEMPLATE GUIDES ROUTER TO ROUT TAMBOUR GROOVE

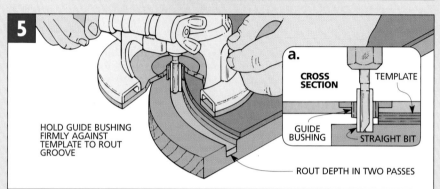

a.

CROSS SECTION TEMPLATE

GUIDE BUSHING STRAIGHT BIT

HOLD GUIDE BUSHING FIRMLY AGAINST TEMPLATE TO ROUT GROOVE

ROUT DEPTH IN TWO PASSES

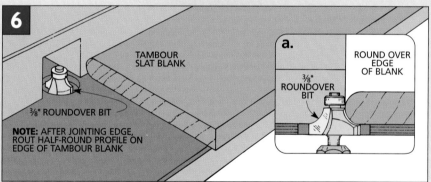

TAMBOUR SLAT BLANK

a.

ROUND OVER EDGE OF BLANK

⅜" ROUNDOVER BIT

⅜" ROUNDOVER BIT

NOTE: AFTER JOINTING EDGE, ROUT HALF-ROUND PROFILE ON EDGE OF TAMBOUR BLANK

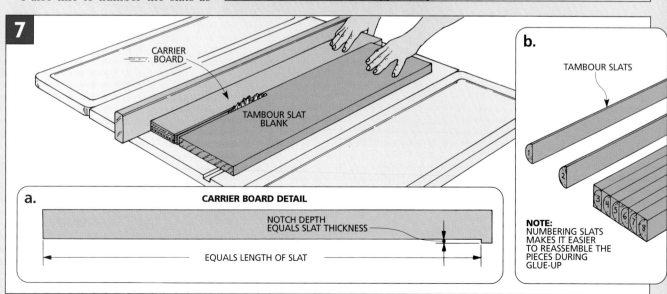

CARRIER BOARD

TAMBOUR SLAT BLANK

b.

TAMBOUR SLATS

NOTE: NUMBERING SLATS MAKES IT EASIER TO REASSEMBLE THE PIECES DURING GLUE-UP

a.

CARRIER BOARD DETAIL

NOTCH DEPTH EQUALS SLAT THICKNESS

EQUALS LENGTH OF SLAT

they're cut, see Fig. 7b. That way they can be reassembled for the best color and appearance. And while you're set up, make some extras. There's always a few slats that will twist or bow.

GLUE-UP

To hold all of the slats and lift rail together, they're glued to a piece of canvas. Trim the canvas so it's narrower than the slats. This keeps the canvas out of the grooves.

I use a couple of coats of contact adhesive to glue the slats to the canvas. A small roller spreads the adhesive quickly. This is easy on a big piece of canvas. But it can be tedious on the narrow slats. So I temporarily assemble a few slats by taping the ends; see Fig. 8.

The tape holds the slats together so there's a large surface to work on. And once you remove it, the ends are free of glue. (Glue on this part of the slats would keep them from sliding freely in the grooves.)

ASSEMBLY JIG. Now the challenge is getting the slats and lift rail installed on

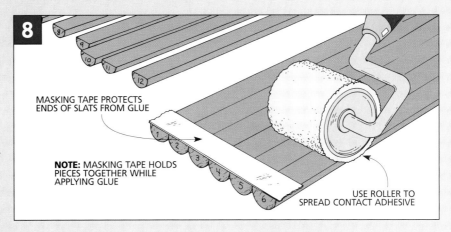

MASKING TAPE PROTECTS ENDS OF SLATS FROM GLUE

NOTE: MASKING TAPE HOLDS PIECES TOGETHER WHILE APPLYING GLUE

USE ROLLER TO SPREAD CONTACT ADHESIVE

the canvas so they're square to each other. Here's where an assembly jig helps; see Figs. 9 and 10. This jig is just a couple of pieces of scrap screwed to a piece of plywood at right angles to one another. These guide boards keep the door pieces straight at the sides and parallel to each other.

I stretch out the canvas first (adhesive side up) so it's flat and tight. Just screw a guide board at one end to hold it in place, stretch it out, and secure the other end with a piece of scrap. Then

using a framing square, install the other guide board square to the first one.

Now the lift rail and slats can be installed on the canvas. Just remember, when they make contact, you won't be able to move them. It's also a good idea to periodically check that the slats are running true; see Fig. 10.

After the slats are all in place, tap them with a mallet to remove any air gaps under the slats. Finally, to complete the door, trim off the excess canvas at the end.

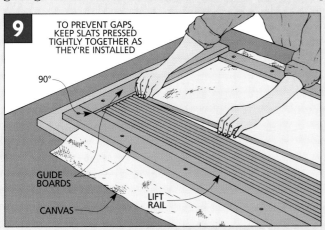

TO PREVENT GAPS, KEEP SLATS PRESSED TIGHTLY TOGETHER AS THEY'RE INSTALLED

90°

GUIDE BOARDS

CANVAS

LIFT RAIL

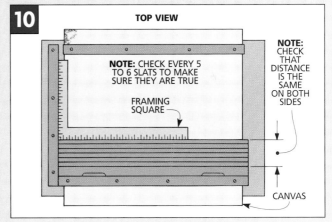

TOP VIEW

NOTE: CHECK EVERY 5 TO 6 SLATS TO MAKE SURE THEY ARE TRUE

FRAMING SQUARE

NOTE: CHECK THAT DISTANCE IS THE SAME ON BOTH SIDES

CANVAS

Troubleshooting Tambour Movement

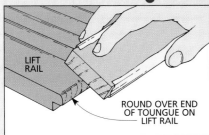

LIFT RAIL

ROUND OVER END OF TOUNGUE ON LIFT RAIL

LIFT RAIL. *When a tambour won't slide freely, check the lift rail. Sharp corners can hang up in the groove. Use a sanding block to round the corners.*

FILE OR SAND ENDS OF SLATS TO SMOOTH ROUGH SPOTS

SLATS. *The slats can also get hung up. Here again, round over the ends. But because the groove is shallow, keep the radius small so it's not exposed.*

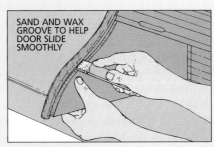

SAND AND WAX GROOVE TO HELP DOOR SLIDE SMOOTHLY

SAND & WAX. *It's always a good idea to sand the groove lightly to remove any chatter marks left by the router. Then apply paste wax so door will slide freely.*

DESK ORGANIZER

This organizer is sized to fit the roll-top desk. But it's designed to look good from any side, so you can put it on a desk or even a countertop.

I don't know what it is about desks, but they seem to be built-in "clutter magnets." Letters, bills, junk mail, you name it — all are attracted to a desk like iron filings to a magnet.

That's what this desk organizer is all about. It has drawers and slots like those you'd find in an old post office desk, so things can be sorted neatly away. (At least in theory.)

Originally, I designed this organizer to slide inside the roll-top desk featured on page 65 (see the photo to the right).

But then I got to thinking, "Why hide it?" It would look great sitting out on top of a regular desk or even on a counter.

But if you expose the back of the organizer, you have to take a couple things into consideration. First, consider the back panel. Since 1/4" plywood has only one good face, I had to veneer the "bad" side since it can be seen if it's not hidden behind a roll-top case.

Also, I thought it would look a little neater if the joinery in the back was hidden. This meant I had to "stop" the dadoes, so they're not visible after the organizer is assembled.

While I'm talking about joinery, take a look at my favorite part of this project: the drawers. The simple design of the box joints seemed to be perfect for this project as were the little cut-outs to use as handles for opening the drawers.

EXPLODED VIEW

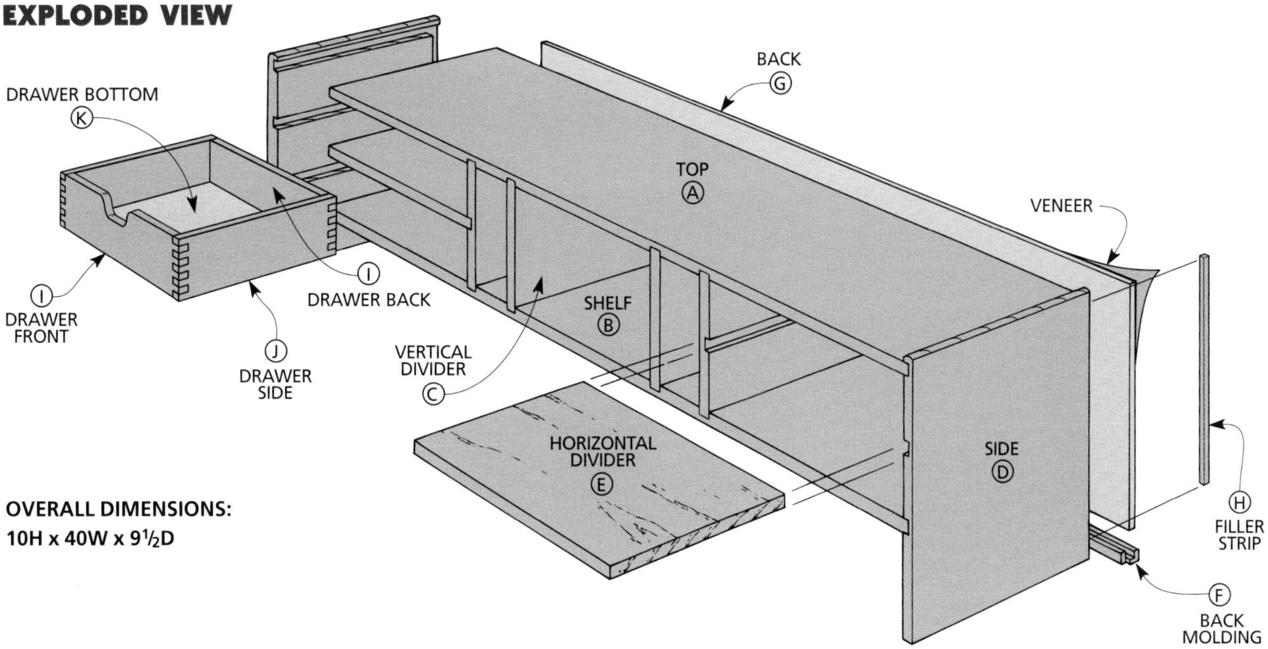

DRAWER BOTTOM
K
BACK
G
TOP
A
VENEER
I
DRAWER FRONT
I
DRAWER BACK
SHELF
B
J
DRAWER SIDE
VERTICAL DIVIDER
C
HORIZONTAL DIVIDER
E
SIDE
D
H
FILLER STRIP
F
BACK MOLDING

OVERALL DIMENSIONS:
10H x 40W x 9½D

MATERIALS LIST & CUTTING DIAGRAM

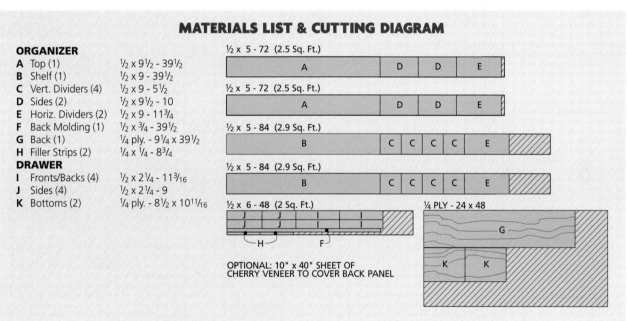

ORGANIZER

A	Top (1)	½ x 9½ - 39½
B	Shelf (1)	½ x 9 - 39½
C	Vert. Dividers (4)	½ x 9 - 5½
D	Sides (2)	½ x 9½ - 10
E	Horiz. Dividers (2)	½ x 9 - 11¾
F	Back Molding (1)	½ x ¾ - 39½
G	Back (1)	¼ ply. - 9¼ x 39½
H	Filler Strips (2)	¼ x ¼ - 8¾

DRAWER

I	Fronts/Backs (4)	½ x 2¼ - 11$^{3}/_{16}$
J	Sides (4)	½ x 2¼ - 9
K	Bottoms (2)	¼ ply. - 8½ x 10$^{11}/_{16}$

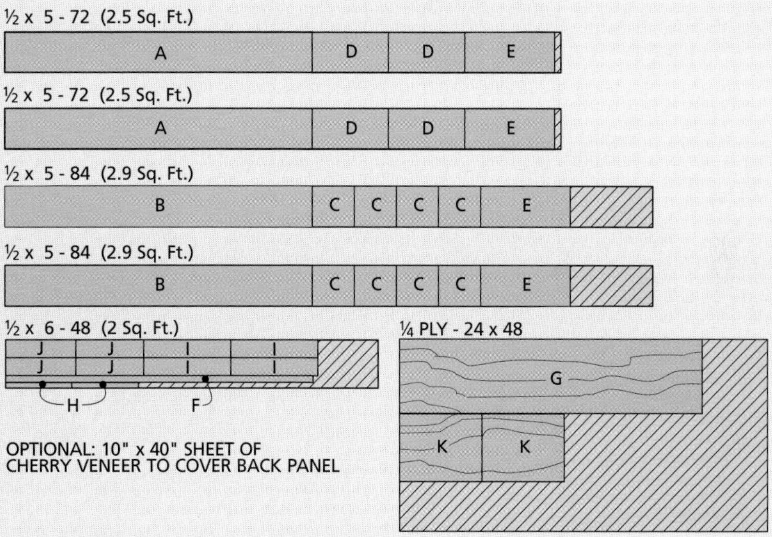

½ x 5 - 72 (2.5 Sq. Ft.)
A D D E
½ x 5 - 72 (2.5 Sq. Ft.)
A D D E
½ x 5 - 84 (2.9 Sq. Ft.)
B C C C C E
½ x 5 - 84 (2.9 Sq. Ft.)
B C C C C E
½ x 6 - 48 (2 Sq. Ft.)
J J I I
J J I I
H
F
¼ PLY - 24 x 48
G
K K

OPTIONAL: 10" x 40" SHEET OF CHERRY VENEER TO COVER BACK PANEL

Veneer

There are three commonly available types of veneer. (I veneered the back panel on the desk organizer).

Standard veneers are $^{1}/_{40}$" to $^{1}/_{32}$"-thick solid wood usually available in 4" to 12" widths and 36" lengths. (Extra width and extra length can often be ordered — at an extra price.) One of the problems with standard veneers is they're subject to expansion and contraction with changes in humidity. This can result in cracking, cupping, and curling.

Flexible veneer was developed to solve this. It's wood veneer that has been laminated to a paper backing to make it flexible and stable. Available in 24" and 36" widths and 96" lengths, it's applied with contact cement.

Finally, *peel-n-stick veneers* are flexible veneers that can be applied without the mess. They have a pressure sensitive adhesive on their backside. You just peel off the backing sheet, lay down the veneer in its final position, and roll it flat with a veneer roller.

For sources of veneer, see page 95.

TOP & SHELF

To build this desk organizer, I started with the top and shelf. Like most of the pieces in this organizer, they're made from $1/2$"-thick stock that's been glued into 10"-wide panels (rough size).

CUT TO SIZE. When the top (A) and shelf (B) panels are dry and planed flat, they can be cut to the same length ($39^1/2$" or a hair less to fit into the roll-top desk). But their widths are different. The top is wider ($9^1/2$") than the shelf (9") because it holds a back panel.

GROOVE FOR BACK. To hold the back, I cut a $1/4$"-deep groove along the back edge of the top panel (A); see Fig. 1a. This groove is cut to width to match the thickness of the $1/4$" plywood used for the back panel (usually a bit less than $1/4$" thick) *plus* a layer of veneer if your desk organizer will be exposed from the back; refer to Fig. 8 on page 82.

DADOES FOR DIVIDERS. The shelf and top are connected by four dividers. These fit in $1/2$"-wide dadoes; see Fig. 1b. To make sure the dadoes align, clamp the shelf and top together and use a hand-held router and a straight-edge guide; see Fig. 1.

But you don't want to rout all the way across both pieces. Otherwise, the dadoes will be visible from the back. So either plunge the bit in or stop the dado when the router bit reaches the groove. Then chisel out the waste; see Fig. 1c.

CUT ARC IN SHELF. After routing the dadoes, all that's left is to cut an arc in the front edge of the shelf. To draw the arc, you'll need to locate the arc's centerpoint in a piece of scrap; see Fig. 2. Then cut it out and sand it smooth.

VERTICAL DIVIDERS

Next, the dividers can be cut to join the top and shelf. There are four vertical dividers (C), and they're all the same size; see Fig. 3.

CUT DIVIDERS. The dividers are identical except for one thing. The two outside dividers also hold horizontal dividers added later. So I routed a $1/4$"-deep dado centered on the height of each vertical divider; see Fig. 3.

When the dadoes are routed, the top, shelf, and vertical dividers can all be glued together; see Fig. 4. Use a framing square to check that the assembly is square. If it's not, you'll have problems when adding the sides.

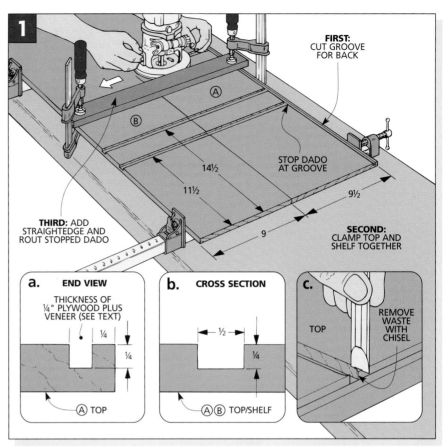

1

FIRST: CUT GROOVE FOR BACK

(A)

(B)

14½

11½

STOP DADO AT GROOVE

9½

9

THIRD: ADD STRAIGHTEDGE AND ROUT STOPPED DADO

SECOND: CLAMP TOP AND SHELF TOGETHER

a. END VIEW

THICKNESS OF $1/4$" PLYWOOD PLUS VENEER (SEE TEXT)

$1/4$

$1/4$

(A) TOP

b. CROSS SECTION

$1/2$

$1/4$

(A)(B) TOP/SHELF

c.

TOP

REMOVE WASTE WITH CHISEL

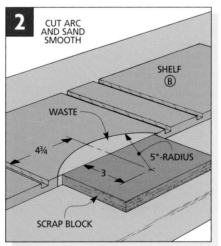

2 CUT ARC AND SAND SMOOTH

SHELF (B)

WASTE

$4^3/4$

3

5"-RADIUS

SCRAP BLOCK

3 VERTICAL DIVIDERS (MAKE FOUR)

(C)

9

2½

5½

CUT $1/2$"-WIDE DADO ON THE TWO OUTSIDE DIVIDERS ONLY (SEE DRAWING BELOW)

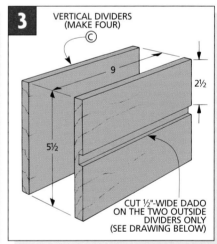

4

TOP (A)

(C)

(C)

(C)

(C)

VERTICAL DIVIDER

(B) SHELF

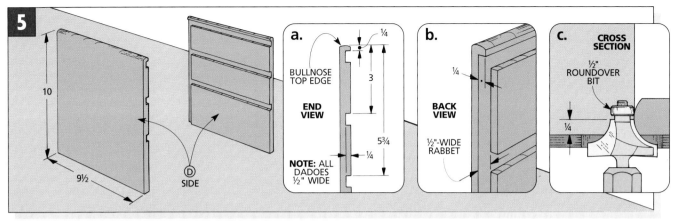

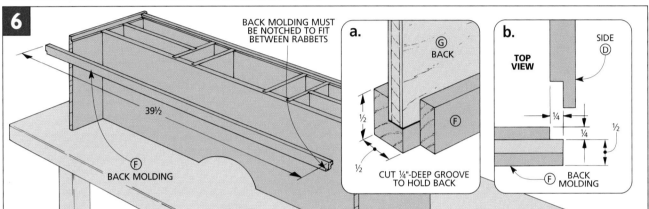

SIDES & DIVIDERS

The next step is to add the sides (D); refer to Fig. 7.

SIDES. Begin by ripping two $\frac{1}{2}$"-thick panels to match the width of the top ($9\frac{1}{2}$"); see Fig. 5. The lengths of the side panels will determine the height of the organizer.

Note: If you're making the organizer to fit inside the roll-top desk, the sides should be just slightly shorter than the desk's tambour opening. (I cut my sides 10" tall.)

Next, rout three $\frac{1}{4}$"-deep x $\frac{1}{2}$"-wide dadoes in each side; see Fig. 5a. The first holds the top panel and is located $\frac{1}{4}$" down from the top edge. The other two align with the shelf and the dado cut on the vertical divider.

To hold the back (and filler strips) added later, each side also needs a $\frac{1}{2}$"-wide rabbet; see Fig. 5b. This rabbet is stopped as it hits the top dado in the side panel.

Finally, to soften the top end of the side panels, I used a $\frac{1}{2}$" roundover bit in the router table to rout a bullnose profile; see Fig. 5c.

HORIZONTAL DIVIDERS. With the side panels complete, it's time to add

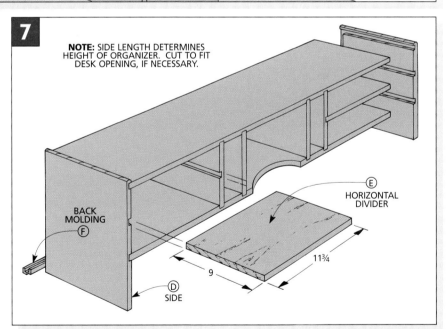

the horizontal dividers (E). The width of these pieces is the same as the shelf (B) (9"). To determine their length, dry assemble the case; see Fig. 7. Then cut them to length to fit between the dadoes in the sides and the vertical dividers. When they've been cut to size, these pieces and the side panels can be glued and clamped to the ends of the case.

BACK MOLDING

Before adding the back, a back molding (F) is cut to fit between the rabbets in the sides; see Fig. 6. To make it fit, I notched the front corners; see Fig. 6b.

Next I cut a $\frac{1}{4}$"-deep groove in the molding to hold the $\frac{1}{4}$"-thick plywood (plus veneer) back; see Fig. 6a.

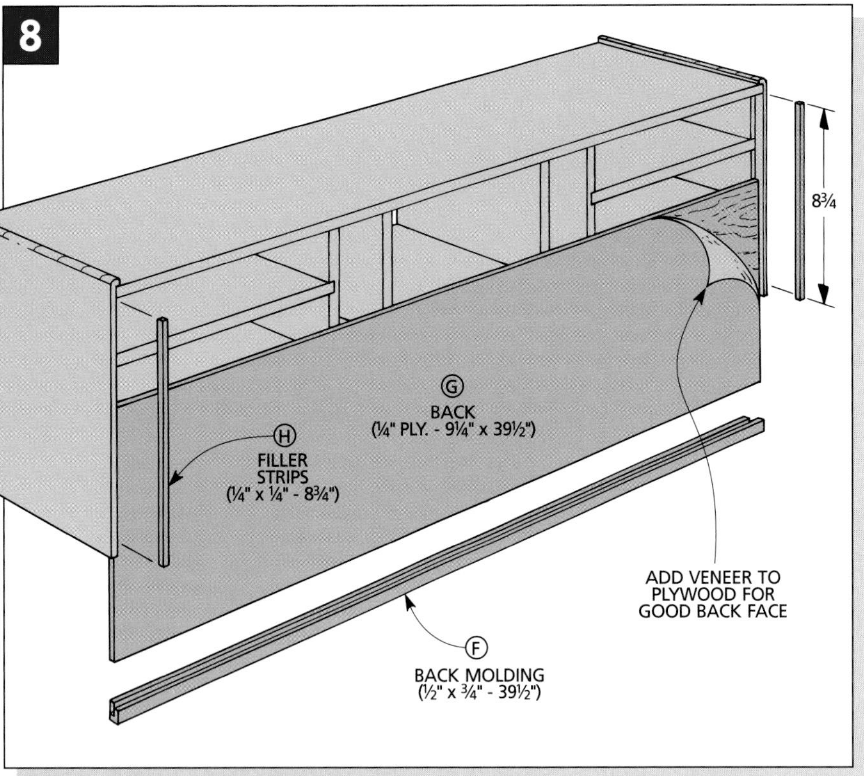
8
8¾
Ⓖ
BACK
(¼" PLY. - 9¼" x 39½")
Ⓗ
FILLER
STRIPS
(¼" x ¼" - 8¾")
ADD VENEER TO
PLYWOOD FOR
GOOD BACK FACE
Ⓕ
BACK MOLDING
(½" x ¾" - 39½")

BACK

Now that the molding is complete, you can work on the back (G); see Fig. 8. Here, I used a piece of 1/4"-thick plywood. (Again, if you are building the desk organizer to stand by itself instead of being placed in a roll-top desk, you'll probably want to glue veneer to the back side before cutting it to size; see the box at the bottom of page 79).

Once the back (with veneer) is cut to size, it can be glued to the back molding and then glued to the back of the organizer; see Fig. 8.

FILLER STRIPS. There's still one more step to complete the back. To finish off the back at the sides, I added filler strips (H); see Fig. 8. These 1/4" x 1/4" strips are cut to fit between the top panel and back molding and are simply glued in the rabbet cut on the sides.

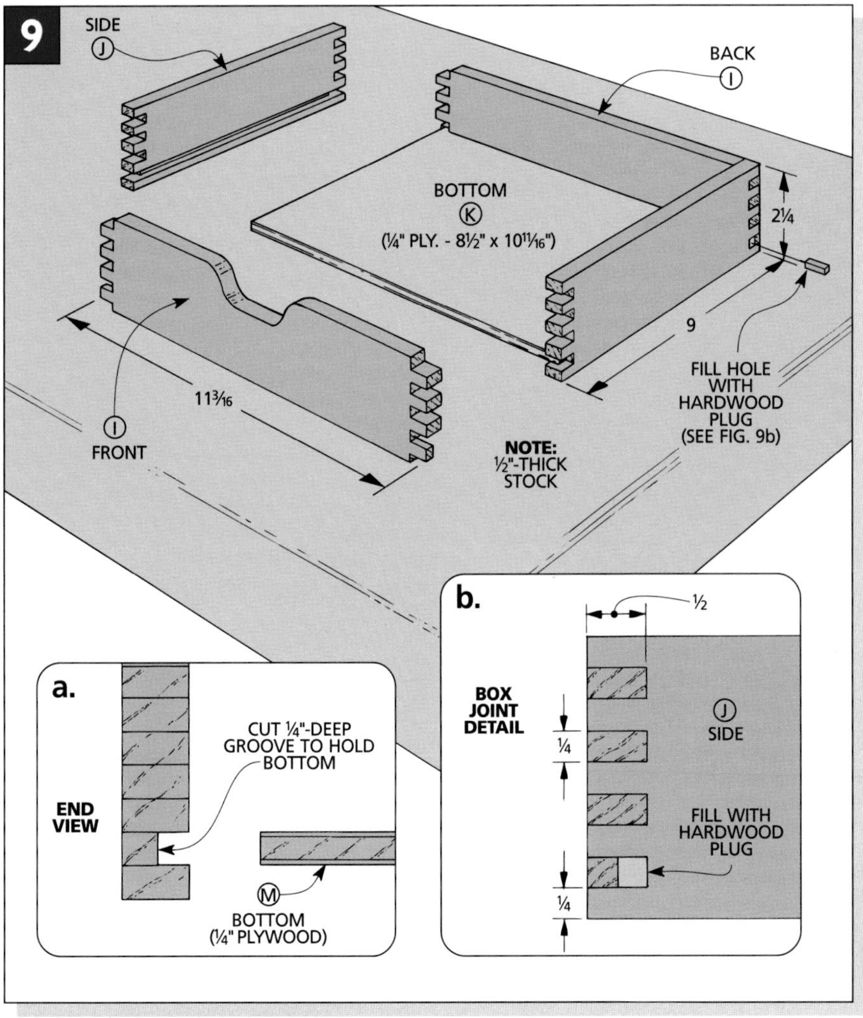
9
SIDE
Ⓙ
BACK
Ⓘ
BOTTOM
Ⓚ
(¼" PLY. - 8½" x 10¹¹⁄₁₆")
2¼
9
11³⁄₁₆
Ⓘ
FRONT
FILL HOLE
WITH
HARDWOOD
PLUG
(SEE FIG. 9b)
NOTE:
½"-THICK
STOCK
a.
END
VIEW
CUT ¼"-DEEP
GROOVE TO HOLD
BOTTOM
Ⓜ
BOTTOM
(¼" PLYWOOD)
b.
½
BOX
JOINT
DETAIL
¼
Ⓙ
SIDE
FILL WITH
HARDWOOD
PLUG
¼

DRAWERS

With the case complete, I built two drawers to fit the organizer. Cut the drawer fronts/backs (I), and sides (J) to size; see Fig. 9. (Allow for a 1/32" gap at each side. But for now, the *height* of each drawer should match its opening.)

The drawer is joined with 1/4" box joints (Fig. 9b), and the 1/4" plywood bottom (K) is held in a groove that's cut in each piece; see Fig. 9a.

Before assembling the drawers, I laid out and cut an opening for a handle on each front piece; see Fig. 10.

Next, cut a drawer bottom to fit and assemble the drawers. Then trim the top and bottom edges very slightly to create a 1/32" gap above the drawer.

There's one final step. After each drawer is assembled, the grooves for the drawer bottom will be exposed on the sides; see Fig. 9b. I cut small wood plugs and inserted them into the square holes to hide the grooves; see Fig. 9. ■

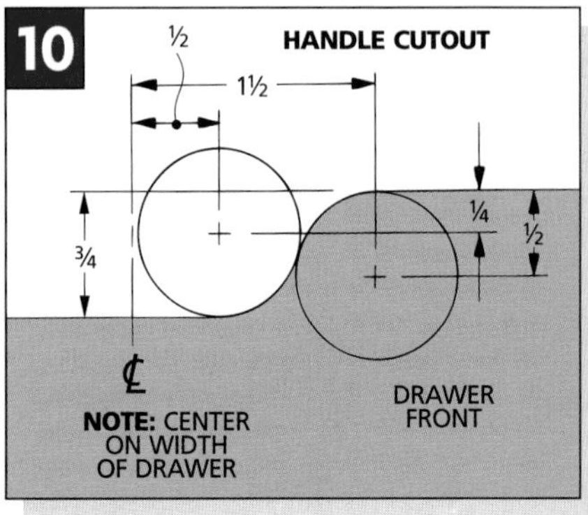
10
HANDLE CUTOUT
½
1½
¼
½
¾
℄
NOTE: CENTER
ON WIDTH
OF DRAWER
DRAWER
FRONT

PEDESTAL DESK

The symmetry of this oak desk makes the building process straight-forward. The pedestals are identical and so are the drawers.

I had already built this pedestal desk from working drawings and then we put together the Exploded View (on the next page). That's when I got worried. The Exploded View looks complicated — even more complicated than the desk I'd just built.

But then I realized one of the great things about a pedestal desk is its symmetry. The pedestals are identical, the panels are identical, even the drawers are the same. This means once you are set up to make a cut, the actual work is fairly easy and quick.

It's not the construction techniques that inspired me to make this desk, it's the classic design. This desk is typical of pedestal desks made in the early 1900's. But some of the joinery techniques and materials I used are new.

JOINERY AND WOOD. For example, I used stub tenon and groove joinery to make the side and back frames. It looks like the frame and panel joinery of a hundred years ago. And the oak veneer plywood for the panels wasn't around that long ago either. But in combination with the solid oak base and frames, it has the traditional look, with greater dimensional stability.

OPTIONS. One of the things you're as likely to need today as a century ago is a file drawer. You can build this desk with one file drawer or as many as four.

Another option is a vanity panel. It encloses the knee space between the pedestals on the back of the desk. While it may keep others from seeing your scuffed-up shoes, it's probably better for keeping your legs warm in a drafty room. In any case, the vanity panel also makes the desk seem more formal.

A final option would be to build a traditional tambour roll-top for the desk. Though it's not shown with one here, you could easily take the design of the roll-top case from the roll-top desk on page 65 and with a few measurement changes make it fit this pedestal desk. (Also see the technique section on building tambours starting on page 74.)

FINISH. To finish the desk, I used Minwax Fruitwood stain, and two top coats of General Finishes' Royal Finish.

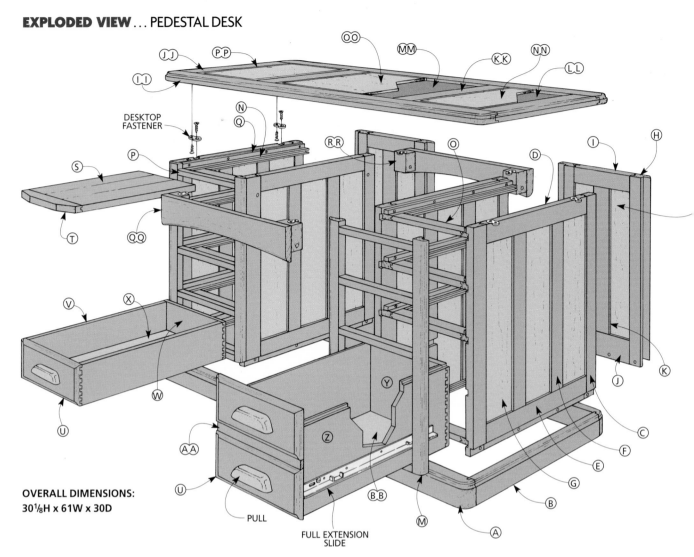

DESKTOP FASTENER

OVERALL DIMENSIONS:
30⅛H x 61W x 30D

PULL

FULL EXTENSION SLIDE

PEDESTAL BASES

I began work on the desk by making the bases for the pedestals. Each base is made up of four pieces: 1"-thick kickboard fronts/backs (A) and ³/₄"-thick kickboard sides (B); see Fig. 1.

DADOES. The base pieces are joined with tongue and dado joints; see Fig. 1a. The dadoes are actually saw kerfs cut across the inside face of the kickboard fronts and backs (A). To do this, adjust the rip fence on the table saw so the distance from the outside of the blade to the fence equals the thickness of the side pieces (³/₄"). Now set the blade to cut ¹/₈" deep, and cut the dadoes using the fence as a stop.

CUT TONGUES. After the kerfs are cut in the front/back pieces (A), cut matching tongues on the ends of all the side pieces (B); see Fig. 1a. Once the tongues are cut, the bases can be glued together; see Fig. 1.

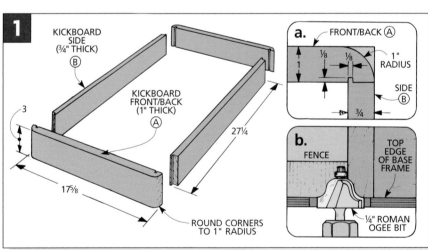

1

KICKBOARD SIDE (³/₄" THICK) B

KICKBOARD FRONT/BACK (1" THICK) A

3

17⁵/₈

27¼

ROUND CORNERS TO 1" RADIUS

a. FRONT/BACK A
1
⅛ ⅛
1" RADIUS
SIDE B
³/₄

b.
FENCE
TOP EDGE OF BASE FRAME
¼" ROMAN OGEE BIT

ROUND CORNERS. A typical feature on a desk like this is large rounded corners. To round the corners, start by drawing a 1" radius arc on the corners; see Fig. 1a. Then rough cut the corners on the band saw and sand them smooth.

ROUT OGEE. The last step on the bases is to rout an ogee on the top edges; see Fig. 1b. To do this, mount a ¼" Roman ogee bit in the router table. Then rout the ogee on the top, outside edges of all four sides.

MATERIALS LIST

BASE		
A	Kickbd. Fr./Bk. (4)	$1 \times 3 - 17\frac{5}{8}$
B	Kickbd. Sides (4)	$\frac{3}{4} \times 3 - 27\frac{1}{4}$
SIDES		
C	Stiles (8)	$\frac{3}{4} \times 2 - 27\frac{1}{8}$
D	Upper Rails (4)	$\frac{3}{4} \times 2\frac{1}{2} - 23\frac{1}{2}$
E	Lower Rails (4)	$\frac{3}{4} \times 3\frac{1}{2} - 23\frac{1}{2}$
F	Muntins (8)	$\frac{3}{4} \times 2\frac{1}{2} - 21\frac{5}{8}$
G	Panels (12)	$\frac{1}{4}$ ply. - $6\frac{1}{2} \times 21\frac{5}{8}$
BACKS		
H	Stiles (4)	$\frac{3}{4} \times 2\frac{1}{2} - 27\frac{1}{8}$
I	Upper Rails (2)	$\frac{3}{4} \times 2\frac{1}{2} - 12\frac{1}{8}$
J	Lower Rails (2)	$\frac{3}{4} \times 3\frac{1}{2} - 12\frac{1}{8}$
K	Muntins (2)	$\frac{3}{4} \times 2\frac{1}{2} - 21\frac{5}{8}$
L	Panels (4)	$\frac{1}{4}$ ply - $5\frac{1}{16} \times 21\frac{5}{8}$
FRONTS/DRAWER GUIDES		
M	Front Stiles (4)	$\frac{3}{4} \times 1\frac{1}{4} - 26\frac{1}{8}$
N	Runners (18)	$\frac{3}{4} \times 1\frac{1}{8} - 26\frac{3}{8}$
O	Rail Supports (9)	$\frac{3}{4} \times 1\frac{1}{4} - 13\frac{5}{8}$
P	Front Rails (9)	$\frac{3}{4} \times \frac{3}{4} - 14\frac{1}{8}$
Q	Guides (16)	$\frac{9}{16} \times \frac{3}{4} - 26\frac{3}{8}$
R	Stops (6)	$\frac{3}{4} \times \frac{3}{4} - 2$
WRITING SLIDES		
S	Panels (2)	$\frac{3}{4} \times 14 - 26\frac{1}{4}$
T	Handles (2)	$\frac{3}{4} \times 2 - 14$
DRAWERS		
U	Fronts (8)	$\frac{3}{4} \times 5\frac{1}{4} - 14$
V	Sides (12)	$\frac{1}{2} \times 5\frac{1}{4} - 23\frac{5}{8}$
W	Backs (6)	$\frac{1}{2} \times 5\frac{1}{4} - 14$
X	Bottoms (6)	$\frac{1}{4}$ ply. - $13\frac{1}{2} \times 23\frac{1}{2}$
Y	File Drwr. Fr./Bk. (2)	$\frac{1}{2} \times 9\frac{3}{4} - 13$
Z	File Drwr. Sides (2)	$\frac{1}{2} \times 9\frac{3}{4} - 25\frac{5}{8}$
AA	File Drwr. Spcr. (1)	$\frac{3}{8} \times \frac{7}{8} - 14$
BB	File Drwr. Btm. (1)	$\frac{1}{4}$ ply. - $12\frac{1}{2} \times 25\frac{1}{2}$
VANITY PANEL		
CC	Stiles (2)	$\frac{3}{4} \times 2\frac{1}{2} - 29\frac{1}{8}$
DD	Upper Rail (1)	$\frac{3}{4} \times 2\frac{1}{2} - 21\frac{1}{4}$
EE	Lower Rail (1)	$\frac{3}{4} \times 5\frac{1}{2} - 21\frac{1}{4}$
FF	Muntins (2)	$\frac{3}{4} \times 2\frac{1}{2} - 21\frac{5}{8}$
GG	Panels (3)	$\frac{1}{4}$ ply. - $5\frac{3}{4} \times 21\frac{5}{8}$
HH	Kickboards (2)	$\frac{1}{2} \times 3$ -26 rough
TOP		
II	Frame Fr./Bk. (2)	$1 \times 2\frac{1}{2} - 61$
JJ	Frame Ends (2)	$1 \times 2\frac{1}{2} - 26$
KK	Dividers (2)	$1 \times 2\frac{1}{2} - 26$
LL	Side Base (2)	$\frac{3}{4}$ prbd. - $26 \times 14\frac{5}{8}$
MM	Center Base (1)	$\frac{3}{4}$ prbd. - $26 \times 24\frac{3}{4}$
NN	Side Inlay Ply. (2)	$\frac{1}{4}$ ply. - $24\frac{3}{4} \times 13\frac{3}{8}$
OO	Ctr. Inlay Ply. (1)	$\frac{1}{4}$ ply. - $24\frac{3}{4} \times 23\frac{1}{2}$
PP	Inlay Strips (12)	$\frac{1}{8} \times \frac{1}{4}$ - cut to fit
QQ	Arch. Supports (2)	$\frac{3}{4} \times 4 - 25\frac{3}{4}$
RR	Support Blocks (4)	$1\frac{1}{2} \times 2 - 3$

HARDWARE SUPPLIES

(110) No. 6 x 1" Fh woodscrews
(8) Wooden drawer pulls (or make yourself)
(28 ft.) ½" Nylon self-adhesive glide strip
(1 set) File drawer slide hardware (optional)
(4) ¼" x 3½" Carriage bolts, nuts, washers
(4) ¼" x 1¼" Machine screws and washers
(4) ¼" Threaded inserts
(8) Desk top fasteners

CUTTING DIAGRAM

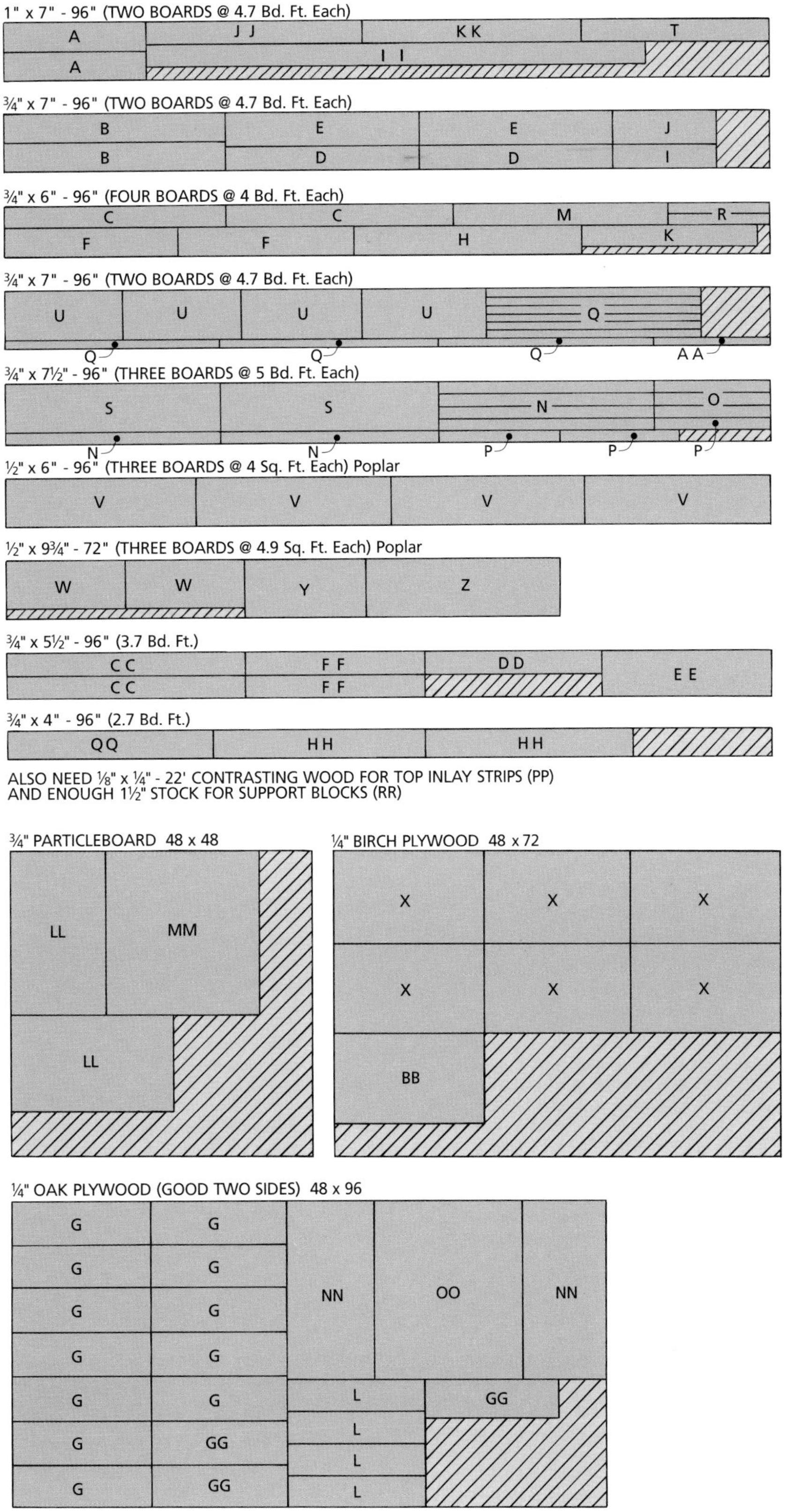

1" x 7" - 96" (TWO BOARDS @ 4.7 Bd. Ft. Each)
A
A
J J
K K
T
I I
¾" x 7" - 96" (TWO BOARDS @ 4.7 Bd. Ft. Each)
B
B
E
E
D
D
J
I
¾" x 6" - 96" (FOUR BOARDS @ 4 Bd. Ft. Each)
C
C
M
R
F
F
H
K
¾" x 7" - 96" (TWO BOARDS @ 4.7 Bd. Ft. Each)
U
U
U
U
Q
Q
Q
Q
A A
¾" x 7½" - 96" (THREE BOARDS @ 5 Bd. Ft. Each)
S
S
N
O
N
N
P
P
P
½" x 6" - 96" (THREE BOARDS @ 4 Sq. Ft. Each) Poplar
V
V
V
V
½" x 9¾" - 72" (THREE BOARDS @ 4.9 Sq. Ft. Each) Poplar
W
W
Y
Z
¾" x 5½" - 96" (3.7 Bd. Ft.)
C C
C C
F F
F F
D D
E E
¾" x 4" - 96" (2.7 Bd. Ft.)
QQ
H H
H H
ALSO NEED ⅛" x ¼" - 22' CONTRASTING WOOD FOR TOP INLAY STRIPS (PP)
AND ENOUGH 1½" STOCK FOR SUPPORT BLOCKS (RR)
¾" PARTICLEBOARD 48 x 48
LL
MM
LL
¼" BIRCH PLYWOOD 48 x 72
X
X
X
X
X
X
BB
¼" OAK PLYWOOD (GOOD TWO SIDES) 48 x 96
G
G
G
G
G
G
G
G
G
G
G
GG
G
GG
NN
OO
NN
L
L
L
L
GG

PEDESTAL SIDES AND BACKS

Once the pedestal bases are complete, the next step is to make the frame and panel units for the pedestal sides and backs. This is a systematic process — each of the panel units is made the same way, in a series of repetitive steps.

CUT TO LENGTH. Begin the process by cutting four pieces of $3/4$" stock for the back upper (I) and lower rails (J) to length; see Fig. 2. Then cut the eight pieces for the side upper (D) and lower rails (E) to length.

The twelve stiles (H,C) for all the frames are the same length ($27^1/8$"); see Fig. 2. Each of the frames is divided by one or two vertical muntins (K,F). And all of these muntins are also the same length ($21^5/8$"); see Fig. 2.

RIP TO WIDTH. With all the pedestal frame pieces cut to finished length, the next step is to rip the pieces to finished width. All the upper rails, muntins, and back panel stiles are ripped to the same width ($2^1/2$"); see Fig. 2. The side panel stiles are ripped a little narrower (2"). And lower rails are ripped wider ($3^1/2$").

STUB TENON AND GROOVES. After all the frame pieces have been cut to finished size, they can be joined together with stub tenon and groove joints.

To begin the joinery, first cut a $1/4$"-deep groove on the inside edge of all of the stiles and rails, and on both edges of the muntins; see Figs. 2a, 2b, and 2c.

Center the grooves on the thickness of the workpiece, and cut the grooves the same width as the thickness of the plywood used for the panels ($1/4$" plywood is usually less than $1/4$" thick).

All the stub tenons are cut the same way and at the same time. I used the table saw with the rip fence positioned $1/4$" from the outside of the blade. To determine the height of the blade, I used a test piece the same thickness as the actual workpieces. Sneak up on the height, cutting on both sides of the test piece until the tenon fits the grooves.

Once the tenon on the test piece fits, stub tenons can be cut on the muntins (see Fig. 2b) and the rails (see Fig. 2c).

PLYWOOD PANELS. After the stub tenons and grooves have been cut on the frame pieces, the next step is to cut the $1/4$" plywood panels (L and G) that fit inside the frames. The panels are all cut the same length as the muntins. To determine their width, I dry assembled a side frame and back frame and cut the panels to fit; see Fig. 2.

ASSEMBLY. With the plywood panels cut to size, the frame and panel units can be assembled. Make sure the four side units are identical in size, and that the two back units are identical as well.

RABBETS. Before the base and panel units can be assembled into the pedestals, joints need to be cut on each panel unit so they fit together and onto the base.

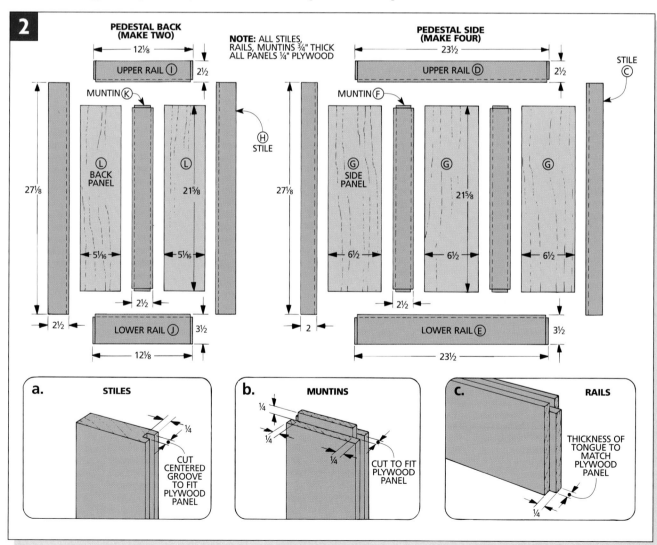

The side and back units fit inside the top of the pedestal base by means of rabbets at the bottom of the units; refer to Figs. 3a and 3c.

To cut this rabbet on the *lower outside* edge of each unit, I used a dado blade. (Note that the rabbet on the side unit is shallower than on the back unit.)

Then drill four $^3/_{16}$" countersunk shank holes through the rabbets; see Figs. 3a and 3c. These are for the screws that will hold the units to the base.

Next, cut a rabbet on the *inside* face of the back units' stiles to join the back units to the side units; see Fig. 3b.

ROUNDOVERS. To complete the work on the back units, rout a $^1/_2$" roundover on the *outside* edge of the back stiles; see Fig. 3b.

DADOES. Next, dadoes can be cut on the inside of the sides for the drawer runners. To cut these, first set up a $^3/_4$"-wide dado blade to cut $^1/_8$" deep. Then lay out the dadoes on one of the side units; see Fig. 3d.

Now cut the matching dadoes on each of the side units before moving the rip fence to cut the next set of dadoes. This way, all the dadoes will align.

RUNNERS. Next I made the 18 drawer runners (N) to fit into the dadoes. (Why 18 runners? I built the desk with six standard drawers requiring two runners each. Plus a file drawer that required two runners, and four more for the writing slides.)

The runners are made from $^3/_4$"-thick stock ripped to a width of $1^1/_8$"; see Fig. 4a. Cut the runners $^5/_8$" shorter than the width of the side units. This way, they won't interfere with the back units when assembling the pedestals.

Before gluing the runners into the dadoes, cut a $^1/_4$"-deep groove in each runner for attaching rail supports; refer to Fig. 7 on page 88. Center this groove on the thickness of the runner; see Fig. 4a.

Now the runners can be glued into the dadoes. Set the runners back $^1/_4$" from the front edge to leave room for front stiles added later; see Fig. 4.

DRAWER GUIDES. There's just one more step before the pedestals can be assembled — cutting and installing drawer guides (Q); see Fig. 5. The guides serve as spacers to keep the drawers tracking straight.

When the guides have been cut to finished size, screw them to the side units; see Fig. 5a. Note: Don't glue the guides in place so they can be removed and custom fit later (if necessary).

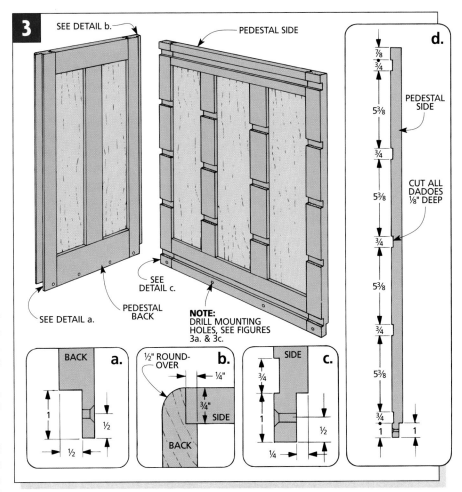

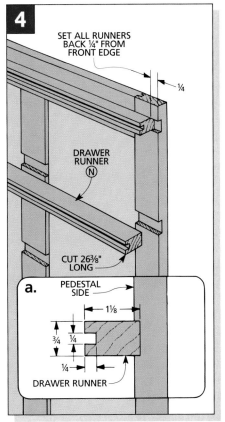

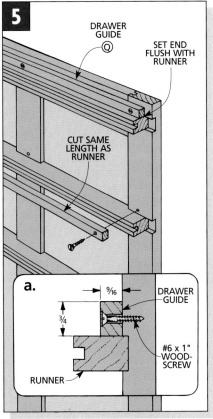

PEDESTAL ASSEMBLY

Once the runners and guides are in place, the pedestals can be assembled.

ATTACH SIDES & BACK. First, screw each side unit to the base from the inside; see Fig. 6b. Then, to install the backs, first spread glue along the rabbets in the stiles. Next slip the bottom rabbet over the top of the base, and clamp the back between the sides. Now drive screws into the base.

FRONT STILES. To cover the front edges of each pedestal, cut four front stiles (M) to a width of $1^1/4$" from $3/4$" stock, see Fig. 6. Then cut them to length to match the height of the sides.

Next, cut a rabbet on the back side of each stile and rout a $1/2$" roundover on the front edge; see Fig. 6a. Now glue the front stiles to the side units; see Fig. 6.

RAIL SUPPORTS. The desk drawers are separated by supports that stretch between the front stiles. Each support consists of two pieces, a rail support that fits between the runners, and a front rail; see Figs. 7 and 8. Note: If you plan to build the file drawer (see page 90), you need only make nine supports.

Cut the rail supports (0) to length to fit between the grooves in the runners. Next, cut a centered tenon on each end of the supports to fit the grooves in the runners and glue the supports in place.

FRONT RAILS. Now cut front rails (P) to length so they fit between the front stiles. Then glue the rails to the front of the supports; see Fig. 8.

DRAWERS

Each drawer is designed to fit in its opening with a $1/16$" gap all around. So, measure the openings and cut the $3/4$"-thick fronts (U) and backs (W) $1/8$" less than these dimensions. Next cut the $1/2$"-thick sides (V) $23^5/8$" long.

FRONT OGEE. Now, rout an ogee on the face of the drawer fronts. I set the fence on the router table to decrease the width of the cut to $3/8$"; see Fig. 12a.

DRAWER JOINTS. I used half-blind dovetail joints cut with a router, $1/2$" dovetail bit, and a dovetail jig to join the drawer sides to the fronts and backs.

DRAWER BOTTOMS. Now, cut a groove for the plywood drawer bottom (X); see Fig. 12b. Then, after cutting a bottom to fit, glue each drawer together.

PULLS. The last step is to screw pulls to the front of each drawer; see page 89.

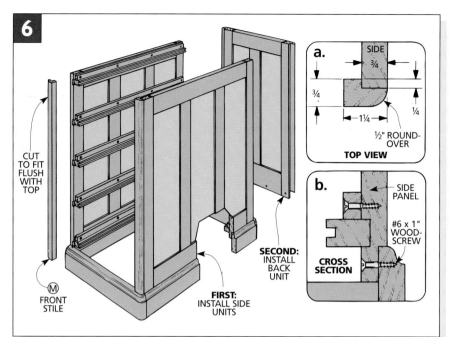

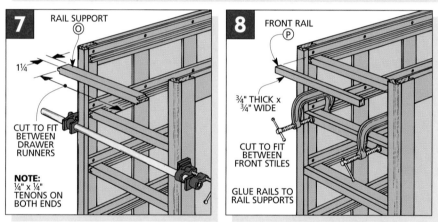

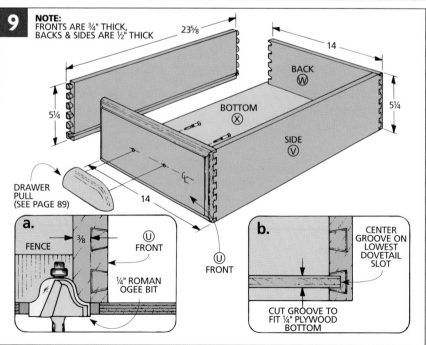

Shop-Made Drawer Pulls

There's a good reason for making your own drawer pulls on a project such as the pedestal desk. If you use stock left over from making the drawer fronts, the pulls will match the drawers.

The drawer pulls I made for the desk started out as pieces of drawer stock that are cut to length and width, then routed to shape.

To make the routing operations safer, I built a jig to hold the blank while routing on the router table; see drawing at right. This also helps to produce pulls that are identical in shape and size.

The neat thing about this jig is that it's double-ended to serve two purposes. One end holds the blank for routing a cove for a finger

slot. Then the workpiece is screwed to the other end of the jig for trimming the corners flush and rounding over the edges.

The jig is simply a pair of 3/4"-thick pieces of scrap cut to the desired length of the pulls (61/4" was what I wanted for the pedestal desk). The pieces are then

glued together with an equal amount of overhang at each end; see drawing below. The width of the overhang matches the desired width of your pulls (for the pedestal desk, 13/8").

Two screw holes through the overhang hold the workpiece while routing

the edge. These holes also serve another purpose — they become mounting holes in the pull.

In order to keep the blank in place while routing the cove for the finger slot screw a pair of 3/4"-thick cleats to the sides of the jig; see Step 1 below.

I cut and sanded a smooth radius on the front corners of the jig to serve as a pattern for the bearing on a flush trim router bit; see Step 5.

Once the jig is built, it's simply a matter of following a series of steps to making the pulls; see below.

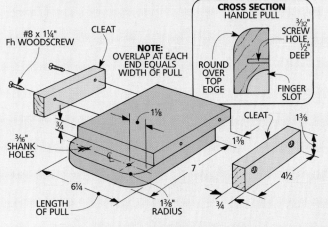

CROSS SECTION
HANDLE PULL

#8 x 11/4" Fh WOODSCREW
CLEAT
NOTE: OVERLAP AT EACH END EQUALS WIDTH OF PULL
3/32" SCREW HOLE, 1/2" DEEP
ROUND OVER TOP EDGE
FINGER SLOT
3/16" SHANK HOLES
11/8
3/4
CLEAT
13/8
13/8
7
61/4
LENGTH OF PULL
13/8" RADIUS
3/4
41/2
3/4

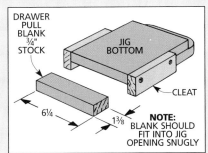

DRAWER PULL BLANK 3/4" STOCK
JIG BOTTOM
CLEAT
61/4
13/8
NOTE: BLANK SHOULD FIT INTO JIG OPENING SNUGLY

1 First, cut the blanks to length and width. Then, to rout a cove for a finger slot, slide one blank into the jig. It should fit snugly between the cleats.

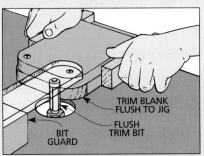

FENCE
5
5
STOP
1/2" COVE BIT
STOP

2 Clamp two stops to the router table an equal distance from the center of the bit. This determines the travel of the workpiece, and the slot length.

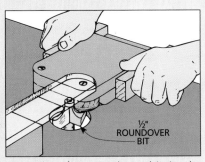

ROUT RIGHT TO LEFT IN SEVERAL PASSES
5
5
PULL BLANK

3 Now set bit to cut full-depth, and position fence flush with the edge of the bearing. Make several light passes from right to left to rout slot.

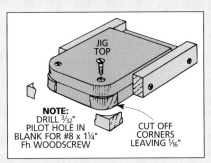

JIG TOP
NOTE: DRILL 3/32" PILOT HOLE IN BLANK FOR #8 x 11/4" Fh WOODSCREW
CUT OFF CORNERS LEAVING 1/16"

4 Use the other end of the jig to shape the front of the pull. First, screw the blank to the jig. Then cut off the "ears," leaving 1/16" to trim.

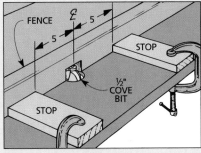

TRIM BLANK FLUSH TO JIG
FLUSH TRIM BIT
BIT GUARD

5 Now, with a flush trim bit in the router, trim the corners and front edge flush with the jig. Do this on all the pulls before going to Step 6.

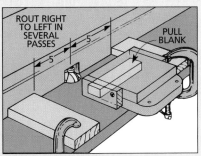

1/2" ROUNDOVER BIT

6 With a 1/2" roundover bit in the router table, raise the bit to full depth. Make several light passes to round over front and ends of the pull.

FILE DRAWER

One of the neat things about the file drawer on this desk is that, from the front it doesn't look like a file drawer — it looks like two regular drawers. To achieve this, the file drawer is built differently than the others.

FALSE FRONT. The first difference is that the file drawer has a ³/₄"-thick false front attached to it. The false front is made of two regular drawer fronts (U) plus a spacer (AA); see Fig. 11.

NARROWER DRAWER. The file drawer is also narrower than the other drawers. There are two reasons for this. First, the file drawer holds hanging file folders that hang on the top edge of the drawer without any hardware; see Fig. 10a. Also, the narrower drawer allows clearance for the full extension slides mounted between the drawer and the sides of the pedestals.

MAKING THE DRAWER. To make the file drawer, first build a dovetail box to fit the large drawer opening; see Fig. 10. I used ¹/₂" poplar for the front, back, and sides (Y) (Z), and ¹/₄" plywood for the bottom (BB). Note: Before assembling the box, cut ¹/₄"-deep rabbets on the top edge of the drawer sides for the hanging file folders; see Fig. 10a.

Next, cut a ³/₈"-thick spacer (AA) ⁷/₈" wide and glue this between two drawer fronts (U); see Fig. 11. Then attach the false front to the drawer, and install the drawer in the pedestal with the extension slides. (See page 95 for sources of full extension slides.)

FITTING DRAWERS

Once the file drawer is installed, you'll probably want to go back and work on the "fit" of the other drawers. Don't expect them to fit properly the first time. Several adjustments have to be made. In order for the drawers to slide

easily — and also look good — they have to fit in three directions: side to side, top to bottom, and front to back; see Fig. 12.

SIDE TO SIDE. To fit a drawer side to side, check the gap between the drawer sides and the drawer guides (Q). There should be a slight gap on each side — enough to allow the drawer to move in and out without binding; see Fig. 13.

If there's no gap, or if the gap is too narrow, the guides need to be removed and planed to fit. If you do plane the

guides, plane each guide an equal amount. Then screw them back into the pedestal and test the fit again.

TOP TO BOTTOM. Now check the distance above each drawer front when the drawer is in the closed position. It will probably be about ¹/₈". To create a uniform ¹/₁₆" gap above and below the drawer front, I stuck self-adhesive nylon glide strips to the top of the runners; see Fig. 12. The strips do two things: they even out the gap, and they make the drawers slide easily.

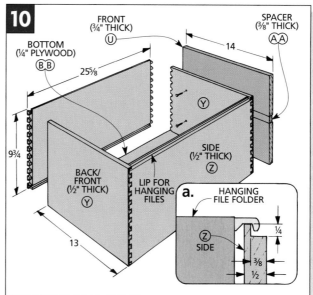

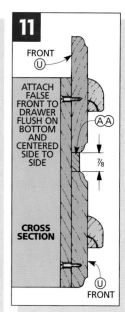

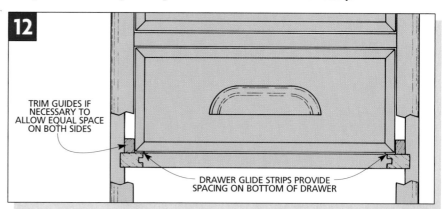

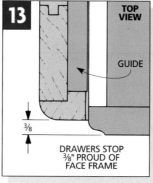

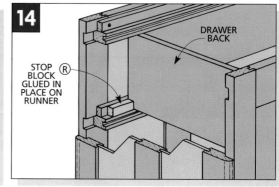

FRONT TO BACK. When the drawer is closed, the drawer front should stick out $3/8$" from the face frame; see Fig. 13. This means you can see the entire molded edge of the drawer front, but the dovetails aren't visible. To prevent the drawer from sliding in further, I glued a small stop block (R) onto the runner behind the drawer; see Fig. 14.

To make it easier to position the drawer while installing the stop block, I made a simple L-shaped gauge; see the tip box at right.

WRITING SLIDES

One of the traditional features of a pedestal desk like this is a writing surface or slide that pulls out from the top of each pedestal.

SLIDES. To build the slides, first glue up stock for two panels (S). Then, trim them to rough length ($26^{1}/4$") and $1/8$" narrower than the opening in the pedestal; see Fig. 15. Now, cut a tongue along the front edge; see Fig. 16.

HANDLES. Next cut a pair of handle (T) blanks to finished dimensions; see Fig. 15a. Then cut a groove along the inside edge of the handles to accept the tongue on the panels; see Fig. 16.

To rout a stopped finger slot on the bottom side of the handles (Fig. 15a), I used a $1/2$" core box bit and stop blocks clamped to the router table.

Then, taper the front corners of each handle, and glue the handles onto the panels; see Fig. 15.

POSITIONING THE SLIDES. Each slide should be positioned in its pedestal so the handle extends $3/4$" beyond the front stiles; see Fig. 17. To do this, measure the depth of the opening and cut the slides to fit.

ARCHED SUPPORTS

Finally, the pedestals can be joined. This is done by a pair of arched supports that bridge the opening between the pedestals. Note: If you make the optional vanity panel (page 92), you'll only need one support.

CUTTING THE ARCH. Begin making the arched support(s) (QQ) by first cutting $3/4$" stock to finished width and length; see Fig. 18. To lay out the curve of the arch, first mark the high point of the curve (1" up from the bottom edge) centered across the back of the workpiece. Then drive a finishing nail into

each of the bottom corners, about $1/8$" above the bottom edge.

Next, spring a flexible wood strip (like a yard stick) between the two nails until it reaches the high point of the curve. Now, draw this curve on the workpiece and cut it to shape.

Finally, round over the bottom edge

with a $1/2$" roundover bit; see Fig. 18a.

SUPPORT BLOCKS. To attach the support to the pedestals, I added blocks (RR) to the back face; see Fig. 18. After cutting these, bore a $5/16$"-diameter hole through each block to accept a carriage bolt; see Fig. 18a. Then glue the blocks to the support.

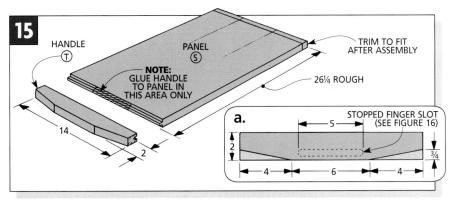

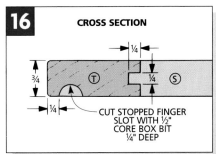

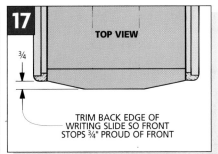

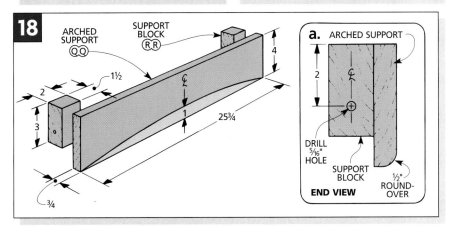

JOINING THE PEDESTALS

Before installing the arched supports between the pedestals, you'll need to drill $5/16$"-diameter holes in the sides of the pedestals for the carriage bolts; see Fig. 19. To locate these holes so they align with the holes in the support blocks, I temporarily clamped the pedestals together with the arched supports in place.

Note: The top of the support should be flush with the top of the pedestal. But the support should be set in 1" from the outside of the pedestal; see Fig. 19a.

Now drill the holes using the holes in the blocks as a guide. Once they're drilled, bolt the pedestals together.

VANITY PANEL

An optional vanity panel between the pedestals encloses the knee hole at the back of the desk.

To build the vanity panel, I used frame and panel joinery with stub tenons and grooves. It's made the same way as the pedestal sides, with a couple differences; see Fig. 20.

LOWER RAIL. First, the lower rail (EE) is wider than the lower rails in the

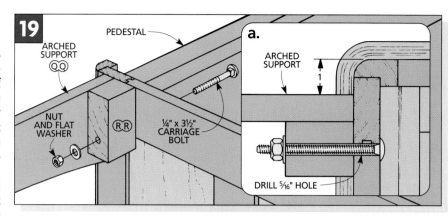

pedestals. This provides more surface for attaching kickboards; see Fig. 21.

NOTCHES. The second difference is a couple of notches. Once the panel is built, notches on the bottom reduce the panel's width so it fits between the pedestal bases; see Fig. 20a.

When you're done building the vanity panel, cut the notches $1/2$" wide and 3" high.

KICKBOARDS. A pair of kickboards hide the notches on the outside and inside of the panel; see Fig. 21. To make the kickboards (HH), first cut a pair of blanks so they're an inch or two longer than the width of the vanity panel ($25^3/4$"); see Fig. 20.

Then cope the ends to match the shape of the pedestal kickboards. (For information on how to cope molding, see page 94.) Finally, glue the kickboards to the vanity panel.

INSTALLATION. I used machine screws and threaded inserts to install the panel between the pedestals; see Fig. 22a. To do this, first drill holes through the pedestals for the screws.

Next, temporarily clamp the vanity panel in place between the pedestals. Then, using the holes as a guide, mark the locations for the threaded inserts on the edges of the vanity panel. Finally, install the threaded inserts and screw the panel in place.

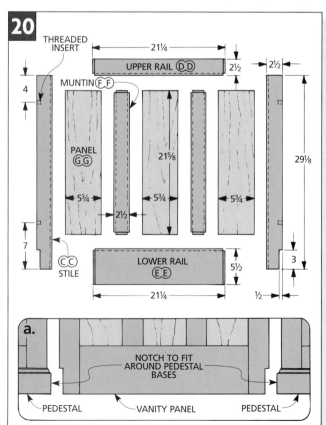

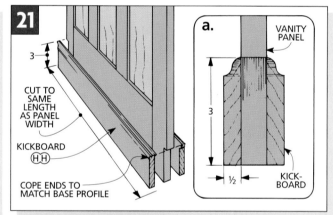

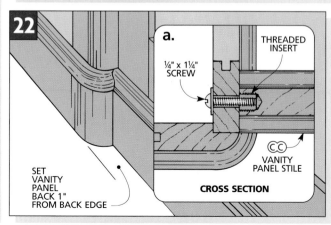

TOP

The final part to build is the top. It's a large frame and panel assembly — but here, the panels and frame are 1" thick.

FRAME. Start by cutting the frame pieces (II, JJ, KK) to size; see Fig. 23.

Next, cut a ½"-wide by ½"-deep offset groove on the inside edge of the front and back pieces (II) and the ends (JJ); see Detail in Fig. 23. Then cut grooves on both edges of the dividers (KK). Finally, cut matching tenons on the ends of the end pieces (JJ) and dividers (KK).

BASE PANELS. Though the top panels are made of a piece of ¼" plywood on top of a piece of ¾" particleboard, I found it easiest to build the frame around the particleboard, and then add the plywood (and inlay strips) after the frame was assembled; refer to Fig. 26. So cut the particleboard base panels (LL, MM) to size; see Fig. 23.

TONGUES. Next, cut tongues on all four edges of the panels to fit the grooves in the frame; see Detail in Fig. 23. Note: The tongues aren't centered on the thickness of the particleboard, but offset so the ¼" plywood will be flush with the top of the frame.

After the frame pieces and panels are cut, you can assemble the top; see Fig. 24.

ROUT OGEE. Once the glue has dried, the next step is to rout a Roman ogee on the outside edges of the top; see Figs. 25 and 25a.

INLAY STRIPS AND PANELS. Now the recess on top of the base panels can be filled with ¼" oak plywood surrounded by thin inlay strips (I used walnut); see Fig. 26.

Start by cutting the inlay strips (PP) ¼" thick and ⅛" wide. Then miter them to fit snugly into the recesses.

After gluing the inlay strips in place, the inlay panels (NN, OO) can be cut to fit inside the strips. (Note the grain direction.) Fitting these is tricky. Start by cutting the panels slightly oversize. Then sneak up on the exact fit. Finally, glue the panels in place.

ATTACH TOP. Once the top is finished, I attached it to the pedestals with "figure 8" desk top fasteners; see Fig. 27.

To mount the fasteners, first drill shallow mortises on top of the pedestals and support blocks (RR) with a Forstner bit; see Fig. 27. Then screw in the fasteners. Now, center the top on the pedestals, and screw through the fasteners into the top; see Fig. 27a. ■

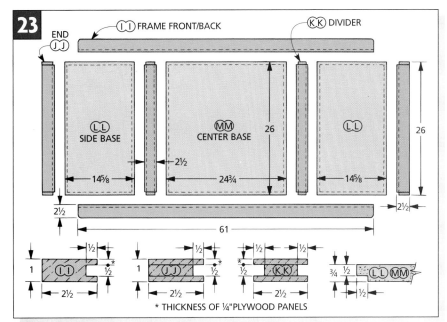

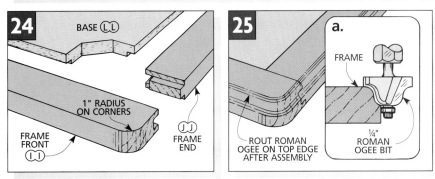

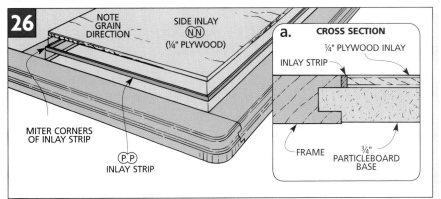

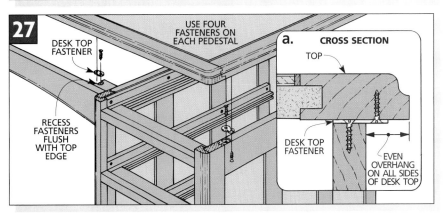

When I was installing the vanity panel on the pedestal desk, I ran into a situation often faced by house trim carpenters — joining two pieces of molding at an *inside* corner. The trick is getting a good, tight fit.

MITERS. Can't you just join the two pieces with a traditional miter joint? On the desk I couldn't do this, since the kickboard on the pedestal runs through and beyond the vanity panel. But even on a typical inside corner on house baseboards there are a couple of problems with using a miter joint.

First, it's almost impossible to find a way to nail or clamp the two mitered pieces together tightly. And, even if you could fit them together tight, there's a good chance a gap would develop in the corner as the wood shrinks and swells.

Since you'll be looking down into the corner, any gap will be noticeable. And, if the corner isn't perfectly square (and often it's not), it's difficult to get a tight-fitting miter joint.

COPED JOINT. On a coped joint one of the mating pieces is cut (coped) to match the shape of the other. The other piece has a square end that's hidden behind the coped piece. Yet from above, it still appears that both are mitered.

The first step in making a coped corner is to attach the square-end piece; "Molding B" in the top drawing at right. (On the pedestal desk, this piece, the kickboard, is a little different than on a typical inside corner since it doesn't have a square end. It runs around the pedestal. But the procedure is the same.)

CUT MITER. From this point, all of

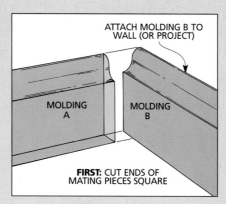

ATTACH MOLDING B TO WALL (OR PROJECT)

MOLDING A

MOLDING B

FIRST: CUT ENDS OF MATING PIECES SQUARE

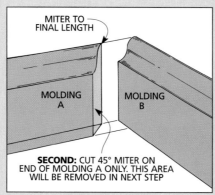

MITER TO FINAL LENGTH

MOLDING A

MOLDING B

SECOND: CUT 45° MITER ON END OF MOLDING A ONLY. THIS AREA WILL BE REMOVED IN NEXT STEP

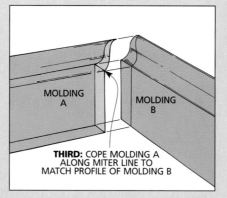

MOLDING A

MOLDING B

THIRD: COPE MOLDING A ALONG MITER LINE TO MATCH PROFILE OF MOLDING B

the remaining work is done *only* on "Molding A" (on the desk, that's the vanity panel kickboard).

First, mark the location of the miters near the ends of the molding; see Step 1 below. (To make these marks on the vanity panel kickboard, I placed the two pedestals on my workbench overhanging the bench top.)

Next, use a table saw or miter saw to make a 45° miter cut just barely outside the pencil marks; see Step 1.

BEGIN COPING. Now the actual coping can begin. For this I use a coping saw with a new blade. (You could use a band saw with a narrow blade, or a scroll saw.) The first section to cope is the straight section; see Step 2.

Shop Note: It's easiest to see the cutting line if the workpiece is positioned so there's a shadow cast on the miter.

When you reach the molded edge, stop. Then make a second cut, this time cutting in from the end of the piece to remove the waste block; see Step 2.

Next is where the tricky part comes — coping the molded edge. The secret is to take your time and cut with smooth strokes; see Step 3. But don't expect a perfect fit with the mating piece when you're done coping.

SAND TO FIT. After both ends of the molding have been coped, test-fit the coped molding (A) with its mating piece (B); see bottom drawing at left.

To get a perfect fit — a tight joint line — you will probably need to carefully sand across the coped ends; see Step 4. Just keep working at it a little bit at a time until the pieces fit together.

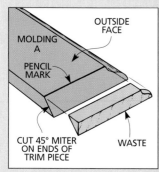

OUTSIDE FACE

MOLDING A

PENCIL MARK

CUT 45° MITER ON ENDS OF TRIM PIECE

WASTE

1 First mark the distance between the pedestal bases on the ends of the kickboard. Now miter the ends.

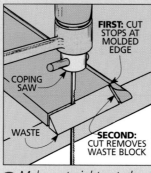

FIRST: CUT STOPS AT MOLDED EDGE

COPING SAW

WASTE

SECOND: CUT REMOVES WASTE BLOCK

2 Make a straight cut along the miter line and stop at molded edge. Remove waste piece before coping the tip.

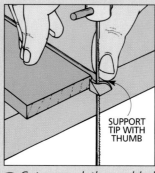

SUPPORT TIP WITH THUMB

3 Cut around the molded edge, supporting the tip with your finger to keep a point on tip of the molding.

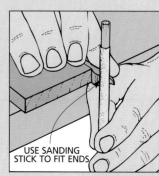

USE SANDING STICK TO FIT ENDS

4 Now test the fit. Use a sanding stick to smooth the end so it fits tightly along the entire joint.

Sources

One of the first things we take into consideration when designing projects at *Woodsmith* is whether the hardware is commonly available. Most of the hardware and supplies for the projects in this book can be found at local hardware stores or home centers. Sometimes, though, you may have to order it through the mail. In the box at right you'll find reputable national mail order sources and their phone numbers.

Also, *Woodsmith Project Supplies* offers patterns and hardware for some of the projects in this book (see below).

Woodsmith Project Supplies

At the time of printing, the following project supply kits were available from *Woodsmith Project Supplies*. These kits include hardware or patterns, but you must supply any lumber, plywood, or finish. For current prices and availability, call toll free:

1-800-444-7527

Queen Anne End Table (pages 20-31)
Full-size patterns of cabriole leg, transition block, and apron profile.
Patterns......................No. 8005–015

Ladder-Back and Formal Dining Chairs (pages 39-50)
Full-size patterns of leg profile, horizontal and vertical back slats.
Patterns........................No. 764-300

Computer Desk (pages 51-59)
Hardware kit ....No. 7109–100
(Note: Doesn't include keyboard hardware; see sources at right.)
Extension Wing (pages 60-64)
Hardware kit..............No. 7109-200

Pedestal Desk (pages 83-94)
Hardware kit.............. No. 779–100
(Note: Includes one set of full extension slides, but doesn't include vanity panel hardware.)
Vanity Panel
Hardware kit................No. 779-150
24" Full Extension Slides
Extra set......................No. 1006-120

KEY: BX73

Mail Order Sources

Some of the most important "tools" we have in our shop are the mail order catalogs kept on the shelf. They're filled with special hardware, tools, finishes, lumber, and supplies that we can't always find at our local hardware store or home center.

I've found that these catalogs have excellent customer service and are only a phone call away. You should be able to find all the supplies for the projects in this book in one or more of these catalogs.

One more thing. It's amazing what you can learn about woodworking just by looking through these catalogs. If you don't have the following catalogs in your shop, I strongly recommend that you call and have each one sent to you. (And, of course, you'll be put on their never-ending mailing lists.)

Woodcraft
210 Wood Co. Industrial Park
P.O. Box 1686
Parkersburg, WV 26102-1686
800–225–1153
A must! Has just about everything for the woodworker. Tools, computer desk (keyboard tray) hardware, finishing, wood, pre-made cabriole legs, and lots more.

The Woodworkers' Store
4365 Willow Drive
Medina, MN 55340
800–279–4441
Probably the best all-around source for general and specialty hardware such as knock-down fittings and computer desk (keyboard tray) hardware, but also has tools, laminate bit, finishes, lumber, turning squares, and veneer.

Woodworker's Supply
1108 N. Glenn Road
Casper, WY 82601
800–645–9292
Excellent source for power tools and accessories (laminate bit and reverse cut sabre saw blades), computer desk (keyboard tray) hardware, turning squares, pre-made cabriole legs, and finishes.

Trendlines
135 American Legion Highway
Revere, MA 02151
800–767–9999
Another complete source for power tools and accessories. Some hardware and supplies.

The WoodsmithShop
2200 Grand Avenue
Des Moines, IA 50312
800–444–7002
Our own source for practical jigs, useful tool accessories, *Woodsmith* project supplies, finishes, lumber, and kits.

Garrett Wade
161 Ave. of the Americas
New York, NY 10013
800–221–2942
The "Bible" for hand tools but also one of the best sources for finishing supplies and high quality power tools. This catalog is filled with useful information and tips for your shop. We got the handle for the Queen Anne end table from their separate hardware catalog.

Constantines
2050 Eastchester Road
Bronx, NY 10461
800–223–8087
One of the original woodworking mail order catalogs. Known for veneers and inlays but also has a good collection of desk hardware, finishing supplies, pre-made cabriole legs, and turning squares.

Adams Wood Products
974 Forest Drive
Morristown, TN 37814
423–587–2942
A source for pre-made legs including cabriole legs and other styles in a variety of woods. Also turning squares in a variety of sizes.